Blue Star Adventure

Cover design and map (p12) by Verso Creative.

Cover photograph shows *Blue Star* heading north towards Cape Wrath, courtesy of Chris Mason, taken from on board the yacht *Wizard*; see chapter 14.

Blue Star Adventure

A Circumnavigation of Britain

Mike Goodwin & Roger Colmer

Publisher: Independent Publishing Network
First Published: 2021
ISBN: 978-1-83853-744-9
Authors: Mike Goodwin and Roger Colmer
Email: michaelgoodwin100@gmail.com or
roger.yotmaster@gmail.com
Please direct all enquiries to the authors.

Dedicated to

Daniel John Goodwin

and

Geoffrey Charles Colmer

Table of Contents

Foreword by Tracy Edwards MBE

In 1989 Tracy Edwards skippered the first all-female crew in the Whitbread Round the World Yacht Race. Her yacht, *Maiden*, finished second in class, winning two of the six individual legs. Before the race *Maiden* and her crew had been written off by the critics as having no hope. Tracy Edwards subsequently became the first woman to receive the Yachtsman of the Year Trophy and was awarded an MBE.

***

Blue Star Adventure is quite frankly a delightful book. Beautifully written in such a personal way it reminded me of so many things I have thought and feelings I have felt when putting to sea. Some of the departures and arrivals felt so familiar in their emotions. The descriptions of the ports, scenery and sailing are just wonderful and it was easy to imagine myself back out there. I loved getting to know Mike and Roger and the many people with whom they shared their journey. It reminded me how blessed we are in the UK to have such a stunning coastline with so many varied and fascinating communities. With the added bonus of raising funds for the Cystic Fibrosis Trust, this book is a must buy and must keep. It will definitely be compulsory reading for the *Maiden* crew in readiness for our UK tour! Thank you to Mike and Roger for allowing us to share your wonderful adventure.

Foreword by the Reverend Bob Shepton

Bob Shepton is an internationally acclaimed yachtsman, having sailed his 33-foot production yacht, *Dodo's Delight*, to the Arctic Circle where, with his crew, he explored the landscape and made the first ascent of a number of mountain peaks. He won the Yachtsman of the Year award in 2013 and in 2020 received the Sailing Today Lifetime Achievement Award.

***

I am quite the wrong person to be writing this Foreword! My sailing over the years has turned more and more into long serious expeditions to remote areas of the world to fulfil some particular objective. But here at last are two people, joined by many others too, sailing for pleasure! Not that the voyage was without adventure and challenge, coupled also with the serious and worthy aim of raising money for the Cystic Fibrosis Trust. But at root it was still... FUN. What a relief!

It also proves another finer point. You do not have to cross oceans and climb huge rock walls to enjoy adventure and meet challenges. These can be found within easy reach much closer. As a hubristic self-styled ocean sailor, I was initially tempted to think nothing much could happen surely, sailing round the coast of Britain? How wrong I was, take for example ...no, no, I won't spoil your voyage of discovery through these pages! That all important ingredient of risk was also present, so important to our wellbeing and for our society, in sharp contradiction to our present shameful risk averse society. Things could still go wrong if not properly managed, or even if they were. All these were amongst the many good things about the trip, such as the way people also took the expedition to their hearts, and were generous in their support. And who has ever heard of marinas and harbours waiving their fees before!

And Mike and Roger were generous too. Here were two people fulfilling a long held dream, planned and prepared for over a long period of time. They could easily have said this is our dream, our project, we will keep it to ourselves, perhaps asking one or two people to help them on the more difficult sections. But another pleasing aspect of the voyage was that it involved so many people.

There can be few circumnavigations of Britain that deliberately loop back up north through the Minch in order to savour the challenges of Cape Wrath and the far north of Scotland, and the delights of the intriguing, historic and scenic Caledonian Canal, twice. A stroke of genius that! As you read through you become aware of the underlying feeling of eagerness and excitement, so refreshing to a jaded old salt. Many experiences were new for the crew, as in the north of Scotland but not just there, and those on board were actually enjoying themselves – this is not allowed, folks - even the suffering or hairy moments, and were looking forward to more! So, did it all go smoothly and to plan? Of course not, but overcoming those times was part of the enjoyment, or so it seems.

It is not altogether true that 'pictures make a book', but they were interesting, informative, well produced, and amusing, and definitely added to the book. I have no hesitation in heartily recommending this book, in celebration of a well-planned and well-executed expedition, and for a good read of a well written book.

And when all is said and done, it was still... FUN.

Map showing our route

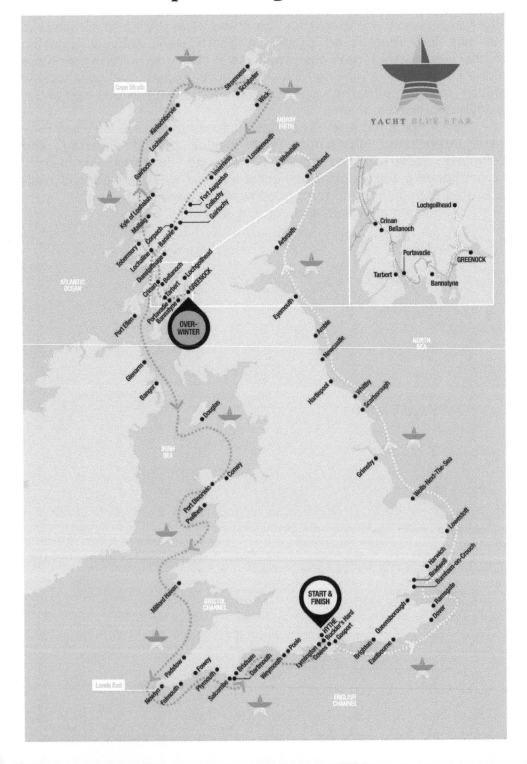

Introduction

*Twenty years from now you will be more disappointed
by the things you didn't do than the ones you did do.
So throw off the bowlines. Sail away from the safe harbour.
Catch the trade winds in your sails. Explore. Dream. Discover.*

Often attributed to Mark Twain or to H. Jackson Brown Jr.

During the summer months of 2015 and 2016 we sailed our yacht, *Blue Star*, around the coasts of Great Britain and Northern Ireland. The voyage would satisfy a yearning that we had to explore and would also be a test of our sailing skills. We had sailed in the UK and overseas. A circumnavigation of Britain was the obvious next step!

We would need a boat – chartering was a non-starter. We found one that was suitable and, although we could have sailed it ourselves, others were eager to come along for the ride. We asked them to donate to charity if they enjoyed their time on board with us. Mike's elder son, Daniel, had cystic fibrosis, and so the Cystic Fibrosis Trust (CF Trust) was our chosen charity.

We ran a daily blog. It included a nautical joke and we have reproduced many of these in this book. We hope this conveys the fun that the voyage encapsulated – we needed a sense of humour; there were many testing times!

We imagined lazily exploring every creek and cranny of the coast. For some reason we envisaged shorts and tee shirts. How wrong could we have been! It soon became apparent that to complete our journey in the time we had set ourselves we would have to make considerable progress each week, but that said, it was not a race and we did not set out to break any records.

We'd heard how beautiful the Caledonian Canal was, and we resolved to include it in our route, but we wanted the challenge of sailing the North of Scotland too. We settled on a figure-of-eight route that included navigating the canal twice!

Our voyage led us through treacherous waters, challenging conditions, beautiful places, hilarious moments and to meetings with some amazing people. This is the story of our *Blue Star* adventure.

Above: *Blue Star* **under sail (photo courtesy of Keith Spilsbury)**

1. Time to go

Ropes released, freedom found,
Halyards hoisted, winches wound,
Pencil, plotter and chosen charts,
Silver spray and hastening hearts,
Our sloop to sea, adventure bound!

Mike Goodwin, 'The Yacht'

Sunday, 17 May 2015. It was time to go. No putting it off. Cancelling was not an option. We didn't want to delay but even if we did, so many friends, relatives and even strangers had gathered to see us off and wish us well. People were waiting expectantly. We couldn't possibly let them down. All the work and months of planning that we had put in could not be wasted. And what about all of the funds we'd raised for charity, through people who'd sponsored us? We owed it to everyone to go through with it. This was, after all, something we'd dreamed of doing and it was now or never! The weather wasn't ideal; there was a cool wind blowing but a slight showing of blue in the sky gave cause for optimism. The project was about much more than sailing around Great Britain in a small boat – it was about adventure, yes, it was about a challenge and about testing ourselves. Could we really do it?

***

We travelled to Hythe, near Southampton, the day before our departure. *Blue Star* had been brought over a few days earlier, in readiness. She really looked the part, standing out from the hundreds of other boats in the marina. We felt an overwhelming sense of pride in her. Her white coach roof and decks were spotless, and the navy-blue hull was adorned with the logos of all our sponsors. At the bow, the slogan 'Cystic Fibrosis A Fight We Must Win'. Around her decks, attached to the stanchions that hold up the guard rails, were yellow banners publicising the charity, as did a host of yellow balloons. The boat was also 'dressed' in bunting. A rope attached at *Blue Star*'s bow led up to the top of the mast with a multitude of triangular, yellow

Cystic Fibrosis Trust flags. A second string of bunting led from the top of the mast to *Blue Star*'s stern. This, adorned with patterns of blue stars, had been made by Mike's wife, Diane.

Family and friends, including Roger's niece, Claire, from Australia and members of Stafford Coastal Cruising Club, had come to support us. They had been excited and pleased to have the opportunity to board *Blue Star* that morning to inspect her. All were very generous in their comments on how good she looked.

Our venue for the farewell gathering, the Boathouse Hotel, looked out directly onto the marina at Hythe, enabling our supporters to see and visit the boat. It was just a short walk to the seafront to see us sail away. The hotel had a number of bedrooms available and incorporated a dining room capable of accommodating all of the people that we envisaged would attend the event. Because it was a small hotel, we had reserved rooms for ourselves, our families and friends well in advance, to ensure we had a convenient base on the day. Others had managed to find lodgings at nearby B&Bs and hotels, but still within walking distance of the marina.

The feeling of expectation was building up. In the afternoon a group of us walked into Hythe, a pleasant town bustling with shoppers and tourists. At the seafront you could see the Southampton ferry arrive and a tiny train travelled the length of the pier.

In the evening everyone had gathered in the restaurant of the hotel; we greeted all guests as they arrived and thanked them for their support. The party was a great success. Everyone sat down to a splendid dinner followed by 'afters' and coffee.

We each spoke about why we wanted to sail around Britain and the difficulties we expected to face. Woolcool, a manufacturer of sustainable packaging, was our main sponsor, and was represented by Managing Director, Jo Morris. She explained that sailing was environmentally friendly and therefore consistent with the company's ethos. The Commodore from Stafford Coastal Cruising Club made us all laugh with amusing tales of his own single-handed circumnavigation of the world. The evening concluded with the cutting of a beautifully decorated 'sail-away cake'.

In the weeks leading up to the sail-away event we did media interviews. Representatives from BBC Radio Stoke visited Mike's house in Stone and broadcast live as he spoke about the challenges presented by the impending voyage, and about his motivation to raise funds for the Cystic Fibrosis Trust. There had been articles in the local newspapers about the project. Roger arranged a similar interview with Radio Solent. There had even been a suggestion that a TV crew might be present to film our departure.

Publicity photographs were taken to raise awareness of the project. Some were taken aboard *Blue Star* while she was being prepared for the trip. Mike and Diane posed in Cystic Fibrosis Trust tee shirts. Other photos were taken at the local dinghy sailing club in Stafford. Several of these accompanied articles published in local newspapers and helped raise awareness. People responded by donating to the charity via our website. One person even enquired about sailing with us as crew, and did eventually join us on board!

As well as helping with sponsorship of the project, Woolcool made available their marketing consultants, Verso Creative. They designed a clever logo for the boat in the form of a blue star that also looked like a yacht. We were extremely pleased with it. Our team shirts sported the logo and a larger version of it appeared on each side of the boat towards the stern.

We sought the sponsorship of employers, in the form of donations to the charity. In exchange, each employer's name appeared on the sides of our boat and on our website. Many businesses were contacted. A handful of employers came forward to support us. These were all found by way of personal contacts. The CEO of Woolcool, Diane's cousin Angela Morris, had no hesitation in supporting us. Woolcool donated by far the greatest amount to our Virgin Money Giving page. Staffordshire University, Mike's former employer, also donated. We purchased *Blue Star* via the yacht brokers Clipper Marine; they were persuaded that sponsoring our project was part of the deal! The IT company Amaze, employers of Mike's son, Daniel, lived up to their name with an 'amazing' donation! They understood how important it is to find a cure for cystic fibrosis. Perhaps they also admired Daniel and the way he lived with the disease. Abel & Cole, a Woolcool client who prepared meals for delivery by post, were also brought on board. The clothing company Next were persuaded to donate too.

Other activities had taken place on the fundraising front prior to our sail-away. Many friends responded with personal donations. Mike's sister-in-law, Susan, made a wonderful *Blue Star* quilt which she raffled off. We arranged to give talks about the *Blue Star* project at local sailing clubs; this too resulted in many generous contributions.

Some thought had gone into the logistics for the sail-away, especially with regard to transport to the marina. Mike had driven himself, Diane and his younger son, Cliff, to the Boathouse the previous day. After the sail-away Cliff would drive Diane home in Mike's car. Daniel, unfortunately, was too unwell to travel and stayed home with his wife, Jess. Roger had also arranged for a lift. The two of us would subsequently be returning home at different stages in the voyage by using various means of transport.

Another part of the planning was the question of who would crew for us? Our intention all along, as one of our fundraising mechanisms, was to invite people to sail part of the voyage with us. We would ask them to consider giving to our charity after they had sailed with us, hoping that they would do so if they had enjoyed their time on board. We didn't want to enter into any commercial agreement with crew, so it would be voluntary, but we suggested a figure that might be appropriate. Crew were sailing with us 'as friends', and we would all share the on-board costs of food, diesel, gas and marina fees. In practice, we were to find that many of the marinas waived their fee because we were sailing to raise funds for charity. This kept costs down and helped increase the personal contributions.

To assist planning our crew, we established a website which indicated who had signed up for particular weeks of the voyage, and which showed where we expected to be for any set week. This gave anyone considering coming with us a chance to choose, to some degree, which part of the coast they would be sailing along. There was no guarantee that we would adhere to the schedule but in practice we were delayed by bad weather on very few occasions.

We ran a blog (svbluestar.blogspot.com) so that followers could receive a report at the end of each day about where we were and what challenges we had faced. We also posted some photographs. Occasionally it wasn't possible to post a report because of poor internet access. The blog linked to our charity page, making it easy for people to donate.

An interesting feature of the blog was a link that located the boat in real time. A follower could see a map on their screen, with an icon to indicate the position of *Blue Star* at that precise moment – at least that was the theory! In practice, because the system worked by tracking Mike's phone, its accuracy depended upon either telephone masts triangulating, or on the GPS within Mike's phone. This worked well for most of the trip but there were occasions when people questioned why we had taken the land route, whether we were ploughing a rut through a field with *Blue Star*'s fin keel or whether we were aboard a low-loader transport lorry!

***

And now the day had finally arrived, after all the hard work to get to the 'start line'. We had been preparing for well over a year, and felt that everything had gone well. We were delighted with the amount of support at the sail-away event. Now it was time for us to deliver.

Mike:

I had slept well and felt 'up for it', but was anxious nonetheless. This project was certainly 'do-able', but it could also go dreadfully wrong! It was certainly not without risk. It would be the most challenging sailing voyage I had undertaken. What if we were shipwrecked, or if *Blue Star* sank? What if a crew member was badly hurt in an accident? Good grief – what if someone was killed! The potential disaster scenarios were numerous and many of them had already played out in my mind in the weeks and months leading up to our departure. I set my fears to one side and focused on getting things right on the day. Feelings of excitement and adventure, but also of apprehension and expectation, were washing over me, and I knew that the only way to deal with it all was to set sail.

Roger:

I was constantly going over, in my head, the maintenance work carried out over the previous three months. Had I checked everything? Did we have the correct spares? Could we cope with running repairs? Fortunately, during the first week on the water we would be close to excellent support services; however, as we progressed, technical support could be scarcer. I was confident in our ability to sail the yacht and achieve our target. As I had frequently worked away from home I was reassured that all would be well during my absence. Something told me that there would be a lot of lawn mowing on my return! Overall, I was excited and keen to get *Blue Star* under way.

We checked the weather forecast early in the morning. A force 5 from the northwest was predicted, and a 'slight' sea state in the Solent. No rain was forecast. There were some clouds however, and the sun would have to work hard to keep them at bay. That would do. We didn't intend to sail further than Portsmouth on the first day, and the weather sounded reasonable for that trip. The important thing was to make a start, especially with everyone coming to see us off. It would have been a great disappointment if we'd had to cancel our sailing that day, but we would have done so if conditions had dictated it to be necessary.

We finished a relaxed breakfast at the hotel and returned to our rooms to complete our packing before giving our thanks to the hotel staff. They had been a big help in reserving rooms and part of the restaurant for our function, even though we had only guessed at the likely numbers early on. We walked outside and onto the marina pontoons with our bags, and met the other crew at *Blue Star*'s berth. On this first leg, scheduled to end at Ramsgate, we were joined by Rob Wilford, a longstanding friend of Mike's, and by Hastings McKenzie from Staffordshire University.

Rob and Mike met years ago when their children played together at Pant Gwyn caravan and camping site in Abersoch. They started sailing together during these holidays. Later, they and other friends chartered yachts together for several years.

Hastings had recently succeeded Mike as a faculty Dean at Staffordshire University following Mike's retirement. He owned a narrowboat which he kept at Aston near the university, but was keen to join the crew of *Blue Star*.

In the marina a great crowd gathered to join with us in a farewell photograph session, much of it choreographed by Cliff. Everyone wanted to watch the crew board the boat. We both planned to complete the whole circumnavigation, but accompanied by different crew for each leg of the voyage. A final photo was taken of the crew for the first leg, standing together on the side-deck of the boat, all wearing their navy 'Woolcool Blue Star GB Challenge' polo shirts. *Blue Star* was not the only one who looked the part! We removed the balloons that would be in the way of the sails and would have made managing our lines difficult. We were ready to go!

Mike kissed his wife, Diane, goodbye. She had supported him throughout, despite 'not being particularly keen' on sailing. She had reluctantly sailed with him on previous occasions, always on condition that the boat would not be too 'tippy', and that she could get off the moment that she had had enough. Naturally, he always gave her these reassurances, but of course they both knew that he was in no position to give them! Still, she would join the crew for the Caledonian Canal stage where perhaps there was a chance that both conditions could be met. Roger kissed Judith goodbye, and Rob and Hastings also said goodbyes to their partners. It was an emotional time but a wonderful send-off.

By now the crowd was moving away from the pontoon, where the crew had just boarded the boat, and were walking over towards the harbour wall where they would be able to watch us put to sea.

Mike was the skipper for the first week of the voyage. We had both equally invested our time and money in the project and would share the skippering duties. The crew were asked to slip the lines and then we were away. We reversed out of our berth and into the lane that divides the pontoons, then engaged forward gear and steered towards the marina exit. The crew took in the fenders and attached them to the guard wire at the stern. They coiled the mooring lines and stowed them in the cockpit locker. We were on our way at last! We had scheduled our departure to coincide with high water and so there was free flow of traffic in and out of the port – no need to use the lock gates. We motored out to sea and held our position a short distance off, pointing *Blue Star*'s bow into the wind whilst the bunting was removed and the mainsail raised, 'Woolcool' shouting out from the large letters attached to the sail. A huge tanker manoeuvred close by, dwarfing *Blue Star*. It seemed to symbolise the enormity of the challenge that we were taking on. Another wave to everyone and we disappeared down Southampton Water towards the Eastern Solent, out to the open sea.

✳✳✳

Joke

Quilting is where you take a number of pieces of lovely fabric, then cut them into pieces, and then sew them back together again. (Susan makes a marvellous job of it.)

✳✳✳

Above: Supporters gather for a photo

Below: *Blue Star* at Hythe before we sailed away

Above: Leaving the marina at Hythe

Below: A large ship symbolises what we have taken on

2. Background to our adventure

Believe me, my young friend,
there is nothing – absolutely nothing –
half so much worth doing
as simply messing about in boats.

Kenneth Grahame, *The Wind in the Willows*

Mike:
My mother was from Amsterdam. She always said that the Dutch love the water so perhaps it is no surprise that I became a sailor. My first 'close encounter' with sailing was with a student friend, John Bennett. It was 1974 and we were both studying Mechanical Engineering at North Staffordshire Polytechnic. We shared lifts each day from Newcastle-under-Lyme to the Beaconside campus in Stafford. John was a sailor; he showed me his GP14 sailing dinghy that he was restoring in his garage. I wasn't particularly impressed at the time; sailing all sounded rather slow and boring. Years later, as an academic, I started to think about how a sailing boat travels upwind and my interest was sparked.

I bought my first boat, also a GP14, in 1987. She needed some work to strengthen the keel which was somewhat soft – a fairly common problem with old GP14s. It was a standard upgrade approved by the class association and involved gluing a thick strip of hardwood on top of the keel, under where the mast was stepped. I spent several days giving the boat a new paint job - cream with coloured stripes at the stern - christened her *Flying Colours* and joined Nantwich & Border Counties Sailing Club.

My boat was relatively old and my skills somewhat lacking but I soon realised just how exhilarating sailing a boat can be. That winter I entered the aptly named 'frostbite' series of races. Thanks to a handicap system, as an absolute beginner, I was thrilled to win the trophy! Several summers of trailing the GP to the sea at Abersoch in North Wales followed.

For me, sailing on the sea was far more exciting than the confines of Doddington Pool, the sailing club base. The seemingly endless coast offered countless opportunities for adventure and the chance to explore. I wanted to see what was behind the next headland, and to prove to myself that I could get there and back under sail. There were a few narrow escapes though.

First was the challenge of sailing from Abersoch Bay round to Llanbedrog, a journey I undertook with Daniel as crew. Getting to Llanbedrog proved easy enough, and we jumped out of the boat and walked for a short while on the sand to convince ourselves that we had indeed arrived! At that point I realised that Diane, sitting on the beach at Abersoch, would be wondering where we had got to! We knew we should get back as soon as possible. However, it was at this point that I first came across the experience of a foul tide. Try as we might to get past the headland back to Abersoch, the tide always seemed to stem our progress. Finally, after what seemed like an eternity of tacking into the wind and tide and getting nowhere, I decided to risk a route which took us close inshore, where theory told me that the tidal stream would be weaker. We sailed so near to the rocks off the headland that I expected disaster at any moment! We eventually managed to get back before our disappearance had caused too much concern, but it had been a close shave.

The second spot of bother was when sailing single-handed on a mission to circumnavigate the St Tudwal's Islands – two small privately owned islands situated off Abersoch Bay. It was a hot sunny day, a gentle breeze blew and the sea was flat. A very relaxing and enjoyable sail took me out to the islands, and around the back of them. It was at this point, however, that the wind disappeared. I sat and waited … and waited. Slowly the tide was sweeping me further and further out into the Irish Sea. I was in trouble. Much to my relief, rescue arrived in the form of a lone speedboat whose driver spotted my waving arms and towed me back. Phew!

Around this time Daniel was honing his sailing skills on his own Topper dinghy. Although it was strictly a one-man boat, we all had great fun with it. It was often a rather overloaded craft taking turns around the bay!

I tired of pulling the heavy GP14 up and down the beach. The boat was sold and replaced with a Dart 18 catamaran which I left in the dunes, among the others parked there. The Dart was easier to manoeuvre on the sand when launching and recovering, and went like a 'bat out of hell' in the slightest breath of wind!

By now it was beginning to dawn on me – if I really intended to explore the coast I needed an engine. A yacht with an inboard engine would be ideal for the kind of trips I wanted. In preparation I read magazines and books about yacht cruising, and signed on to a Royal Yachting Association (RYA) course to obtain my Day Skipper theory certificate. A practical course with the Island Sea School at Port Dinorwic completed my first sailing qualifications.

I arranged a taster-day sail on board a yacht out of Cowes. Although it wasn't a great success - the skipper had a bad back - it was enough to convince me that I wanted more and I seized every opportunity to build my experience. Thanks to Dan's networking, we crewed on *Jay Jay*, a J24 based near Cardiff, taking part in several weekend races off Penarth. Aboard *Jay Jay* we crossed the Bristol Channel to Weston-super-Mare, and rounded several small islands. Another time we crewed on a Contessa 32 out of Pwllheli.

By the summer of 1999, I'd persuaded Rob that it was a good idea to charter a yacht with me. We booked a 32-foot Westerly Fulmar from a base at Gosport, paid our charter fee and travelled down for the week. Climbing on board, this was the first time I was going to be in charge of a yacht. It seemed huge! I had become a capable dinghy sailor but this was something else. Nervously, and very slowly, we reversed out of the marina berth and went to sea. The week was a success. We circumnavigated the Isle of Wight, and my confidence grew.

Rob and I enjoyed sailing together with our sons and I arranged more yacht charters. I scoured the yachting press and spotted an 'ad' for what claimed to be the cheapest yacht charter on the Solent! Surely this had to be a good choice, didn't it? The company owner, John, had several ageing boats. We became familiar with many of them over the years, and discovered that maintenance was 'questionable'.

On one charter we found so many parts of the boat were malfunctioning or becoming detached that we had great fun making a comic home video showing these, proclaiming that we loved the challenge of working with a boat that was falling apart beneath our feet. It would, after all, be very boring with a state-of-the-art vessel where everything worked perfectly!

When executing a tack while a crew member was indisposed, the boat suddenly leaned over the other way and he ended up flying through the heads door, ripping it off its hinges in the process!

One summer John suggested, at handover, that I might need to regularly pump some grease into the stern gland during the week. Unfortunately, this went forgotten until the end of the week. We were returning to Southampton after cruising off the French coast when Cliff came to me looking rather worried, saying the floorboards were floating, was this OK?

One year, while cruising off the Normandy coast and heading for Cherbourg, we'd just rounded the headland at Barfleur against a contrary tide when the wind died. No problem, we'll put the engine on. Nothing happened, save for the click of the key. Richard Bradford, another friend and regular crew member, went below to investigate. I stayed on deck monitoring our slow drift backwards as the tide took us towards the rocks, considering a radio call to the French coastguard. We might have set the anchor, and it might have held, but the light was fading and it wasn't the ideal place to spend the night. From below, Richard gave a gasp and exclaimed what a total mess the engine wiring was. He located a loose piece of wire that seemed to go nowhere and speculated on where it ought to go. After a brief discussion we agreed that he should 'attach' the wire in situ using a pair of mole grips, seemingly the only means at our disposal. The engine immediately gunned into life at the next turn of the switch and so relieved was Cliff that he flung his arms around a stunned Richard! The mole grips remained exactly where they were for the rest of the trip, for fear of rendering the engine useless again. On our arrival back at Cowes we gave John the 'benefit of our advice'. Apologetic, he arranged for 'an engineer' to visit the boat to correct the 'spaghetti-wiring mystery'. The chap arrived and raised the companionway steps to inspect the engine. On seeing the electrics he scratched his head and proclaimed that he was more of a motorbike man and didn't know much about boat engines!

The reader would be forgiven for wondering why we persisted in chartering John's boats. The fact was they were extremely competitively priced and, whilst the maintenance was not top notch, there was never any unacceptable risk to life.

John retired from the yacht charter business and his boats were sold off. I looked for another boat and found *Andiamo*, a First 38, based initially at Ocean Village in Southampton and later at Northney Marina in Chichester Harbour. *Andiamo* was privately owned by Geoff who had a PhD in electrical engineering. I was very pleased to charter her on a regular basis. She was a fast boat, maintained to an excellent standard, especially compared to the boats we had been used to. Our only observation was that the electric circuits seemed to have so many fuses that it appeared sometimes one fuse was installed to protect another! We enjoyed several summers sailing her around the Solent and across to France. At one point she easily outperformed a larger French boat in a 'race' from Fecamp to Honfleur.

It's particularly satisfying to calculate tidal height and finding it to be spot on in practice. Whilst sailing the Normandy coast we were searching for the entrance to the river which leads to Carentan. The river is little more than a ditch at low water, so we approached at high tide. The calculations suggested that we needed to find the entrance within the next 15 minutes or forget it as an overnight stay. We did indeed find it in time, and passed over the bar with just half a metre of water under the keel, exactly as calculated!

On another occasion we were exiting the harbour at Honfleur. To my shame I hadn't planned the exit before entering the harbour, and didn't appreciate quite how shallow it would be in the lock. On approaching I thought things didn't seem quite right and went below to quickly calculate what the depth under the keel would be once the water had been let out. The answer ... precisely zero! We couldn't delay; we needed to return home, so we pressed on into the lock. I kept my eye on the depth sounder as the water level dropped. As the lock gates opened, the bottom of the keel was just touching the mud. We used engine power to push through the mud and out into the river Seine. That was a close one!

At a meeting of the Engineering Council I found myself sitting next to a man who had a senior role at Shell. We chatted and discovered that we both shared an interest in sailing. Roger was keen and available to crew on my next adventure across the Channel! It proved to be an 'interesting' trip. We set out from Chichester Harbour in *Andiamo*, the plan being to head for the Channel Islands. The forecast was for a force 6 – not likely to be the most comfortable sail. We set out anyway and found ourselves close-hauled in a moderate sea. Had we continued we would probably have all been sick, so we altered course until the boat's motion felt more acceptable and found that we were heading for Fecamp! So be it! Fecamp became our new destination and onward we sailed. We split ourselves into watches. After a sleep I came on watch at around midnight to find us somewhat overpowered and the wind gusting force 8. We shortened sail and carried on, finally entering port before dawn. *Andiamo* behaved impeccably but most of the crew felt it had been far from their best sailing experience – except for Roger who thought it had been the best sail he had ever been on!

Roger introduced me to Nick, a charter operator working out of Lymington. We hired many of Nick's boats. Several times we competed in the 'Round the Island Race' (the Isle of Wight), the largest yacht race in the world in terms of entries. With hundreds of yachts massed at the start, it requires a huge amount of skill and concentration to navigate a path amongst all the competitors and come home unscathed!

I was lucky enough to compete in the Fastnet Race in 2003, as a crew member on board *Highland Daughter*, a privately-owned Bavaria 42. The skipper, Gordon, had offered places to individuals willing to pay for a berth. We had some great sailing, some heavy blows and were becalmed under the sun in the Irish Sea, where we all went swimming! It was a marvellous experience and I'm so glad to have had the opportunity to compete in such a famous yacht race. Today, places on the Fastnet Race are in extremely high demand.

An interesting escapade was the time Rob and I agreed to help deliver a yacht from Palma to Naples. The owner had just bought the boat and was lending it to his friend who was to skipper it around Italy, taking in paying guests. The forecast when leaving Palma was for gales but the new owner had a plane to catch in Sardinia and was determined to set sail. Rob and I were on night watch when thunder clapped and lightning flashed, turning the black sky violet and white in every direction. It was a beautiful and impressive sight, but rather alarming too as we prayed for the bolts of electricity to miss our mast. The next day the gales persisted and we were eventually forced into Mahon on Minorca when the headsail sheet snapped, the skipper intending us to leave as soon as new rope was bought. When Rob and I threatened to abandon ship and take the next flight home he relented and we stayed a night in Mahon. Thereafter the trip was a delight and the owner was still in good time for his flight.

By 2013 I was planning early retirement and looking for a bigger sailing challenge. I'd read of yachts circumnavigating Great Britain and was getting very enthusiastic about the idea, even contemplating a single-handed attempt, much to Diane's horror. I decided to put the proposal to my usual crewmates. The response was a resounding silence from all but one. Only Roger was 'brave' enough to join the challenge.

Roger was 'in'. Great! Diane was a lot happier too. A charter would not make financial sense though. We would have to buy a yacht. We quickly agreed to share costs, ownership and skippering of the boat, and the project could also raise funds for the Cystic Fibrosis Trust. We 'just' needed to find a boat.

***

Roger:

Whilst living in the Middle East in the 1970s, I had a few hours in a Laser and some experience in a GP14. It was only after retiring much later that I had the time and opportunity to return to sailing and take it up seriously. Many years spent roaming the globe searching for oil and gas meant that hobbies had to fit into a suitcase and the uncertainty of assignments never allowed for long-term commitments where hobbies were concerned. This new third age, post full-time employment, meant there were many activities to explore and after some thought I signed up for an RYA Competent Crew course on Southampton Water. This turned out to be a magical and life-changing experience; the combination of good company, some cerebral activity and pulling bits of rope seemed to be a great way to spend time. The instructor should also take credit for the engaging and interesting way in which the course was delivered – sailing was fun!

Over the following years the RYA syllabus was studiously followed, passing through Coastal Skipper and eventually reaching RYA Yachtmaster Offshore level. Not actually owning a boat, I was dependent on friends to offer local crewing opportunities and trips further afield through Lymington Town Sailing Club. A very generous member (Peter) took me on many trips across the Channel and around the South Coast. In 2005 I participated in the Middle East Yacht Rally. This was before the current geo-political chaos in the region. Sailing from Western Turkey along to the eastern border and then down to Syria, Lebanon and Israel was a fantastic experience. From Haifa we sailed back across the Mediterranean to Western Turkey. This long trip not only provided many interesting historical aspects but also some challenging sailing.

Having the opportunity to crew for a variety of owners and skippers meant that a range of skills could be observed and practised. There are often a number of ways of doing things on board and normally the wishes of the boat owner/skipper take precedence. However, with little previous experience I had taken my cues from the excellent RYA training programmes I had been on, and also several books. Sometimes my understanding and practices were at odds with the skipper's. One skipper had the practice of 'joining the dots' when it came to plotting the passage on a chart. In some cases little attention was paid to what we might sail over or into, never mind the optimum route considering tides!

In most cases where there was a difference of idea or practice a constructive chat over a beer after tying up would sort out the issues. From my offshore experience in the international oil and gas business I was fully aware that there may come a time where jumping ship was the right thing to do if the safety and risk factors were too high. This only occurred once when we were about to sail into Syrian and Israeli territorial waters. The skipper thought it would be wonderful to capture the experience via a small video camera mounted at the mast head. Having worked in this part of the world I had to advise 'no' as I felt that the risk of being arrested as a spy was too great. Had he insisted, I would not have been on hand to witness the outcome. Eventually the camera was not installed, common sense prevailed.

From the mid-2000s onwards chartering enabled us to explore new places and gain further experience. Together with Judith and friends, yachts were chartered in the UK, Turkey, Greece, Croatia and the British Virgin Islands. After meeting Mike we also had an annual sailing week together with friends Jean-Francois and Joan. There was a competition during these fun weeks on the water to charter larger and larger yachts. We learnt the hard way that some charter yachts are not always well maintained. Sharing ownership of a yacht with Mike would enable us to make sure that everything was in good order for the major test that we had set ourselves.

***

Planning the route for our circumnavigation and the crew who would sail with us proceeded apace, but in parallel we began our search for the right vessel. The sailing experience we had accumulated during our years of chartering helped to shape our ideas about the specification and type of yacht we desired for our adventure. We gradually narrowed it down to a 37-foot Bavaria because of its spacious accommodation, popularity, resale value and relative simplicity to sail. Our challenge then became one of finding a suitable yacht.

After scouring the 'Boats for Sale' columns of yachting magazines and numerous websites we found several which we felt were worthy of investigation. The first was on the East Coast and seemed to be ideal. We contacted the broker and agreed a date for a visit – Roger driving from the South Coast and Mike from the Midlands. We inspected the boat and indeed it lived up to our expectations and seemed to be in excellent condition. We raised the question of price, emphasising that we needed the boat for a charity adventure and the broker committed to talking with the owner. Within a few days the answer came back that there was no possibility of lowering the price. A long and involved story followed about the owner's impoverished state and why there was no room for manoeuvre. It was a nice boat, but not worth the money.

Our second attempt was a yacht moored in Bristol; again, the specification looked good and the price was within our range. We met the broker on board and although the boat showed signs of neglect there was nothing which a good dose of elbow grease would not solve. We engaged in a discussion about the price only to be told again, no movement. We were beginning to question our strategy; as with most commercial negotiations, there should be some room for compromise. This boat wasn't worth the price asked, bearing in mind the work required.

A third boat was identified in Gosport so Roger went with his wife, Judith, to have a look. Externally the yacht seemed in poor condition; they asked the broker for a look inside. The interior matched the exterior which was not very promising! The biggest surprise came when they started opening lockers. Every conceivable storage area was filled with bottles of alcohol. Was the boat owned by a modern-day smuggler or maybe someone who just liked a drink? This one was a non-starter.

Finally, our fourth attempt proved to be successful. Called *Santa Bettina* and berthed on the Isle of Wight, she was a 2006 model and in excellent condition. We understood from the broker, Clipper Marine, that the owner had just ordered a larger Bavaria and was thus keen to complete the transaction. Contrary to our previous experience, there was room for a slight price adjustment, making both parties feel satisfied. With our wives, we made a visit to see the boat before the final decision and the deal was done!

With the yacht's ownership transferred, we arranged registration and insurance and changed her name to *Blue Star* as she had a navy hull and she would be our 'star'! We would start our adventure in early May which gave only a couple of months for preparation.

Roger, living on the South Coast close to where she was berthed, organised the upgrades and was able to carry out some of the work personally. Service technicians were used for much of the work but it was important to oversee what they were doing. We thought about 'single point failure' – which one item would put us into trouble or stall our progress? This guided our preparation and helped to make sure we had the right spares on board. The Bavaria 37 turned out to be more suitable than we had hoped. She was simple to maintain, had easy access to all components and was supported by a comprehensive spares service. We replaced the seacocks and saildrive seal, and had a professional rigger check the wire stays supporting the mast.

With all the major items serviced, work commenced on the installation of up-to-date electronics. The old chart plotters in the cockpit and at the chart table were replaced by modern touch-screen units. A new digital radar was fitted and an Automatic Identification System (AIS) installed which would display the position of other vessels on our cockpit chart, useful in poor visibility. We equipped the boat with an Emergency Position Indicating Radio Beacon (EPIRB) which would summon help from rescue services if needed.

The remainder of the work focused on the minor points picked up in the surveyor's report. We strengthened the straps holding down the batteries and renewed the anchor windlass mounts. Down below, the 240-volt electrical sockets were all changed from the original continental style to British.

For cosmetic reasons it was decided to replace the plastic trim around the stern. Removing the old one was incredibly time-consuming, especially taking off the old glue. After a couple of days, Roger, with the help of Ian, his brother-in-law, had the hull ready for the new strip. Fitting this was like wrestling a 15-kilogram anaconda about four metres long and was definitely a two-man job! About one third of the way through, the yard supervisor told them to stop the job as he wanted to move the yacht – a reasonable request – but there was no way they could halt the application of the 'snake'. After some plain talking the he understood that they were the owners and not just a couple of contractors trying to fight an uncontrollable reptile. A couple of hours later, new rubbing strake fitted, the yacht was moved.

The jobs' list continued to get shorter as the launch date approached. Diane equipped the galley and attended to the soft furnishings. Given the time we were expecting to spend on board, we wanted a degree of home comfort! Some safety equipment was kindly sponsored by Nick. The six-man life raft, mounted in a cradle on the coach roof, was acquired as a rental item, saving on capital costs. A new handheld VHF radio and a comprehensive toolkit were added before launch. The final touch was two coats of anti-foul before going back into the water.

Tuesday 21 April 2015 was an exciting day, the launching of *Blue Star*! Nick came along to help us celebrate. Our pride and joy was lowered into the sea and we hastily checked for water ingress. There was none. Good! After motoring round to her new marina berth we christened her with a bottle of champagne.

Margaret and Geoff Haylock travelled from Stafford to join us for a test sail in the Solent, but soon after their arrival the forecast talked of a severe storm, force 8 gusting force 9 – a worrying sign given it was early May. The storm arrived, crashing into the South Coast and meant that despite the Haylocks' arrival we could not get out on the water. The yacht was moored at the head of the River Hamble and should have been well protected from the elements. However, such was the strength and ferocity of the storm that we almost had to clip on just to move about in the cabin! Notice of the gale was confirmed by Carol Kirkwood from the BBC who went on to become the 'Patron Saint of Meteorologists' for *Blue Star*. Fortunately, we were comforted by a large selection of homemade cakes which Margaret had made for us. Margaret and Geoff had to wait until later in the voyage before they got their sail with us.

Eventually we got out on the Solent for sea trials. Rob's partner Madeline and her friend, Ginny, joined us for a weekend, and later we were also joined by Jean-Francois and Chris, friends of Roger. *Blue Star* sailed like a dream and we were delighted.

There was one time when we gave ourselves a little fright, and a stern talking to! When out with Jean-Francois and Chris we were all fascinated by the new touch-screen multi-functional display chart plotter. Nothing so modern as this had been seen on the yachts we had chartered previously. Whilst investigating a particular 'magic' function, all heads were glued to the screen. With two chartered engineers, one chemical engineer and a former 747 senior captain on board we were all deep into an erudite technical conversation at the helm when suddenly a very large, yellow, tanker mooring buoy near the BP terminal slid majestically down our starboard side just a few metres away without a murmur. Whoops! In our excitement with the new toy we had all forgotten Rule 5 of the 'Collision Regulations' - the need to keep a good look-out at all times. Given our collective level of sailing qualifications, excuses about the buoy being masked by the headsail were not appropriate; this was a sobering reminder of the basics.

Another 'exciting' moment was when we first engaged the autopilot. On pressing the 'Auto' button, instead of simply continuing on her current course, *Blue Star* attempted a sharp and rapid 180-degree turn. It was totally unexpected. We were in the middle of the River Hamble amongst a few million pounds worth of boats and it was sheer good fortune that we didn't collide with any of them. A quick visit from the technician who had installed the new chart plotter, incorrectly wiring the autopilot, and the problem was fixed.

All that remained to do was stock up on supplies, and fill up with fresh water and diesel. We were ready to go!

***

Joke

A very nervous first-time crew member asks the captain, 'Do yachts like this sink very often?'

'No', replies the captain, 'It's usually only once'!

***

Above: Mike and Daniel with *Flying Colours*

Left: Mike's Dart 18

3. Hythe to Dover

It is pleasant and dreamy, no doubt, to float
With `thoughts as boundless, and souls as free':
But, suppose you are very unwell in a boat,
How do you like the Sea?

Lewis Carroll, 'A Sea Dirge'

Although the sun shone as we exited Hythe marina, clouds threatened. Our short-sleeved polo shirts were soon covered by another layer. The wind took us in the direction we wanted to go, but it was not a warm wind – an omen of things to come! Our destination on this, the first day of our voyage, was Portsmouth. Not a great distance to cover but it was important to have left Hythe at the planned time. It was a blustery day and we had noted the earlier weather forecast that warned of gales the following day. With all of the excitement and activity leading up to our departure, we weren't going to push hard today. It was predominantly a comfortable, downwind sail. The four of us chatted in the cockpit and took turns to helm. We followed a course that avoided the deep-water shipping channel used by the cruise ships and tankers. Once around Gilkicker Point we were soon entering Portsmouth Harbour. We radioed ahead and found a berth at Gosport Marina.

The following day Mike's blog read: 'Progress – none expected today. One crew member (Rob) sick with stomach infection. Weather – gales and rain. Outlook grim. Whose idea was this?' Rob spent most of the day close to the heads where he could vomit as 'tidily' as possible! The rest of us went for a walk, shopped for milk and groceries, bought newspapers, read and watched TV. We did a few jobs – Roger was hauled up the mast to clean the spreaders and attach halyards from which we could fly courtesy flags. We also hoisted Mike's Vice-Commodore ensign from Stafford Coastal Cruising Club.

The marina at Gosport had two interesting features. The first of these was the old lightship, the Mary Mouse 2, which had been transformed into a novel shower block and bar. The second was the little navy vessel *Medusa*, moored next to the lightship. It had been used to guide the landing craft to Omaha beach during the D-Day landings. A small boat but with a big place in history!

We all felt somewhat fraudulent. For all of the trumpeting of our grand circumnavigation and our wonderful send-off, we had not travelled very far. Things were already going awry!

By Tuesday Rob was feeling better, which was a relief. It was still blowing a cold wind but the sun was making a decent effort. The forecast was a force 6 from the west. Another yacht left the marina in the morning with three reefs in its mainsail. We decided that we would leave after lunch, despite some misgivings about the conditions that we might find outside the harbour.

In order to reassure crew in circumstances such as these we often tell them, 'We can just go out and take a look and if we don't like what we find we can return!' Now we tried the same tactic on ourselves but still felt apprehensive. Although large waves were forecast, the wind would be from the west so it would be behind us as we sailed to Brighton, our next stop. A downwind 'run' would be the most comfortable point of sail. We motored out of the harbour and beyond, past the old sea forts that guard the Eastern Solent and we unrolled our headsail. Immediately, the boat was powered up and we were moving at over six knots, the normal cruising speed for *Blue Star*.

For yachts navigating eastwards along this part of the coast there are two possible choices for rounding Selsey Bill, the peninsula that projects into the English Channel between Chichester Harbour and Bognor Regis. One might argue that the safest route is to head well offshore, beyond the rocky shallows and out to the Owers south cardinal buoy which marks the extent of the shallows. Unfortunately, that route adds several extra miles to the journey – the Owers being seven miles southeast of the Bill. We chose, instead, the alternative route through the Looe Channel, inshore of the rocky shallows area. In strong wind against tide conditions, ferocious waves can be generated in the Looe Channel and these can spell trouble for small boats. Fortunately, we had planned our passage so that the tide was in our favour and in the same direction as the wind. Even so, there remained for us the problem of finding the area with sufficient depth. It is marked by red and green buoys, between which yachts must pass in order to navigate the deepest water. The marks were partially obscured by the waves and we had to pay careful attention to ensure that we spotted them in good time.

Once past the Looe Channel we were able to alter course further to port and head straight towards Brighton. Our speed had been building steadily and with the course alteration the wind was now almost directly from behind. *Blue Star* accelerated to eleven and a half knots, by far the fastest we had sailed her. In fact, it proved to be the fastest sailing we did in the entire circumnavigation. The sailing was exhilarating, though a little unnerving, so we rolled away some of the headsail in order to reduce speed and improve control. We shot past Bognor Regis, Littlehampton and Shoreham in no time at all. Arriving at Brighton Marina we found a berth near the exit walkway and close to the showers. It had been a memorable sailing day. We'd travelled at a tremendous speed but it had been rather 'up-and-down' and very cold. In the end we were relieved to arrive.

It was a chilly night. Mike 'slept' in his clothes with a thick quilt. The other crew also commented on how cold it was. This was not part of the plan!

On Wednesday it was Mike's turn to be ill. Very ill. So ill in fact that he didn't want to put to sea, despite good sailing conditions. Apologising to the crew, he suggested they might like to spend a day ashore and leave him to nurture a much closer relationship with the heads. It was a dismal day for him, but by the evening, starting to feel better, he summoned up enough energy to take a shower. The rest of the crew, meanwhile, had a pleasant day ashore, wandering around the shops near to the marina and taking the narrow-gauge railway into town.

By Thursday morning there was still a strong wind blowing but we were fit and ready to resume our journey. Brighton Marina gave due recognition to our quest to raise funds for charity and didn't charge us for our stay. We were very grateful.

We left the marina with some commotion. The wind was blowing very strongly and pinning us to the pontoon. Ordinarily this would not have been a problem, we would simply have motored forward against a bow spring which would have the effect of forcing the stern away from the pontoon despite the wind. We would then have swiftly engaged reverse gear before the stern was blown back. On this occasion, however, we were on the far end of an almost closed 'box' of pontoons, with many other boats around and very little room to manoeuvre. We were concerned that we would be blown onto one of the other yachts once we had engaged reverse gear. We discussed our strategy. One option was to warp the boat into a suitable position for escape – that is to use ropes and winch the boat into an acceptable orientation. After some discussion we decided that this was not necessary, a huge amount of trouble and too time-consuming. And so it was, for entirely the wrong reasons, we decided that a bow spring would fit the bill perfectly! On the first attempt we were almost certainly going to blow back onto the yacht behind as we tried to reverse out. We aborted the operation at the very last moment. We also tried using a stern spring to get the bow pointing out; that attempt was aborted too when a collision with the boat in front seemed inevitable. After a further meeting of the ship's officers (Mike and Roger) we decided on a third attempt using a bow spring once more. This time we gave it full throttle, both in getting the stern pointing out and swiftly engaging reverse gear. Simultaneously we used the bow thruster to encourage the boat to turn stern to wind. Our trajectory took us very close indeed to another yacht and our high engine revs prompted people nearby to watch our work. It was a close-run thing and could easily have ended in a monumental bill! This time we got away with it. Hopefully the onlookers were impressed with our boat handling and judgement. Still, another time perhaps the warping method might be worth further consideration. You live and learn. In any instance we were on our way again, at last.

The trip to Eastbourne, our next destination, was far less demanding than the trip to Brighton. The sun put in an appearance as we sailed past Newhaven. Newhaven is predominantly a commercial port from where cross-channel ferries depart, bound for Le Havre and Dieppe. The passing yacht needs to be prepared to take action to avoid a possible collision but no such action was called for this time.

We sailed on towards the high, white cliffs of Beachy Head. They jut out from the coast, forming a headland where tidal currents are sometimes reversed as you pass from one side to the other. We were careful to take this into account in our planning.

Beachy Head is a very picturesque part of Britain's coast, equally impressive and in some ways similar to the white cliffs of Dover. The highest chalk sea cliffs in Britain, at 162 metres above sea level, stood majestically towering above us. We passed the lighthouse that is built on the rocky shoreline at the foot of the cliffs, a white column with a broad red stripe around it. We could just make out the insect-like silhouettes of people walking the clifftop. It was a sobering thought that many people chose this site to end their lives by jumping. Ironic that so much tragedy besets such a beautiful place.

From Brighton to Eastbourne is only 19 miles, so it had been an easy day for us. Getting into Eastbourne Marina entails passing through a sea lock at the end of a dredged channel, the lock opening every half hour. It is one giant marina divided into four pools that are linked together by mini canals. We were instructed to moor at a location which luckily was convenient for the shower block. The marina is a modern complex, featuring high-rise apartment blocks, restaurants, shops and a nearby supermarket. An interesting feature is that at high water the sea level outside the lock can be higher than inside the marina – in the unlikely event of the sea lock failing to hold back the tide, the ground floor of the surrounding apartment blocks would be flooded!

Friday, 22 May, Roger had to leave the crew for a few days to attend a family gathering. Rob was 'promoted' to first mate. We left Eastbourne with just the three of us on board bound for Dover. It was a sunny day and a force 3 wind drove us along the flat sea past Hastings (the town not the crewmate!) with its quiet seafront homes and pier, and on towards the next headland at Dungeness.

The seafront at Dungeness features several miles of cobble beach, holiday cottages and a nuclear power station. More recently, wind turbines have been built close to the seafront. The old lighthouse, obscured by the power station, still stands, despite being decommissioned. The new lighthouse is closer to the sea. This stretch of the coast is rather bleak, but nevertheless a popular holiday area. There is warm water from the power station and a nearby sewerage outlet; together they create an oasis for sea life!

After the headland we were able to sail directly for Dover, passing the port of Folkestone. By the time we arrived, the tide was running strongly in our favour and we had to use full engine power to avoid being swept past the harbour entrance. Dover is one of the busiest ports in the world with a constant flow of craft, mostly car ferries crossing to and from France. The French port of Calais is only 21 miles away, this being the narrowest stretch of the English Channel.

Yachts are required to contact port control when two miles away and await permission to enter. Once through the western entrance, an inner seaway to the left is partitioned off from the main area by a concrete wall; yachts need to take this lane to access the marina. We had an on-board dinner and went for a shower. The showers at Dover Marina were portacabins, not particularly impressive but adequate.

The question of showers and toilets was one which *Blue Star*'s crew became obsessed with during the voyage. Although we had a heads cabin on board, it was rather cramped. There was inevitably a certain lack of privacy, with thin 'walls' separating the cabins. We felt particularly aware of this when we had ladies on board. We were always very pleased when we put in to a port with clean spacious toilets and showers. We even considered constructing a 'league table'!

Roger had planned to re-join the crew at Ramsgate, our next destination. In the morning the passage plan to Ramsgate was discussed with Rob and Hastings. We would be sailing past the notorious Goodwin Sands (nothing to do with Mike!), shallows on which many a ship has foundered. It is an area that needs to be treated with great respect. As we prepared to depart, down came a thick mist and the weather turned generally damp and 'yuk'! Visibility deteriorated significantly. Suddenly the thought of negotiating the Goodwin Sands didn't seem a good idea. The trip was cancelled at the eleventh hour. Hastings had planned to leave the crew at Ramsgate but now, after helping us with the refuelling, he left from Dover instead.

Hastings:

It was great to attend the launch event. It was inspirational to see so many people committed to the *Blue Star* venture for such an important cause. After that great send-off, I had then had to cope with returning to sailing after several years away from the sport. Roger and Mike were both skilled hands and it led to one of the most relaxing and enjoyable weeks of sailing that I've experienced. We made our way round the South Coast, waters I'd last sailed during my time in the Royal Navy, so for me it was also a bit of a nostalgia trip. I was sad to leave the boat in Dover but it had been a great week. I knew then that the combination of Mike's and Roger's sailing skills and excellent preparation would lead to the success of the project and it was an enormous pleasure for me to have been just a small part of it.

After Hastings' departure we discovered that the drain from the holding tank had become blocked. In the past, toilets on yachts discharged directly into the sea. Modern yachts are built with holding tanks into which the sewerage is pumped from the toilet. These need to be emptied when several miles offshore. Ours was full! It had not drained and the outlet was blocked! The volume of paper used when Rob and Mike were sick was probably to blame. Small pieces of toilet paper can usually be pumped through marine heads. From this point on, however, we insisted on toilet paper being disposed of separately.

Now we turned our attention to fixing the holding tank.

Mike:

Phase 1 - *Blue Star* had an inspection hatch on the tank which could be unscrewed. It was going to be an easy task to open this and fish out any obstruction. Not so! The first problem was that the 'fluid' level inside the tank was above the level of the inspection panel. Any attempt to unscrew it would result in a substantial helping of sewerage being deposited on the cabin floor. Hmmm! There was a holding tank pump-out facility adjacent to the fuel station. With the boat alongside it we unscrewed the stainless-steel cap on our side-deck, inserted a giant hosepipe and switched on the pump. A very impressive sucking noise could be heard. It took a while, because of excess air, before any 'fluid' was extracted. Eventually, though, the pump did its job.

Phase 2 – Check that everything works. We pumped more water into the holding tank, expecting it to flow out. Unfortunately, we could see that the fluid level was rising. We hadn't cleared the blockage. Drat!

Phase 3 – There was a fluid-level sensor at the top of the tank. We needed something to poke down the hole into which it screwed, to clear the blockage at the bottom of the tank. It needed to be firm enough to poke with, but flexible enough to bend a little around corners. But what?

I set out for Dover town centre, a 'man on a mission'. Despite my best efforts I failed to find a hardware store to supply the required implement. Wandering around Poundland, feeling gloomy, I spotted the 'something' I was looking for. It was a 'Little Miss Princess Twirling Baton' - a plastic baton with a bell, a nice coloured ball attached to one end and lovely coloured sparkly streamers! I wasn't too fussed about the bell or the streamers but the plastic baton might just come in handy for another function. I proudly showed my purchase to Rob but received back a blank stare.

Phase 4 – Togged up in protective suit and rubber gauntlets, I made an assault on the blockage with my baton. It didn't quite reach the outlet. We were going to have to remove the inspection hatch.

Phase 5 – After much persuasion with mallet and drift we got it to move the smallest amount. Eventually, persistence paid off and the hatch was off. I still couldn't reach the blockage but ... with the 'trusty twirling stick', and a few more pokes, the outlet was located. A little slurping noise ensued. One more, big prod and whoosh! Blockage cleared! Hurrah for the Little Miss Princess Twirling Baton! But where was it? Oh no! It had slipped out of my hand and was still in the tank, blocking it up. Fortunately, the lovely ball on the end had prevented it sliding into the outlet and it was retrieved.

We cleaned up everything, disinfected every surface we could see, and disposed of the suit and gauntlets. I think I was reasonably clean but went for a shower anyway. Thank goodness that 'simple' job was done!

✳✳✳

Joke

Two guys set up a business making yachts in their attic. Sails are going through the roof!

✳✳✳

Left: Mike 'togged up' ready to clear the heads with his 'twirling baton'

4. Dover to Harwich

It was a quarter to six, on the morning in June
When the little ships took to sea
Loaded with men of all nations
The 'Vanguard', to set the world free

Anonymous, 'Little Ships'

Sunday, 24 May. Crew-change day and still in Dover rather than Ramsgate. Rob left for home, intending to join us again later in the voyage, and new crew arrived in the form of Steve Gould. Steve was an IT consultant who had sailed with us before, always extremely helpful and fun to sail with. Roger was back for his first week of the voyage as skipper, Mike stepping down to first mate.

It was satisfying being the skipper, forming a passage plan and working with the crew to see it through. It is where the buck stops though; it's the captain who is held accountable in law, so it is a position of responsibility. We enjoyed it when the other was the captain too. Freedom from being in charge means not worrying as much! Invariably, whoever was first mate would check the passage plan. If they reached the same conclusion about tidal heights, tidal streams and other information it would give us extra confidence.

In the evening we decided to pump more water through the holding tank to check that it was still working, expecting to see it drain freely once the valve was opened. Oh! B ...! Blocked again! It would have to wait until the morning.

Monday, another assault on the holding tank. Perhaps a twirling baton was not the choice of professionals in this business. We needed a 'proper' piece of hosepipe. The only place in town selling hosepipe was closed. In Halfords we espied a syphoning tool which incorporated a length of plastic hose.

Mike, this time kitted out in washing-up gloves and plastic bags, thrust the syphoning tool into the tank. It refused to play its part. He was now close to despair. Steve and Roger, using their initiative, came up with the perfect solution. Lurking innocently behind the rubbish bins was ... a STICK. Cut to size, the stick was put to work and ... hey presto!

45

The slurping and whooshing sound we all loved to hear. Tank empty. We were so pleased with the performance of the stick that it was added to our ship's tools and stored in the cockpit locker for the remainder of the voyage.

At last we were ready to go, and go we did. The conditions for navigating through the Goodwin Sands had improved. We would be able to see the buoys that indicate the safe routes – better than relying solely on navigation by electronics. Ramsgate lay about 15 miles away, so nothing too arduous. Since the advent of GPS, navigation is much safer but still requires great care, especially where we were about to sail. Even in recent times yachts have been stranded on the Sands and needed assistance. We did not plan to be one of them.

We left Dover early in the afternoon, radioing port control for permission to pass out to sea, exiting the eastern entrance under engine and mainsail. Following the coast to the east, the first five miles is generally unproblematic. A decision must then be made as to which side to pass round the large 'South Calliper' of the Sands.

To the east lies clear deep water, but this is also closer to the commercial shipping lanes and results in a far longer passage to Ramsgate. To the west, hugging the coast, about half a mile wide and west of the 'Brake' section of the Sands, lies the Ramsgate Channel. It is suitable for small craft but requires careful calculation of tidal heights during the passage. The charted depth, being only around two metres, leaves very little to spare! We opted for the middle route, the Gull Stream, passing between the shallows of South Calliper and Brake.

Bearing left, our course took us to the Goodwin Fork south cardinal buoy and then the red buoy, Downs, which marked the entrance to the Gull Stream. We continued 'buoy hopping' until we reached the red mark called Brake. From here the Gull Stream continues in a north-easterly direction, ideal for deeper draught commercial vessels, but now to the west of it there was enough depth for us to navigate safely. We headed north and after about three miles reached the buoys, arranged east to west, that guide shipping into Ramsgate Harbour.

Ramsgate was a main ferry terminal for the transport of cars and people to Belgium until the collapse of the service in 2013. The infrastructure of a large commercial ferry port was still very much in existence, including the procedure requiring us to radio ahead for permission to enter, despite there being no large vessels around. We could not help but be bemused by this, although there are plans to restore the ferry service.

Our visit coincided with the 75th anniversary of the evacuation of the British Army from the beaches of Dunkirk during the Second World War. In May 1940 the situation seemed hopeless as German forces closed in on the Allies. The Royal Navy was unable to get ships close enough to the shore to enable the troops to embark. All seemed lost until Churchill launched 'Operation Dynamo' in which owners of small vessels with shallow draught were asked to form a fleet of boats capable of evacuating large numbers of men from the beaches. Almost the whole of the British Army was saved as, over eight days, more than 800 'Little Ships' repeatedly ferried servicemen from the beaches to naval vessels offshore, whilst under enemy fire from land and air. An astonishing achievement!

To mark the anniversary, many 'Little Ships' re-enacted the crossing to France and had now returned and gathered in Ramsgate. We had been warned that because of the re-enactment there would be no room at Ramsgate. However, we found the marina busy, but no busier than many South Coast marinas and we had no great difficulty in finding a berth.

We were captivated looking at the 'Little Ships' in the marina. One in particular left us awestruck. The 54-foot long *New Britannic*, an old open-decked motor vessel, had not ventured far from the coast around Ramsgate before 1940. A small board next to her explained:

'In May 1940 New Britannic under Capt. Walter Read, his 15 yr old son Joe & deck hand, Bill Mathews, rescued 3,000 British & Allied soldiers off the beaches of Dunkirk.'

It was an incredible story. We guessed that many of the other vessels gathered in Ramsgate that day had similar stories behind them. We could not help but marvel at the heroism of all involved.

On Tuesday there was brilliant sunshine as we departed. We were bound for Queenborough on the River Swale, which loops around the Isle of Sheppey from the Thames to the River Medway. We delighted in the brisk wind powering *Blue Star* along. It lasted an hour. After that, a course change put the wind on the nose, useless for us. On came the 'iron horse' to help out but at least the sun continued on what became a fascinating day.

Once in the Thames Estuary, instead of heading directly to Queenborough, we navigated past the derelict Red Sands Fort, an example of a 'Maunsell fort'. Seven steel towers, armed and armoured, were built out at sea to defend the capital against German air attack during World War Two. Each tower, mounted atop four huge steel legs, looked like some beast from H. G. Wells's *The War of the Worlds*, silent and menacing. The towers were once connected by metal walkways, but these have long since collapsed. We ghosted past them, dwarfed by the structures that were now almost entirely orange-red with rust, deserted and desolate. It was sobering to think about what life must have been like for servicemen stranded out in the Thames Estuary and under attack from the air! After the war the fort was decommissioned although subsequently, in the 1960s, it was used by several pirate radio stations. Moves were once made to remove what is left but were dropped on the grounds of cost, and so it remains, a sinister reminder of the past.

A delicious bacon and egg lunch was served up by Steve as we motored on further. Working our way to the south bank of the Thames we entered the River Medway. Here lies the wreck of the liberty ship SS *Richard Montgomery*, yet another reminder of the war. Liberty ships were of simple design, intended for low cost, mass production so they could be used in numbers to keep Britain supplied during the war. SS *Richard Montgomery* left Philadelphia in August 1944 loaded with over 6,000 tons of munitions. She anchored in the Thames Estuary to await the formation of a convoy to Cherbourg, the port having come under Allied control in July 1944. The harbourmaster ordered that she berth at the Great Nore anchorage. In a gale she dragged her anchor and ran aground on a sandbank, breaking her back as the tide went down. An effort was made to remove the cargo but it was abandoned after the ship broke apart; it was considered too dangerous to resume the work. The large amount of unexploded ordnance on board means the vessel is listed as a 'dangerous wreck'. She has an exclusion zone around her marked by a series of yellow buoys. According to one report, if the ship were to explode, a 300-metre wide column of water and wreckage would be blown three kilometres into the air. It would also cause a tidal wave five metres high and damage nearly every building in nearby Sheerness! Spontaneous explosion of the ship is still considered to be a possibility, albeit a remote one. As we navigated through the entrance to the Medway, the three dark, rusted, barnacled masts, tilting at an angle out of the sea, gave the scene a chilling air of danger.

The Medway continues inland towards Chatham and beyond, but that was not our route. A short distance past the wreck we turned left into the River Swale. Queenborough was now visible. Here the industrial landscape gave way to housing and commercial property. The town lay to our left; to our right was deserted marshy scrubland.

Queenborough Harbour has many moorings, some available for visitors, and we were soon tied up. A lady in charge of a small dinghy with an outboard sped towards us. Yvonne, a volunteer from the yacht club, ran the water taxi and would ferry us to the main pontoon once we were ready. From there we could walk ashore. A short while later we were strolling through the town and sampling the beer at a pub, seated at the outdoor tables overlooking the Swale. A brilliant red sky lit the world as the sun set.

A local told us about the 'unused marshy land' on the other side of the river. Over 200 years ago, floating prison ships were moored off Sheppey. Men and boys who died of contagious diseases whilst aboard the ships were buried amongst the marshes on Deadman's Island. Their corpses were entombed in unmarked coffins, in six feet of mud, and are being slowly uncovered by the tide. The public are not allowed to land on Deadman's Island (who would want to!). There is no plan to re-bury the dead, their remains being slowly washed away by the sea!

We returned to *Blue Star* in good time, before Yvonne knocked off. Back on board Steve cooked a tasty stir-fry meal which we consumed gratefully! We were not aware of the macabre history of Deadman's Island when we picked up our mooring buoy just off the marshland, but we certainly thought about it as we tried to get to sleep that night! Was that tapping noise we could hear just the halyard blowing against the mast, or something else?

At 0800 hours the following morning we dropped the mooring buoy and motored back towards the Medway and the Thames, bound for Burnham-on-Crouch. It was bright with a good wind in the Medway; we hoisted sail enthusiastically and made our way out to the Thames, whereupon all signs of wind disappeared! It became another motoring day, but very pleasant all the same. Over towards the north bank we spotted what looked like a large pinnacle of dark rock in the middle of the Thames and we scoured the chart to check what it might be. We couldn't identify it so we went closer to get a better look. As we did, the 'rock' transformed into the silhouette of a Thames sailing barge, complete with large mast and sails!

Following the coast, we passed the town of Shoeburyness. A Ministry of Defence (MOD) firing range is based nearby and Roger radioed to check it was safe for us to pass. 'Yes and no' came the reply. Very helpful! An explanation followed – we should proceed and if firing was imminent then a guarding motor launch would soon be alongside to warn us. That at least would prevent us getting a shell through our mainsail! We motored on and were not visited by the patrol boat.

At Foulness Point we turned to port and into the River Crouch. It was busy, with several other craft passing up or down the river. About four miles upriver is a junction with the River Roach. It looked like a scenic setting and ideal for a lazy day at anchor, but we hadn't got time to linger. Onward we motored for another few miles before arriving at Burnham Yacht Harbour to starboard. It was a tight turn into the marina and some nifty manoeuvring was needed to get into our berth, but we were soon relaxing with a celebratory drink!

Strong winds were forecast for the earlier part of Thursday and so in the morning we ambled into the town and picked up supplies. Walking past one of the houses we noticed a rather splendid laburnum tree. We were most amused with ourselves when we realised that it was a 'Burnham laburnum'!

We chatted with a couple of 'old sea dogs' on the hard. When they learnt of our next destination, Bradwell, they told us about a handy shortcut which would save us hours. Back on board we re-studied the charts. Indeed, there was a gulley, but of unknown depth and unclear location! It cut north through the sandbanks towards the end of the river and would certainly be navigable at a high spring tide. After a team consultation we decided that, for us, it would be risky without detailed local knowledge. We didn't intend running aground and we stuck with our plan to pass around the Sands.

We moved on after lunch, but it was an effort to get out of our berth because of the wind and the tight spot we were in. Nevertheless, with carefully organised lines we warped the boat into the position needed for departing. (Perhaps we had learnt from our Brighton experience!) Finally, we slipped lines bound for Bradwell, around 18 miles away.

It was a blustery day. We followed the river downstream to the mouth of the Crouch. We passed a 'pole' projecting from the sea on our port. We speculated that it might have marked the location of the shortcut, but we were not tempted. At the river mouth, once past the sandbanks, we turned north to Sales Point and then into the River Blackwater.

Bradwell nuclear power station stood guard at the river mouth and a short distance upstream was the entrance to the marina. There was little room to manoeuvre inside, no staff around and no reply to our VHF call. Eventually we found a berth. How to plug in to shore-power and gain access to the shower block? Thankfully there were some very helpful skippers on the other boats.

Arriving at Bradwell reminded us of our earlier visit to see a different boat, before we bought *Blue Star*. The boat was good but the price was wrong and the deal didn't go through. The boat was still 'For Sale'! Perhaps the owner had no real intention of selling.

Mike:

I recall my trip home after viewing the boat. It began at a rail terminus, a remote station in the middle of nowhere. There was only one other man in the carriage as my travelling companion, with a large fierce-looking dog. We glanced at each other and nodded 'good morning'. Man and dog got off a few stations later and the ticket collector came by to see that I'd paid. 'Did you realise who you were travelling with?' says the collector, making conversation. 'No' says I, 'Who was it?' The man was once the most notorious armed robber in the country. He spent many years in prison but was now a reformed character. My knees trembled a little and I was glad I hadn't given cause for offence!

Gales were forecast for Friday morning and so we decided not to sail. Instead, a walk into town sounded like a good idea. Bradwell Marina is some distance from the village, so it was a long hike along country lanes. We found a small store and were able to pick up supplies. Back at base Steve cooked us yet another meal, chilli, and we called at the marina restaurant to taste their coffee and puddings. The cat residing there bounded over tables, chairs and customers, but was very friendly and loved attention. It had rained for much of the day. Staying put had been the correct decision.

51

Steve was proving most adept in the galley, which was excellent! During our voyage we encouraged all crew members to join in with the domestic activities. The preparation of meals was felt to be crucial. The general organisation was for each crew member to cook one evening meal. With typically five on board and one evening reserved for a meal ashore this worked out well. With our diverse crew, some, like Steve, had great culinary skills and some were not sure what happened between the supermarket and the plate! We did sometimes 'allow' the real cooks to practise for more than one evening to everyone's delight. The bonus of being the chef for the evening was that you were excused washing-up duties. Those with experience in caravans proved most adept at efficient utilisation of the boat's galley. With just two burners, no grill and only a small oven, it was all about planning and juggling the individual components of the meal.

Saturday. The rain of the previous day had passed and given way to sunshine once more, but a cold wind blew. A pattern was evolving of regular cold winds blowing from the direction in which we wanted to travel. Although there were odd days that didn't follow this trend, it was nonetheless one which was to plague us for much of the first year of our voyage.

Our destination, Shotley Marina off Harwich Harbour, lay 32 miles away. We put on the engine once more. We could have tacked to and fro against the wind and under sail alone but it would have taken much longer to get there. It proved to be an easy 'sail'. A few miles off Clacton-on-Sea the wind dropped down a gear while the sun strengthened and we polished off the remains of the chilli from the previous evening, taking turns sitting down below where it didn't blow cold. We sailed on past the sleepy seaside towns of Frinton-on-Sea and Walton-on-the-Naze. A short while later we were through the sea lock at Shotley Marina and safely berthed.

From the marina we could look out across the River Stour to Harwich; behind the town lay the North Sea. To our left was the River Orwell, joining with the Stour as the two rivers flowed out to sea. On the opposite bank of the Orwell huge silhouettes of strange-looking animals dominated the skyline as the sun went down, the modern cranes of Felixstowe Docks. Felixstowe is the busiest container port in Britain, handling four million containers per year, from three thousand ships.

Shotley was the first stopping point. We left *Blue Star* and returned to our families. It would be two weeks before we resumed our voyage.

***

Joke
Two men in a kayak were out on the sea. It was rather cold so they decided to light a fire in their kayak. The craft caught fire and sank. It just goes to show you can't have your kayak and heat it!

***

Above: The *New Britannic* which rescued 3,000 British and Allied troops off the beaches of Dunkirk in 1940

Above: Red Sands Fort in the Thames Estuary (photo courtesy of Russ Garrett)

Left: Steve knocks up bacon sandwiches for the crew

Above: Yvonne takes us ashore at Queenborough

Below: Sunset looking from Queenborough across the River Swale

5. Harwich to Grimsby

It is not the going out of port, but the coming in,
that determines the success of a voyage.

Henry Ward Beecher

Mike:
Whilst *Blue Star* was at Shotley, Diane and I used the boat as a base for touring the area. We discovered that a 'classic' car rally was being staged on the seafront, a regular event. A trip down memory lane, we saw an Anglia, a Capri, a Triumph Stag, an early Volvo and many others, all in exceptional condition! We visited Flatford Mill, Dedham, Aldeburgh, Orford Ness and Woodbridge – all very charming places.

I carried out some work on the boat's engine, examining the water-fuel separator and doing the regular maintenance checks. Unfortunately, or perhaps fortunately, I spotted a water leak from the engine, a regular drip into the bilge. The cooling water pump was identified as the culprit and the nearby 'Marine Services' fixed it by replacing the bearings and seals, carrying out an excellent job. *Blue Star* was ready to go again!

***

On Sunday, 16 June we travelled back to resume our voyage. We had three new crewmates. Chris, a retired 747 pilot, had sailed with us in the Solent as we familiarised ourselves with our new boat. We had also sailed with Chris during the occasional charter and knew that he would be helpful and fun to have on board. Geoff and Margaret Haylock were fellow members of Stafford Coastal Cruising Club. They had spent a few nights on board *Blue Star* soon after we bought her. We had planned to take them for a sail in the Solent as part of our sea trials. Unfortunately, the weather had been so bad that we never left the marina. Now they had come to spend a week with us, which was great! We all gathered together in the afternoon and loaded our kit onto the boat. Later, Margaret cooked a delicious hot meal for us all!

The next day we decided to explore the Rivers Orwell and Stour instead of continuing the journey north. It was too good an opportunity to miss. We locked out of the marina and turned into the River Orwell. With the wind behind us it was a very pleasant sail and in sunshine too! The river afforded excellent views, the riverbank being lined with green fields and trees. We passed the Royal Harwich Yacht Club on port, close to Woolverstone Marina. Beyond, the river passes underneath the A14 Orwell road bridge with plenty of clearance for masts, and onwards to Ipswich. At Ipswich Docks we rolled away the headsail and motored back downriver against the wind, enjoying a picnic lunch on deck whilst under way.

Back near Harwich, sail was set once more as we left Shotley Marina to starboard and headed up the River Stour. The Stour had a different character altogether – large mudflats on each side and an industrial heritage hinted at by several old, abandoned wharves. By the time we reached Wrabness Point the weather was beginning to change and rain was felt occasionally. We turned on the engine and motor-sailed back to Shotley. It had been an enjoyable day, capped off by a pasta Bolognese dinner followed by strawberries, cream and shortbread biscuits, all prepared by Margaret!

Tuesday. We departed the marina at 0930 hours. As we were passing through the lock we were summoned quickly back to the marina office. What could be the problem? The staff had remembered that we were circumnavigating Britain for charity and wanted to re-calculate our bill for the two-week stay at the marina. The initial payment was made void and a new invoice presented instead, totalling zero pounds! A wonderful way of showing support for us.

In the river mouth there were a few ships passing out to sea, having exchanged their cargo at Felixstowe. We gave them a good offing and headed out behind them. Once at sea we followed the East Anglian coast heading north. There was very little wind and so it was engine on. We were heading for Lowestoft, about 50 miles away. Our route took us past the River Deben Estuary and along the shingle coast towards Aldeburgh and then on past Southwold.

We decided on bacon sandwiches for lunch, Mike doing the honours. The swell was building up and creating unpleasant conditions for anyone down below trying to cook. Still, up on deck the sandwiches were met with universal approval!

A couple of hours later Lowestoft came into view. There was a tide running and large waves had built up as we prepared to enter the harbour. The pilot book warns 'do not attempt an entrance in strong east or northeast winds, especially with wind against tide' when 'heavy seas can build up'. We had got wind at this point in the passage. It was from the north, but fortunately not too strong. Even so, the waves were making life difficult!

Mike:
There is a potentially dangerous sandbank off Lowestoft – Newcombe Sand – which first has to be negotiated. We took the advice of the pilot book, picking up the East Barnard cardinal buoy and then proceeding north to the red lateral buoy, Newcombe Sand. Leaving that to port we turned due west to point towards the harbour entrance. At least that is what our chart plotter told us – but where was it? We knew it must be there but we couldn't see it. There seemed to be just a sea wall lining the coast with no harbour entrance! But there must be one! It would be damned inconvenient if the authorities had decided to move it!

We decided to proceed slowly, as though the entrance was exactly where it was supposed to be, all the time being bounced around by the waves. The pilot book explains that conditions can be 'lively' and we were certainly seeing that! Slowly the entrance came into view and we breathed a sigh of relief. We were still not out of the woods though. It looked incredibly narrow. The harbour walls seemed hard and threatening; a large wave might dash us against them. It would be a desperate situation if the engine were to fail us part way through our entry. Anyway, we had to go for it! With full engine power we made it through. We could breathe easily again. Inside the harbour, it was rather compact, with little room for manoeuvring a yacht. We managed nonetheless, turning hard to port to enter the Royal Norfolk and Suffolk Yacht Club Marina and tie up. It was late afternoon but we were in!

Roger recalls:
The approach to Lowestoft Harbour on the Suffolk coast looked on the chart to be fairly straightforward. As a historic port, strongly linked to the fishing industry in days gone by and supporting the offshore gas business in recent years, it was well founded. However, we had been beating up the coast for several hours against a northerly wind on the nose! We now had the challenge of entering a narrow, east-facing

harbour entrance. With the sails stowed it was important to set up the boat to cater for the wind and the current. Mike was at the helm, and with our 30hp engine working hard we passed safely through between the rocky walls to berth in the shelter of the yacht club. Although it was mid-summer, the yacht club was quiet and without too much nautical atmosphere. I can, however, report that the club facilities were excellent!

The East Coast has always been a raiding ground for foreign powers and so it was in June 1665, when during the Second Anglo-Dutch War, a conflict took place about 40 miles east of Lowestoft. With Mike's Dutch heritage and Roger's English lineage it was appropriate to look up this piece of naval history. A fleet of more than 100 Dutch ships commanded by Lieutenant-Admiral Jacob van Wassenaer attacked an English fleet of similar proportions led by James, Duke of York. The English were deemed to have won. However, two years later under a new commander, Michiel de Ruyter, the Dutch sailed right up the Thames and very embarrassingly wrought havoc with the English fleet in the Medway.

With a single overnight stop planned in Lowestoft we were pleased to welcome friends, John and Linda Brook, on board for an evening drink. John would be joining us for a week further up the East Coast.

The following day we set out north once more, bound for Wells-next-the-Sea on the Norfolk coast, a distance of 66 miles. The wind was from the west, force 3 to 4, which suited us well initially, putting us on a beam reach. We blasted along in the early sun, sticking close to the shore and finding a route between the mainland and the wind farm off to starboard. We saw service boats taking maintenance staff out to the turbines and watched as they disembarked onto the structures, seemingly a hazardous exercise! Following the coast, we slowly turned to head in a westerly direction and so most of the afternoon was spent motor-sailing against the wind. The weather deteriorated later, a fine and persistent rain setting in.

We had discussed the option of visiting Wells; Roger was not too enthusiastic, having lived nearby and knowing something of the hazards; however, he was persuaded. The timing would need to be right. Things were getting a little tense in the cockpit as we were all checking our watches – we needed to arrive at the entrance just before high tide to be certain of sufficient depth to pass up the river. Were we going to make it? If not, there was no alternative harbour that could offer shelter to a fin-keeled boat of our draught, so another 60 miles at sea, through the night, would be facing us. Not really what we wanted. Finally, as high water approached so did the channel that led to Wells, bang on time. Phew!

We shaped up to pass over the bar, keeping Bob Hall's Sands to port and Cockle Hole to starboard, inching our way carefully in with Roger at the helm in full concentration mode and with pilotage plan on the console. The entrance is acknowledged to be challenging with the well-buoyed approach being constantly adjusted by the shifting sands. With dusk arriving we motored up the narrow channel, initially with plenty of water below us. We were simply passing between the red and green lateral marks out at sea, but they guided us ever closer to the sandy shore! Was there really enough depth for us to navigate the way the marks indicated? Surely, we would run aground on the beach! We found ourselves negotiating an ever-narrowing path which twisted this way and that. Once past the beach, amazingly without incident, flat marshland and scrubland were at deck level on each side of the river. On the right we could see a footpath as holidaymakers were walking from the river entrance back towards the town. At one point the channel was so narrow that we could almost step off the side-deck of the boat and onto the field alongside us. The bends in the course were incredibly sharp, so that turns of almost 90 degrees on the spot were required several times! Eventually, the waterway opened out to a harbour basin where there was enough room to turn and come alongside the marina pontoon. Despite our doubts and apprehensions we had done it!

The 'river' that we had just navigated is strictly not a river. There is no freshwater stream draining into Wells from land. Instead, reliance is made on the sea to scour out any silt from the channel that leads to the town, a mechanism that requires some assistance from man! There is also still a sand bar which must be crossed by visiting craft. Prior to crossing the bar we had called up the harbourmaster for an update on conditions and to advise him of our arrival. We were pleasantly surprised, on nearing the quay, to see him waiting to take our lines. After nearly 11 hours at sea it is so heartening to have a kind reception! That evening there was a dinner organised by Sarah Wright, from Stafford Coastal Cruising Club, who had come down with her friend from the Midlands to see us. All in all, a very convivial welcome.

The following morning, a rest day for us, we awoke to the vista of the entrance channel at low water – probably more accurately looking like a wide muddy ditch. Had we really sailed up that? Noteworthy were the channel markers hanging off the mud banks. There had indeed been no margin for error! In the afternoon we walked out to the observation point near the beach and could see more of the topography and challenges. There we spoke with the staff at the local National Coastwatch station and learnt that help was regularly needed to assist holidaymakers who left it too late when returning from the beach on the other side of the river, finding that a rising tide had cut them off.

Back at the marina we were interested to see another yacht departing just as the tide was flooding. A few hours later they were back. Unfortunately, they had run aground on the bar when their engine failed and they'd taken on a considerable amount of water. They had broadcast a mayday and told of how it felt like an eternity before help arrived. Finally, they had been towed back to the quay and had a busy day of drying out and making repairs to their engine. A salutary warning for us!

Having seen the misfortune of our fellow sailors the day before, we spent extra time and care in checking the tide and weather for our departure. We were headed towards Grimsby on the River Humber. As we departed, at a respectable hour, Sarah came to the quayside to wave us off and wish us 'bon voyage'.

Motoring down the river (ditch?) towards the sea, maximum concentration was needed once again to stay in the deep water. At the river bar, large, breaking waves threatened a grim day but we anticipated that they'd die down once away from the land. It would certainly be a very uncomfortable trip if they didn't, and it would very quickly be too late to change our minds and re-enter Wells! Fortunately, our anticipation proved right and very slowly the sea state improved. The wind was still 'on the nose' and so we continued motor-sailing.

We had to rework part of our passage plan whilst at sea. The charts showed a wind farm under construction north of Wells, with a navigable route between it and the land to the west. We found that the development extended much further west than was indicated and there was no obvious inshore route. Our revised path took us to the east instead, adding to our journey somewhat. The wind was forecast to remain force 3 gusting force 4 from the northwest, so we knew that the engine would be needed for the majority of the 60 miles to our destination. Even though this was mid-June the wind had a keen edge to it which meant we all had multiple layers of clothing and wet-weather gear to keep warm. After several hours we were due east of Skegness and the sea state settled a little more – sufficient for us to brew up and eat the sandwich lunch which Margaret and Geoff had prepared before leaving Wells. Suddenly life seemed much better!

This part of the North Sea, off the Lincolnshire coast, has become one of the major wind farm development areas with technical support services based in both Lowestoft and Wells-next-the-Sea. These are a major contributor to renewable energy in the UK and valuable for the environment. However, sailing past, it was difficult to equate them with the term 'farm'. Instead of grazing cows, gambolling lambs and green pastures, they are stark, imposing structures. They would not make a good Constable painting. Some have a 500-metre exclusion zone. Five miles off the coast of Skegness, the Lincolnshire wind farm, commissioned in 2013, has 75 turbines. The adjacent Lynn and Inner Dowsing wind farm has 54 turbines. Further to the east are the Race Bank and Docking Shoal installations. Modern 'green' technology was certainly making its presence felt on this part of the coast!

Keeping outside of the marine exclusion zones and away from the various service boats in the area was the biggest challenge of the day. The highlight of the day was lunch and the lovely homemade cakes which Margaret served up!

Our only other distraction was a change in the pitch of the engine noise which, with so many engineers on board, was studiously investigated at various throttle settings. Net result: nothing found, no conclusions, just relax and motor on!

There was very little to interest us on the flat East Coast. Roger went below mid-afternoon for a one-hour siesta and later came back on deck claiming to be warm and refreshed! Later in the afternoon Mike suggested that he make a bacon sandwich snack for everyone. There were no dissenters and the sandwiches, together with a fresh cup of tea, soon appeared on deck.

We worked our way closer to the shore, watching it slowly get bigger as we ploughed on. This long, low, sandy coastline stretches from Skegness to Mablethorpe and on to Cleethorpes at the entrance to the Humber Estuary. There, we finally had a flat sea! Ahead of us, on the other side, Spurn Head was clearly visible. A long spit of land, it stretches out southwards from the mainland and marks the northern seaward edge of the river. As the wide mouth of the Humber came into view we radioed the Vessel Tracking Service (VTS) to announce our intentions.

After gaining clearance we turned west and entered the river, leaving Spurn Head behind and passing Bull Sand Fort, the larger of two forts built during the First World War to defend the mouth of the Humber. The octagonal concrete and steel structure was originally equipped with large guns and spotlights. The armoury was upgraded during World War Two to help guard against the threat of motor torpedo boats entering the estuary. Whilst easily visible, the forts are marked by north and south cardinal buoys.

The Humber Estuary is of the order of three miles wide, albeit with shifting sandbanks which have to be carefully negotiated. Our destination, the Humber Cruising Association Marina, is 'picturesquely' located in No.1 Fish Dock, some five miles upriver.

It did seem strange, after sailing in Southampton Water with its large tankers, cruise liners, container ships, ferries, hovercraft and many pleasure craft, to have to call up to enter this broad, relatively quiet waterway.

Motoring up the river we were called by VTS who were monitoring our position, presumably by way of our AIS. They informed us that we were in the wrong position and advised us to halt and allow a ship to pass in front of us. This we did, although we found it puzzling, as there appeared to be plenty of deep water for both the ship and ourselves. After the ship had passed we turned to port and entered the docks. Double-checking later, we had indeed been in the correct position in the channel and still did not understand the concern. Later when exiting the river we used the same route and did not hear of any objections.

Access to the fish docks is through a lock. We expected it to be closed as we had arrived earlier than expected. We were delighted therefore to find the lock gates open to the free flow of vessels! However, we had not bargained on the water level being considerably higher in the river than inside the dock, far bigger than one would expect for free flow of traffic through a lock. The sea was racing through the lock and into the marina at a high rate of knots! We motored towards the lock gates and then found that it was too late to escape the clutches of the current that was suddenly flushing us through. Moments later we were propelled like a cork out of a bottle into the inner harbour. Our speed through and out of the lock was impressive. Thankfully, the helmsman, Mike, had still managed to keep us positioned precisely mid-lock, not even close to touching the sides, as we surfed through. We almost had to prise his hands off the wheel as we came into still water on the other side. We passed through No.3 Fish Dock into No.1 Fish Dock where we found a berth.

The marina was functional and not overcrowded. On the quayside was the Humber Cruising Association clubhouse. All around were tumbled-down derelict warehouses, presumably once used for processing fish. Now it all looked a rather sad and depressing eyesore. Clearly a major investment was needed to rejuvenate it.

The area is surrounded by hundreds of years of maritime history and tradition, the old fish dock having been completed in 1856. The clubhouse was very welcoming and seemed to be populated by 'grizzled old salts' who were busy planning their next trip across the North Sea to the Netherlands, Belgium, Scotland or even further afield. The following day we looked around the marina at the boats moored there. We wondered which one might be carrying the intrepid sailors at the bar on their long journeys! Or was it just the alcohol talking last night?

The region's maritime heritage was manifested by the gentle background odour of fish. Grimsby's development as a fishing port in the late 19th century was astounding. From the 1850s until 1891, its fleet expanded from one vessel to 800. The arrival of the railway in 1848 had much to do with the town's success, making it easier to transport goods to and from the port. Today the picture is very different. The government lists only a handful of fishing vessels over ten metres in length based at the port. It is a similar story at other East Coast ports. Lowestoft, which once boasted that you could walk from one side of the harbour to the other across the decks of the boats, now has only a few fishing vessels over ten metres registered there.

One of the architectural features to the west of the fish docks is the Hydraulic Accumulator Tower, built in 1854 for the Grimsby Dock Company. When navigating in the river and seeking the entrance to the docks it is helpful to use the tower, visible from several miles away, as an indicator. The square brick-built tower, over 60 metres tall, was constructed to provide high-pressure hydraulic water power to drive the lock gates and the cranes. It was superseded in 1892 by an electrically driven oil-hydraulic system that provided eight times as much power.

Grimsby has been the setting for many movies over the years. In 1937, *The Last Adventurers*, a black and white film about a skipper's daughter who falls for a humble fisherman, was filmed here. Apparently, it has many scenes of storm-lashed seas and shipwrecks. Not quite what we wanted to hear with the prospect of heading further north! More recently, *Atonement*, a British romantic war drama based on Ian McEwan's 2001 novel, was partially shot in Grimsby. The film starred James McAvoy and Keira Knightley and the Dunkirk street scenes were shot at the Grade II Listed Grimsby ice factory next to the docks. One can see why these buildings were eminently suitable!

Roger:

The following day was used for cleaning and maintenance and I thought this would be an excellent opportunity to pump up the tender and give the outboard a run. We had acquired the outboard second-hand at a very reasonable price from an old sailor in Lymington who was hanging up his 'oilies'. The tender was inflated, the outboard manoeuvred into position on the transom, fuel checked, bailer and oars prepared, lifejacket on and off I went. The docks seemed to be totally deserted. There were no craft at the lock or waiting to enter, just a couple of old trawlers against the quayside that didn't appear to be operational. All this was against a background of derelict or semi-derelict former warehouses. This vacant, inactive area made the ideal space to test the outboard and to check the tender.

All went well; there were no other vessels, either commercial or recreational, moving in the docks. After ten minutes I motored back to *Blue Star* only to be greeted by a gentleman in uniform clutching a clipboard and a VHF radio. I was told in no uncertain terms that I had violated harbour bye-laws by taking the tender into No.3 Dock without permission. Seeking to understand the issue and risks, we had an amicable, if somewhat awkward, conversation; however, I still felt suitably chastised at having contravened the local bye-laws! As we were planning to head home that day I felt it prudent not to push the matter further – who knows, we may have had the boat impounded or the crew put in the local stocks, especially as this was our second brush with officialdom at Grimsby! We secured the boat and departed for home on 21 June for a break, intending to return and continue our journey on 18 July.

Joke

In a narrow harbour entrance a red yacht hit a blue yacht - they were marooned!

***

Above: Blue Star on the quay at Wells-next-the-Sea

Below: Looking out to sea from Wells close to low water (the 'ditch' is to the right in the photograph)

6. Grimsby to Hartlepool

I must go down to the seas again, to the lonely sea and the sky,
And all I ask is a tall ship and a star to steer her by;
And the wheel's kick and the wind's song and the white sail's shaking,
And a grey mist on the sea's face, and a grey dawn breaking.

John Masefield, 'Sea Fever'

This leg was a great sail and we were fortunate to have an interesting and lively crew on board. Mike's cousin, David Allis, joined us from New Zealand, travelling further than anyone else to sail with us on *Blue Star*. Roger's friend, John Brook, who had served in the Royal Navy Reserve aboard minesweepers, provided a great source of nautical anecdotes and the local Yorkshire experience, having been born in the county. Kevin Sneddon, another member of Staffordshire Coastal Cruising Club completed the ship's complement. A retired former technology teacher, Kevin was a most useful person to have on board.

Mike:

I had been really looking forward to David joining the crew. His father, Theo, was my mother's younger brother. Both died some years ago. During the war, Theo had been sent to a workcamp when Holland was overrun by the Nazis. Mum struggled through the occupation and met my father when the Allies advanced into Amsterdam. They married and came to live in England where I was born. After the war, Theo was in the armed forces in the Dutch East Indies, now Indonesia. After demob he decided to live in New Zealand rather than return to Holland. David was born a Kiwi a few years after my birth. We had only met briefly during a few short visits he'd made to Britain. This was a chance for the two of us to get to know each other.

Roger:

In the 1990s I was a General Manager for Shell, extracting gas from the North Sea. John was an executive in a contracting company, building offshore platforms. We became very good friends as well as business colleagues. John kindly donated a bosun's whistle to *Blue Star*. Mike and I were looking forward to being piped aboard but sadly no one seemed to know how to play it!

With new crew we departed Grimsby on 20 July, slipping lines at 0900 hours bound for Scarborough. Out in the River Humber the wind blew in from the east and we motored against it, carefully adhering to the rules about shipping lanes in the river. We certainly did not want to be admonished again by Humber VTS! It was a simple passage downriver, this time leaving Spurn Head to port and passing out into the North Sea.

At this point an unexpected surprise – another wind farm, not marked on our new charts, the latest available, but blocking our planned path nonetheless! We must have missed a chart update notice. The inshore route past the installation did not seem navigable and so we had to head further out to sea to pass around it. Navigating along the edge of the exclusion zone, the VHF radio suddenly burst into life – someone was calling *Blue Star*. We answered the call only to receive a warning that we were in danger of navigating into an area that was off limits. Our third reprimand whilst in the vicinity of Grimsby! Feeling somewhat indignant we agreed to move a little further away.

Once past the wind farm we were able to work our way back towards our original route, passing Flamborough Head, an imposing headland projecting into the North Sea from the mainland just north of Bridlington. It's a chalk headland with sheer white cliffs plunging into the sea. Green shrubs clung to the steep slopes higher up the cliffs. Closer to sea level, rock stacks and arches. All very picturesque.

Navigating a short distance offshore we found ourselves surrounded by hundreds of birds, some soaring overhead and many floating on the sea until we sailed too close. Gannets, kittiwakes and puffins live and breed on the cliffs. It was a joyous moment to be at sea alongside the beautiful, majestic landscape and such rich wildlife. This was one of the highlights of our voyage. To cap it all the wind arrived to push us along and the sun showed up too. Marvellous stuff!

It could not last, however, and presently the wind disappeared and so did the sun, giving way to rain showers. We pulled up our sprayhood and the hoods on our jackets and turned on the engine to ensure that we arrived at our destination in good time. We were reminded of Simon and Garfunkel's 'Scarborough Fair' pop song and played it with our on-board iPod, and our spirits remained high.

An hour out of Scarborough we had a text message from the Commodore of Stafford Coastal Cruising Club. He was in the area and wondered what time we would be in port. It was evening when we entered the harbour and edged into a berth to see him waving to us and shouting 'WELCOME BLUE STAR!' How thoughtful of him. Unfortunately, he had to dash off and we weren't able to buy him a pint, but we were delighted by his support.

On arrival our 'Chef of the Day', Mike, had a tasty hot meal ready in the galley for when we'd tied up. Scarborough is still a quintessential English seaside town with a broad sandy beach, donkey rides and a great selection of arcades and funfairs. Built on limestone cliffs, it is probably the largest holiday resort on the Yorkshire coast. Many fishing boats were tied up in the harbour, but the town also has growing digital and creative industries. After dinner we walked ashore and along the promenade to taste a little of the atmosphere.

Mike:

Roger had us all up bright and early. Of the two of us, he was the 'lark' and I the 'owl'. I came to accept his inevitable early-morning steps on deck as I awoke in my cabin. Likewise, he lived with my late evening rustling of the newspaper and boiling of the kettle. Our body clocks were certainly at opposite ends of the spectrum in this regard, but despite such idiosyncrasies we worked well as a team.

We needed to leave at 0700 hours to make the best use of the tide for the passage to Whitby. Right on cue, the rain started, but thankfully soon stopped. A rainbow formed over the town as the wind from the south pushed us along past colourful beach huts, spectacular cliffs, rock formations and luscious vegetation. It was a wonderful feeling to be blown by the wind, close inshore, as we passed such stunning views. Excellent sailing!

We arrived in time for lunch. A bridge swings open to enable yachts to access the marina further upstream in the River Esk. We tied up at the pontoon just seaward of the bridge and waited for the operator to return from his lunch break and let us in. The town boasts an excellent marina with helpful staff and we easily found a convenient berth.

Whitby is a gem of a town, set in a stunning part of the North Yorkshire coast and with a history that compels the visitor to enquire more and stay longer than they intended. A stay here had to include a visit to the ruins of the old abbey on the headland. The abbey was used from the year 657 but was closed by Henry VIII during the dissolution of the monasteries. The walk to the ruins on the headland was very pleasant in the sun, and our reward was a commanding view over the North Sea and the dramatic architecture of the 'double' harbour wall below, guarding entry to the river. Two straight walls project outwards from the river banks, almost meeting out in the sea and hence making the entrance narrower than nature intended. Further out to sea, two extra curved walls give more protection and reduce the impact of waves striking the inner walls.

The ruins of the abbey told a story of long ago, originating in Anglo-Saxon times. The town now plays host to a regular Goth music festival and many Goths were walking around the abbey and the town in their black clothing and sporting their characteristic black hair and black make-up. They certainly gave the town a distinctive atmosphere!

Bram Stoker's famous novel, *Dracula*, is set in Whitby. In the story, Dracula's ship is wrecked and he comes ashore and sets about sucking the blood of the locals! Stoker himself visited Whitby and its abbey. The spooky ruins, steeped in religion, with bats flapping around church belfries, inspired him to write about the infamous vampire. Many visitors to the town forget that Dracula was not real!

Whitby is also known for its black 'jet' gemstone which can still be found on the seashore and excavated from the nearby cliffs. Jet is produced by the compression of decomposed wood. It's used in ornaments and jewellery and sold in many of the shops. It came to prominence during the reign of Queen Victoria who, after her husband Prince Albert died, dressed predominantly in black, with black jewellery, for the remainder of her life.

Captain James Cook (1728–1798), the legendary master mariner, was a trainee with a local shipping company. The house in which he lodged with his master is now the Captain Cook Memorial Museum. As sailors we were duty-bound to take a look! Cook sailed to the Baltic in the trading ships *Endeavour* and *Resolution*, both built in Whitby. Later he joined the Royal Navy where he was a ship's captain, sailing to the Eastern Coast of Australia in order to explore and survey it. He is widely recognised as one of our greatest-ever surveyors, sailors and explorers.

Roger had visited the town some weeks before as part of a reconnaissance mission, on a short break with Judith. Now he paved the way as tour guide. That evening, on his advice, we all made our way to the Fisherman's Wife, a delightful restaurant overlooking the sea. He'd judged it to serve one of the best fish and chip suppers on the coast!

On our way back to the boat that evening we passed a tattoo parlour and a 'cunning plan' began to form. We asked a passer-by to take a photo of us all outside the shop, intending to send the photo to our families with a suggestion that we had all been tattooed. We would await their reaction.

The following morning the idea took another twist. We went into the town and found a delightful young lady doing face painting for children on the promenade. Among her box of tricks she had some small blue stars … the plan started to come together! Soon the whole crew was lined up to have their photo taken once more, this time each of us sporting a lovely blue star on our upper arms. The ultimate team bonding. Pictures were taken and posted on email and a variety of social media. We were greeted by a mixed response. For some a storm of outrage … 'How could we', 'What on earth have they done'. Mike's daughter, on the other hand, thought it was great. We all became very attached to our 'tattoos' and were disappointed when, after a few days, they disappeared in the shower.

Fun and games over, we set sail for Hartlepool, 26 miles away, on the morning of 23 July. We hoped to drop the hook in Runswick Bay and brew up for 'elevenses'. John had recommended the bay, five miles north of Whitby, because of its spectacular coastal setting. Sadly we were unable to anchor there because the multitude of fishing-pot markers left insufficient room for a visiting yacht. Nevertheless, we were able to appreciate the splendour of the setting. The sheltered, exceedingly pretty bay hosts the red-roofed village of Runswick which stretches down to the sandy beach. Behind it stand cliffs with fir, oak and fruit trees. Once the base for a small fishing fleet, the area is now a destination for holidaymakers who are 'in the know'! John was able to locate his friends' house up on the cliff overlooking the bay, give them a call and wave to them. Meanwhile a brew was served up as we slowly motored around. After tea and biscuits we raised sail once more.

Like so many other times we found ourselves headed by the wind and we turned to the on-board engineering to propel us along.

During the final few hours the wind picked up somewhat and the sea state became rather lumpy. We were in Tees Bay, not far from our destination. Determined to do some sailing before the day was through, we turned off the engine, set some sail and tacked to and fro against the prevailing wind. Here the River Tees enters the sea and upriver is the town of Middlesbrough. Beating across the bay, eventually Hartlepool was in sight. We passed through the sea lock and entered the marina. It was modern and pleasant and we berthed without any problem.

We were now ahead of schedule and had a day in hand. Hoping to give this crew a good day of sailing before they left, we set out to sea the following morning. Once out, we sighted dolphins and they came to join us, playing around the boat and keeping us company. They seemed to be having fun, surfing and diving!

Sadly the wind disappeared and we decided to explore the River Tees. We radioed the port authority to let them know of our intentions. Middlesbrough is the main conurbation on the river and is a large post-industrial town. Its base was in steelmaking, shipbuilding and chemical industries. In the last 50 years much of this has declined. We decided to take a look. Several tankers were anchored off the river mouth, presumably waiting for permission to come alongside one of the quays. We weaved our way around them and headed upriver. Many deserted industrial buildings defined the shoreline and most of the quays were empty. We did, however, see flames shooting out from one of the complexes, presumably related to the steel industry. The presence of ships in the river showed that some industry was still active. Even so, the impression was that what had once been a mighty manufacturing region was now struggling to exist. It was a depressing thought. The town does still have a construction industry and a manufacturing sector, and new employment in the digital technology sector is growing.

After surveying the river we motored back to the marina. There we discovered that the shore power adaptor, loaned to us by the office, wasn't working. Kevin and John proved themselves jolly useful chaps, making an excellent job of rewiring it.

That afternoon we visited the Hartlepool Historic Dockyard, a museum where one of the exhibits is the ship HMS *Trincomalee*. She was built in 1816 in Bombay and was a Royal Navy frigate, entering service in 1847. The museum has been themed to recreate a seaport of around the year 1800. We found it to be fascinating.

We ended the week with dinner on board *Blue Star*, our last dinner with Kevin, John and David who would be leaving us the next day. We had very much enjoyed their company.

Mike:

It had been great to spend time with David. Strange that, despite living on opposite sides of the world, it was as though we already knew each other. We found that we had a lot in common and it was uncanny that family blood had made us quite similar. I do hope that we can meet up again soon.

***

Joke
Q. How does a dolphin make a decision?
A. Flipper coin!

***

Below: The ruins of the abbey at Whitby

Above: The crew at Whitby, Blue Star tattoos all round!
(from left: Mike, Roger, David, Kevin and John)

Below: HMS *Trincomalee* at the museum in Hartlepool

7. Hartlepool to Eyemouth

Before the morning broke, the 'Forfarshire' struck upon a rock,
And was dashed to pieces by a tempestuous shock,

...

And nine persons were rescued almost dead with the cold
By modest and lovely Grace Darling, that heroine bold; ...

Max Plowman, 'Grace Darling'

It was Saturday, 25 July. We were looking forward to the arrival of Lisa Carpenter from Stafford, and of Jim Sheegog and his son James from the United States. Lisa heard about the *Blue Star* project when publicity photographs were shot at her local dinghy club. She was keen to experience sailing the sea in a larger vessel. We reserved the fore-cabin for her. Jim was a former colleague of Roger's from their days working for Royal Dutch Shell in The Hague. Roger had sailed aboard Jim's ketch *Shamrock* on the American Atlantic Coast. When Jim heard about the *Blue Star* project he and James had flown across the Atlantic to support us and to experience sailing the British Coast. Jim was a chap of giant proportions. His son was of at least equal stature. They just about squeezed onto the single bunks in *Blue Star*'s saloon.

Woolcool had kindly organised for a consignment of meals to be delivered to us in Hartlepool. Packed in their insulated, environmentally friendly boxes, the meals kept us going for days. A salmon and leek pie was selected from the 'goody box' for dinner that evening.

Setting out for Newcastle on Sunday, we departed Hartlepool at 0900 hours. There was some sun, cloud and very little wind. On exiting the sea lock we were somewhat surprised by the swell that confronted us – waves of up to two metres were rolling in from across the North Sea. There had been no mention of this in the forecast. Although the waves were not breaking, the motion wasn't pleasant. We soldiered on, hoping that they would die down as the day wore on, which thankfully they did.

Jim and Lisa took turns on the helm and momentarily there was some confusion about the reading from our depth gauge. 'Was there really

25 miles of sea under our keel?' Lisa asked, jokingly. We explained that the 'm' stood for metres!

We pressed on under engine and mainsail, passing the beaches that stretch through Peterlee and on to the town of Easington Colliery. Coal is no longer excavated there, the mine having closed in 1993, but the town's name retains its association with the industry that once thrived. Further north, Seaham was also once a colliery town, as with so many settlements in the Northeast. The importation of cheap coal from Eastern Europe led to mine closures in the 1990s. Efforts have been made to rejuvenate the area and most of the Durham coastline is now designated a 'heritage coast'. In 1992 the area won an 'Outstanding Achievement in Regeneration' award.

With 18 miles behind us we were approaching Sunderland. The city was once known for its shipbuilding and mining. Today, the Japanese carmaker Nissan is a major employer and the banks of the River Wear are zones of rejuvenation.

The Sunderland International Air Show was in full swing. Many different planes zoomed overhead performing aerobatic manoeuvres. They twisted, turned, swooped and dived as they circled over the city. The entertainment was great to watch from the sea. The wind filled in enough for us to turn off the engine and sail. So much better without the throbbing noise from beneath our feet! Several other yachts and dinghies were circling around. They had all come to enjoy the sailing whilst watching the aerial show from the water.

One of the other yachts, *Romteskip*, was heading towards Newcastle with us and so we decided to race her.

We sailed on, passing the Souter Lighthouse north of Whitburn, a white column with red band and red top, rising above the land. Commissioned in the 1870s, the lighthouse was the first in the world designed to be powered by alternating electric current. It was decommissioned in 1988 and is now owned by the National Trust.

We were neck and neck with *Romteskip*, definitely still in the race! With such light winds, 'playing' our sails to get the best of every breath of air was essential. The crew on the other boat were continually adjusting their sails too.

Another three miles and we were approaching the Tyne Estuary. There are large harbour walls which protect the river mouth and we turned to port between them to enter, just ahead of *Romteskip*. We had won! Fancy that! (Did the crew of *Romteskip* realise they had been in a race?)

It was a busy, bustling river, and with several shallow areas to deal with. We needed to concentrate on our navigation now. The shallow areas were well marked, helping us avoid them without any problem. We motored onwards upriver. To our left was the town of South Shields, and to our right, beyond the mudflats that bordered the river, North Shields. It was clearly another post-industrial area. There were several old quaysides, some apparently unused and desolate. We passed small craft moorings on port, and further upstream the ferry embarkation points for passengers travelling between North and South Shields.

The city of Newcastle upon Tyne is about ten miles upriver. It would probably have been an interesting trip, but access to its marinas is dependent on the state of the tide and on bridge opening times. Instead, we decided on Royal Quays Marina, only two miles upriver and on the north bank. We entered, again via a sea lock. Alongside us was *Romteskip*, having caught up with us as we waited for the lock to open. The marina is based in the former Albert Edward Dock. Surrounding the marina were housing estates, a few shops and parkland. It was a pleasant place to stay.

No sooner had we tied up than the heavens opened. Torrential rain looked like it was set in for days. The forecast was not encouraging either so we decided on a short stopover. Unfortunately, the weather deteriorated further and it looked as if we would be there for some time. It was incredibly disappointing, given that Jim and James had flown more than three and a half thousand miles from the States to do some sailing. Not wanting to disappoint the crew more than was necessary, Roger organised some trips to local points of interest. Mike was feeling a little under the weather with flu-like symptoms and took the chance to catch up with some quiet time on board.

Roger:

The first day of the onshore tour took in the sights and sounds of Newcastle including a lovely old pub where we had lunch. The following day, still poor weather, so a second tour was planned, this time to Durham. We set off by train for a day visit to this lovely old city, on the banks of the River Wear. The morning was occupied by visiting the Cathedral and then, after a pub lunch, a walk back up the hill to see some more of the historical sites. Unfortunately, on the way down the

77

narrow, wet, cobbled street, disaster struck. Jim slipped and broke his ankle. This entailed a full blues and twos ambulance ride to the local hospital where he underwent surgery. Knowing this was going to incur a rapid change of plans, we arranged for James to check into a hotel near the hospital. There was no way they could continue with the sailing. They prepared to travel back to the States once Jim had recovered sufficiently. Naturally the mood was very sombre. Having jetted all this way only for this to occur was a massive disappointment for them, and also for the rest of the crew.

By day three the weather had still not improved and at this point Lisa decided she didn't want to stay with us any longer. It was unclear when more sailing might take place and she had the opportunity to compete in a national dinghy racing competition in Brixham. Understandably, this had more appeal than hanging around with us! We escorted her to the train station and bid her farewell.

Lisa:
It seemed like a real calamity of events that unfolded! We had some great times too though, even if we didn't get to sail much, what with the weather and misadventures. The food and company were amazing and it was a pleasure to spend time on the *Blue Star*. I would love to go big-boat sailing again.

Afterwards we visited Jim in hospital, taking him his personal possessions. We made sure that he had a suitable plan for travelling home once he had been discharged, thanked him for his support, apologised for not taking better care of him and said our goodbyes.

By Thursday there were signs that the weather had improved, and the forecast was no longer ominous. The rain had stopped and we were getting somewhat frustrated being holed up at Newcastle for so long. On 30 July we set sail for Amble with just the two of us on board, the first time since starting out from Hythe. It did feel a little strange. Part of our planning had been a conversation about what if there were only the two of us? We were confident that we could handle the boat, but this would be the first time. The layout of the boat and the shared experience of the two of us proved more than adequate. Our first test was negotiating the lock out of the marina, but with Mike on helm and Roger managing lines all went well.

We'd made a sandwich lunch, negating the need to prepare food while at sea. We also watched our 'delightful friend' Carol Kirkwood's weather forecast on the BBC, as was our wont. Carol explained that the day would be cloudy, which we weren't too fussed about, but her graphics also showed some very large squiggly lines out at sea off the Northeast Coast. She did not make any mention of the 'squiggles' though, and we chose not to think too much about them. Several online forecasts for the area were consulted too, as was our usual practice.

There were other vessels manoeuvring in the river and we joined the flow of those heading downstream. Eventually we exited the river mouth and worked our way past the harbour walls, turning north as we did so. Although the weather had improved, the sea was still very 'lumpy' and the wind 'on the nose'. We experienced a chilly northerly wind for most of the journey up the East Coast. The large waves meant it was hard work but we wanted to make progress and decided to press on. Perhaps the 'lumps' would subside.

We advanced slowly, passing Whitley Bay, and after eight miles the port of Blythe was on our left. We had identified it as a possible port of refuge in our passage planning, so a decision now had to be made. Despite the discomfort caused by the sea state we both wanted to continue the journey. Surely these waves wouldn't last much longer?

Under mainsail and motor we 'bobbed' onwards, up the side of a wave then down its back. And repeat. Amble lay over 15 miles further north of Blythe, but we had got this far so why not press on? The waves did not subside as we had hoped. They grew bigger, huge rollers from across the North Sea. Up and down, up and down we went. What we initially estimated to be two-metre waves grew to three metres, then four metres. Some waves we estimated to be five metres high, perhaps larger. It is fair to say that we were anxious as well as queasy! We had never sailed in waves this size before. We had found Carol's 'squiggles'! The waves weren't breaking; if they had they definitely would have given us something to think about. Although not actually seasick, neither of us was too keen to spend very long down below, although we did manage to brew up and have a quick trip to the heads.

Just to the east of Amble lies Coquet Island. The charts show a narrow navigable route between the island and mainland, but with such large waves to contend with we decided to stay offshore and pass outside the island. Once north of Coquet we turned to port and could see the entrance to the harbour at Amble. Rising and falling rhythmically to the demands of the waves, we worked our way to face it and, still some distance off, dropped the mainsail to prepare for a possible entry. We could see people walking along the harbour walls, their coats pulled tightly around them as they braced themselves against the wind. The huge rollers, having for one moment passed under *Blue Star*'s hull, were now crashing against the harbour wall and sending spray everywhere, much of it over the wall. We wondered about the sense of attempting to go in under these conditions. Frankly, it looked menacing! But what then? We held our position for a while, watching the waves smash into the walls ahead, and thought things through.

We decided to call up the harbourmaster for advice about entry under these conditions. No reply. Perhaps the marina might be able to help? We tried the marina office. 'Of course, it will be fine, come on in.' they said. (Later we found that they could not see the conditions at the harbour from the marina office. Perhaps they just wanted more customers?) In the end it was always going to be up to us.

We decided to go for it. But we had better get it right. If we allowed the waves to push us off course we could very easily end up as matchwood, broken into small pieces. With the waves arriving from behind us, we set off, aiming at the centre of the entrance. There were no other vessels going through. Why was that? The people walking the sea walls seemed to pause to watch the action unfold. A few waves passed under us and broke on the wall once more, a small section of them rolling on into the harbour. Then a large wave picked us up and we surfed at speed down the front of it. No going back now. What did fate have in store ...? Our pace picked up. Another wave ahead broke against the wall, sending spray high into the air. Adrenalin pumped through our veins and, still surfing down the giant wave, we shot ... straight through the centre of the entrance. Phew. That was close!

We expected the people on the sea wall to burst into a round of applause at the sight of such impressive boat handling, such bravery. But no. They just seemed to turn away and continue their walking. Did they not realise what heroes we were? What warriors of the sea they had witnessed? Well, perhaps we were neither of those, but it certainly felt like an enormous achievement to have finally arrived at Amble.

Next, we had to find the marina. The harbour plan showed it to be three quarters of a mile up the River Coquet on port side. We picked our way carefully to avoid other boats and the shallows that were shown on the chart, continuing upriver. A quick radio call to the marina office once more confirmed our arrival and we were soon alongside in our allocated berth. Finally, we could relax. It had been a very demanding passage but very satisfying to have made it successfully.

After securing the boat we brewed up and planned a meal ashore. Whilst preparing the tea, a slight whiff of ... something ... was noted ... in the refrigeration department. A fridge stock-taking exercise followed which revealed that we had an excess of cheese on board! We decided, with only two of us on board, we would never use it all. We took a large pile of packets, all still in date, to the marina office and presented it to the staff there as a gift from *Blue Star*. We hinted to them that perhaps we could be given special 'charity' rates when making our payment the next day!

Walking the streets of Amble in the evening was very pleasant. Peaceful and quiet, the therapy that our nerves needed. We made our way to The Wellwood Arms, seeking the gourmet dinner we felt we deserved. As we ate a slap-up meal we reflected on our experiences of the day.

The weather forecast still looked poor in the morning and we settled for exploring the local area. A road and footpath led alongside the river and took us to the village of Warkworth, two miles away, passing the nature conservation area and Warkworth Castle on the way. There, we found several hostelries and selected Masons Inn in which to taste the offerings and ponder our next move.

Later in the evening, after an on-board 'Woolcool pie' dinner, we visited Coquet Yacht Club where we were given a very warm welcome, and where one kind member bought us both a pint. We were very impressed with the reception.

The next day things looked brighter, the forecast had improved considerably and the wind had shifted to the west, which looked encouraging. We departed early and, still with just the two of us on board, had a cracking sail to Eyemouth. Another yacht left port with us, heading in the same direction, but *Blue Star*, under full sail and on a beam reach, soon 'left her for dust'! It was a flat sea, and although the wind was cold the sun shone between the clouds from time to time. We simply 'blasted' along, making a steady six knots and reaching eight knots on occasions!

The coast over on our port side was rapidly passing by, and an impressive panorama it was too! Sandy beaches, rock formations, several seaside villages and Dunstanburgh Castle. The castle dates back to the 1300s, exchanged hands several times during the Wars of the Roses in the 15th century and even had a role to play in World War Two. Today it is managed by English Heritage.

After 20 miles we found ourselves approaching the Farne Islands, the centre of which lies over three miles offshore. They are a group of up to 20 very low-lying islands, some of which are covered by the rise of the tide. We were amongst them almost as soon as we had spotted them, such is their low profile. Rather than skate around them we set a course through the centre, enabling us to fully appreciate their rugged splendour. The islands were once inhabited by monks and hermits but today there is no permanent population, except for National Trust rangers who manage them. The islands are a protected bird sanctuary and a breeding ground for seals.

Grace Darling features in the islands' history. Grace was 22 years old and the daughter of William Darling, one of the keepers of Longstone Lighthouse on the islands. In 1838 Grace and her father, in a rowing boat, rescued nine people from the wreck of the *Forfarshire* which had run aground on the rocks in thick fog and a howling gale. The rescue attracted a great deal of attention and Grace became a national heroine.

On the mainland coast, close to the Farne Islands, lies Bamburgh Castle. This castle dates back to the year 420! Destroyed by Vikings in 993, it was rebuilt by the Normans. In Victorian times the industrialist William Armstrong bought the castle. It is still owned by his family today and is open to the public.

Soon we were abeam of another jewel of the Northeast Coast. Holy Island, also known as Lindisfarne, is joined to the mainland by a causeway that covers with the tide. It dates back to the 6th century when it was an important centre for Celtic Christianity. After the Viking invasions and the Norman Conquest a priory was rebuilt there. The small castle on the island dates back to the 16th century. Today Lindisfarne has a small population, three pubs, a hotel, a post office and a number of holiday properties. It attracts many tourists.

South of the island there is an anchorage which we considered visiting. We sailed on by, on the grounds that it was somewhat exposed to the wind. We needed to make up for lost time, having been delayed by bad weather in Newcastle. In an ideal world we could have anchored for the night and taken the dinghy ashore. It would have been a spectacular stop!

Mike:

In the imaginary tee-shirts and shorts sailing world – the one we'd been using when planning the voyage – all of the crew, including Jim, James and Lisa, would be sitting on deck as we sped past Lindisfarne. It reminded me of one of my favourite pop groups, also called Lindisfarne, who hailed from the Northeast. We could all have been singing along together as we passed by. Now, with just Roger and I on board, a duet did not seem such a good idea. Still, I sang the words quietly to myself:

> Run for home!
> Run as fast,
> As I can!
> Whoa! Runnin' man!
> Runnin' for home!

We all enjoyed listening to music when sailing, and often we sang too! It kept everyone's spirits high.

We were not running, as the band advised, but *Blue Star* was still keeping up one 'hell' of a pace, cutting her path through the sea. The exhilaration of this day of sailing has never left me.

Ten miles further on we were off Berwick-upon-Tweed. The town changed hands several times during the many centuries of fighting between Scotland and England. It last changed hands in 1482 when it was captured by the troops of Richard of Gloucester, later Richard III of Leicester car-park fame! Many of the population still feel a strong affinity for Scotland.

We'd contemplated stopping overnight but we would have had difficulty remaining afloat at low water. Anchoring off was considered too insecure, with potentially changeable weather and sea conditions. We sailed straight on past. In any case it would have been a shame to call a premature halt to the wonderful sailing that we were enjoying. We were still flying along!

The beauty and historical significance of the coastal features certainly gave us much to appreciate during this leg of the journey. What a way to visit all of these places, if only fleetingly! This was how we had envisioned the whole circumnavigation would be. We reflected on how unfortunate it was that our other crew members had not been able to enjoy this amazing experience. It proved to be one of the best passages of our entire voyage. We were certainly due a good day after the disaster in Newcastle and the difficult passage to Amble.

Eyemouth was a further nine miles beyond Berwick. The town is at the mouth of a river, Eye Water. It is principally a fishing port but also has many yachts based at the marina. There is a visitor centre and an early-morning fish market.

The route in is not without challenge. A north cardinal mark indicates the edge of submerged rocks and skerries which need to be given a wide berth on port – but not too wide, for there are rocks and sandbanks on starboard too. Leading marks on the shore must be lined up by manoeuvring into the correct position and then kept in line during the approach. At the last moment a turn to port gets you into the harbour.

On arrival, now in Scottish waters, we rafted up against a rather unseaworthy-looking vessel, the *Admiral Collingwood*. It was rumoured to have once been a youth-training ship – a long time ago! Not feeling too confident about our mooring, we contacted the local lifeboat station and explained our charitable undertaking. They kindly offered to keep an eye on our boat whilst we went home for a couple of weeks.

An interesting feature of Eyemouth was the number of seals that came to feed in the harbour, attracted by the scraps thrown to them from the fishing boats tied up there. The seals' presence has become a tourist attraction. Several men were dangling fish on the end of a pole and line in order to attract them and to persuade them to 'jump' out of the water for a photograph!

After a night's sleep, we informed the harbourmaster when we intended to return. We took a taxi to the railway station and caught the train home. In spite of the problems we'd encountered it had been an excellent end to the week!

Joke
Q. Which vegetables are not allowed on board a yacht?
A. Leeks!

***

Above: Seals in the harbour at Eyemouth

8. Eyemouth to Inverness

*He that will not sail until all dangers are over
must never put to sea.*

Dr Thomas Fuller

It was nearing the end of August and the annual public holiday, but the weather on the East Coast of Scotland was unseasonable. We had endured cold north winds for many of the passages so far and it looked as if we would again have the same conditions. Roger was not able to join the crew for the trip out of Eyemouth as he had pressing business at home. On board were Mike as skipper, Rob Wilford, returning for a further week, now promoted again to first mate, and Jan. Originally from the Netherlands, Jan was a friend of Roger's from their Shell days. They had known each other since 1971. Jan lived in Aberdeen so it was a short trip down to Eyemouth for him.

Mike:

Rob and I arranged to meet en route during our travels north. As it turned out we met up with Jan at the station in Eyemouth. He'd taken the same train during the last part of the journey. The three of us shared a taxi to the harbour and unloaded our bags onto *Blue Star*. We were tired after our travel and wanted to relax. We had little in the way of supplies on board so we walked the short distance into town, found a café and talked about the trip to come. We put together a shopping list and collected groceries from the supermarket before returning to the boat.

In our absence, the outside of the boat had become a mess, covered in all manner of leaves, bird excrement and general muck. Jan and I got to work hosing and scrubbing while Rob put together a hot meal, after which we felt a lot better.

Monday, 31 August. After Rob's bacon butty breakfast, we topped up the tanks and carried out the usual engine checks. We intended sailing to Arbroath, a distance of 50 miles across the Firth of Forth. The Firth is a huge triangle of sea that cuts into the eastern side of the Scottish mainland, narrowing down close to the nation's capital, Edinburgh.

The weather forecast looked promising and we needed to get going whilst there was still plenty of deep water outside the harbour – we noticed that a fishing boat inside the harbour was already aground! We slipped our lines, turned *Blue Star* around to face the exit and were soon on our way, carefully looking over our shoulder as we left the port in order to keep the leading marks lined up.

We soon found that the wind had too much north in it for us to sail so we tried to furl away the genoa and motor-sail, with just the main raised. The furling mechanism jammed, leaving the large white piece of fabric to flog itself to death. Jan, with many years of experience, volunteered to go forward to see what the problem was. He soon worked some magic and the sail was furled away, enabling us to progress. The sea state was kind to us and the sun gleamed down. We were enjoying ourselves, even if the wind wasn't playing fair!

About 20 miles into the trip Jan pointed out the iceberg over on our port side. Something sounded not quite right. We were rather off course if we were encountering icebergs! The 'iceberg', about nine miles away but clearly visible, was Bass Rock, standing about 100 metres tall and one mile off the southern coast of the Firth. It is privately owned and is uninhabited by man. It is, however, inhabited by a large colony of gannets whose guano gives the rock its brilliant white colour!

Later, off to starboard we passed the Bell Rock Lighthouse, built on stone that lies just below the surface of the water. Good job there's something to mark the shallows! In Arbroath we were to learn more about the construction and operation of the lighthouse.

The wind headed us further, causing the mainsail to flap. It was promptly dropped and we proceeded under engine alone. When the wind returned it was from the east, giving us the chance to have a cracking sail, over seven knots on a flat sea! As we ate a sandwich lunch, prepared by Rob, the wind weakened. By mid-afternoon it had gone completely and we had to finish the passage by motoring again.

We radioed ahead to the marina to announce our arrival and, on entering, found there were plenty of berths to choose from. Soon we were tied up and discussing dinner. We made use of the spacious facilities. They were clean and there was also a community room with a free library for sailors to use. All in all, very convenient.

Mike:

To catch the tide the next day we needed to exit the sea lock at 0600 hours. I went to chat with Bruce, the marina manager, to let him know our intention. He replied in his fine Scottish accent.

'Aye, thar's a wee problem with that, so there is.'

'Oh?' I said.

'I dunnae work that early and there's noo'an else a open the lock gates ferr yee.'

Drat! That left us with the option of leaving on the afternoon high water. I calculated that we might make it to Stonehaven before dark. The forecast for later wasn't good, so we needed to be in port by evening. I telephoned Stonehaven for advice, and to see if I could reserve a suitable berth.

'Well Serr, the warta is nice and flat here at presen', but there's a force 6 expecked and thart'll soon pick the sea up. Ya doon wannae be sailin' in that, surely? E'en if you got here, with these spring tides yer'd prabbly be agroun' at low warta.'

And so, with such great encouragement all round, we decided to stay put!

A walk into town for groceries and a coffee was necessary. On our return we bought 'Arbroath Smokies' (a local delicacy of wood-smoked haddock) for lunch. They were very good! With the ship's supplies replenished, we read the news and checked the forecast again. No change. Rob made some flapjacks, also very good! We gazed out from the marina wall to view a millpond sea and a windless air, and wondered why we hadn't sailed. In the evening Roger arrived to join the crew, and we all dined on Rob's pasta bake! We always enjoyed Rob's on-board meals.

The met office forecast the following morning was not at all promising. We tried a different website but the same 'doom and gloom' was on offer. Another day in Arbroath! Jan took the opportunity to hop on a bus and go home to Aberdeen. He'd stay there until the weather showed signs of improving.

Our enforced stay provided us 'Sassenachs' with an opportunity to explore the town and learn something of its history. Whilst there was evidence of an Iron Age settlement, the town documentation starts with the founding of Arbroath Abbey in 1178. During the industrial revolution the town prospered from the flax and jute industries. Further expansion came with the new harbour built in 1839 and by the 20th century Arbroath had become one of the largest fishing ports in Scotland. The town became renowned for the Arbroath Smokie.

It is claimed that, in a nearby village, barrels of haddock were inadvertently set alight. Loathe to dispose of their catch, locals plucked up courage to sample the fish, and found it to be tasty. The Arbroath Smokie was born. Alternatively, the process of smoking fish could have been brought across from Scandinavia. Today, some 15 businesses produce the Smokie, which has protected status under European rules. The fish are prepared with intense heat and smoke, a process which normally takes about one hour. Against this historical background we bought three more Smokies from a local stall and indeed they were delicious!

On the sporting front the town is proud of its record for scoring the highest number of goals in the Scottish Cup back in 1885. We did not mention this to Jan since the result was: Arbroath 36 – Aberdeen 0.

A short stroll from the marina is the Bell Rock Signal Tower. Now a museum, it tells of the construction of the lighthouse that we had passed when sailing to Arbroath. It was built between 1807 and 1810 by Robert Stevenson on the Bell Rock, also known as Inchcape. Legend says it is so named because in the 14th century the Abbot of Arbroath installed a bell on it to warn nearby ships. The bell lasted only a year before it was stolen by a Dutch pirate!

By the 19th century, up to half a dozen ships foundered on the rocks every year! John Rennie was contracted to build a lighthouse with Stevenson as his assistant. Stevenson's notes gave little credit to Rennie and the two families fell out. It is now accepted that both made a significant contribution.

Lighthouse keepers communicated with staff at the tower using a signalling ball. If all was well they hoisted the ball to the top of a pole on the lighthouse roof. The tower would do the same to its ball, meaning message received. If the ball remained down, indicating an emergency, assistance would be despatched.

It is said that when the wife of one of the lighthouse keepers had given birth, a dress or a pair of trousers would be flown from the signal tower mast to indicate the gender of the new-born infant!

We explained our trip to the staff at the signal tower. They invited us to attend a ceremony the following day, 'Merchant Navy Day'.

The weather showed no sign of abating in the morning. We hatched a plan for some sightseeing. First, we would take up the invitation to attend the Ensign Ceremony at the signal tower, honouring all merchant seamen who lost their lives in World War Two. The date of the ceremony marks the sinking of the merchant ship SS *Athenia* by torpedo, with the loss of 128 lives, just hours after Britain declared war on 3 September 1939. She was en route to Montreal and the captain felt she was far enough west to be safe from attack by U-boats. Unfortunately, the Germans had positioned U-boats in the Atlantic in anticipation of Britain declaring war. It was a moving ceremony, made even more memorable by the cold biting wind on the exposed headland.

For afternoon entertainment and education we went by train to Dundee, 17 miles away on the Firth of Tay, to see polar explorer Robert Falcon Scott's ship. RRS *Discovery* is a barque-rigged steamship built specially for Antarctic exploration. Launched in 1901, she was the last traditional wooden three-mast ship completed in the UK. Built in solid oak, there was minimal metal to confuse magnetic compasses, essential for surveying and navigation. In places the hull was over two feet (60cm) thick, designed to withstand being frozen into pack ice and crushed. The ship had formidable strength and excellent insulation against the cold. At the time, she was widely considered the strongest wooden ship ever built. She had no portholes as they would have weakened the hull. Instead, 'mushroom vents' allowed air and light to the interior.

We were struck by the open bridge. Given the atrocious conditions they would have encountered, it is hard to understand why no weather protection was provided ...

Ships of wood, sailed with zeal,
Crewed by good men of steel.

Discovery's mission, from 1901 to 1904, was with the British National Antarctic Expedition led by Scott. This was the great age of polar expeditions with keen competition amongst nations. Later, the British Terra Nova Expedition took place between 1910 and 1913 in Antarctica. Led by Scott, it had various scientific objectives, building on the knowledge and experience of the previous voyage. Scott wanted to be the first to reach the geographic South Pole and together with four companions he arrived at the pole on 17 January 1912. They found that the Norwegian team led by Roald Amundsen had preceded them by 34 days. Much has been written about the terrible conditions they endured on the return trip back from the pole and the heroic actions of the team members. Scott and his entire party died.

We had been port-bound for three days by this time and it seemed far too long. Indeed, it is said that 'harbours rot men and boats'! Little things were starting to irritate us. The only large shower cubicle ashore had a broken fixing. You had to hold the sprinkler whilst washing. We didn't care to start with, but now it was annoying. It seemed time was passing with nothing achieved. We were impatient, and we wanted to enjoy some sailing!

Jan came back from Aberdeen the night before we left and we slipped out of Arbroath early on Friday, 4 September towards Peterhead. Our journey took us past Montrose which we'd identified as a possible port of refuge. The Royal National Lifeboat Institution (RNLI) there had kindly agreed we could use their jetty if needed. Although the weather was not pleasant, with a keen north-easterly wind, we pressed on. After what we had learnt the previous day about polar explorers, surely, we could cope with a little northerly breeze?

We continued north past Stonehaven and Aberdeen. The almanac states that pleasure yachts are not welcome in Aberdeen, given the volume of commercial traffic. It's one of the main ports supporting the offshore oil and gas industry. However, we could no doubt have entered if necessary. Some 40 miles north of Arbroath, and still 24 miles to run, we pushed on, although by now we were motoring.

The weather had not improved and we struggled to find a heading which would take us smoothly through the waves, which were gradually increasing in size. We were now very conscious that both the wind and tide were set against us. The grey sky met with the grey sea. The air was bitterly cold. We took turns sheltering behind the sprayhood to get what relief we could. It blew up to 25 knots as we slowly moved further north. On the cliffs, Slains Castle, another inspiration for Bram Stoker, overlooked us. Was this an omen?

We were still hours south of Peterhead, motor-sailing with double-reefed main. The rain had started and blew almost horizontally into our faces, stinging them. We took turns to helm, with our hoods up, with high collars covering our mouths and as much face as possible. Just a slither of an opening to look out from. To top things off a mist rolled in, reducing visibility to a few hundred yards. The waves were still growing, thwarting our progress, and even with higher engine revs we were doing only three knots over the ground. Then the smoke alarm went off! What else could go wrong?

Roger:

A short distance south of Peterhead are a series of rocks, the Meikle Mackie and the Skerry, which we needed to avoid at all costs. I was helming as we approached the harbour entrance, aware that all the elements seemed to be combining against us: wind, tide, sea state, hazards and nerves! I needed to steer a course of 300° to pass into the harbour, whilst making allowance for the elements pushing us towards the southerly breakwater. We were being rolled by large waves, the side-decks well below the water, a very unpleasant experience. After what seemed like a lifetime we were through into the harbour. What a relief! Although the sea state had subsided, the gusting winds were still keeping up their relentless drive.

Prior to our arrival at the marina the authorities had given minimal advice about where to berth. We motored towards the pontoons and found one which was empty, looking quite accessible under the conditions. The wind was so powerful that close quarters boat handling was difficult. Just as I was lining up to come alongside, the wind took the boat in every direction except the one I wanted. With the engine working hard and the bow thruster coming to our rescue, we reversed free. The only alternative was a hammerhead pontoon further up, which might be easier to moor against. This time I did manage to bring the boat alongside, but not without a small 'coming together' on the starboard quarter which put a 'souvenir' on the boat. Pride was slightly more dented than the boat. We were all ready for a hot meal and an early night.

Now in the marina we discovered the reason why the smoke alarm had sounded. We had boiled the kettle and the flame had accidentally scorched the cooker cover. The alarm had ceased soon after it began but left us worrying about the cause. Mystery solved!

The following morning the weather had improved slightly, but not enough to tempt us out to sea. In fact, the forecast for the next few days was not good and so Jan decided that he would leave us here and head back to Aberdeen. We enquired about diesel and were told 'Monday'. Not helpful considering today was Saturday. We thought we still had enough to get to our next port. We tried to use the laundry near the shower block but that too was closed until Monday!

Looking around that morning we were impressed by the massive harbour breakwaters which we had negotiated the night before. For a long time the town authorities had recognised the importance of a safe harbour and a stout entrance. To this end a prison was constructed close to the town, providing convict labour to build the breakwaters. Work started in 1886 and continued until September 1956 – with stoppages for the two world wars! A special heavy-lift rail-mounted crane named 'Titan' was used to aid construction. The use of forced labour by convicts was abolished in 1949, before the construction was completed.

We decided to venture into Peterhead town. It was a pleasant place and made memorable by the discovery of a café serving excellent coffee and scones. The rating for the scones was high and we decided we would come back again. In fact, scones became a firm favourite of the crew; we would seek out opportunities to track them down at each port we visited. However, in discussion with this café owner we learnt that she was closed on Sunday, and Monday too, because it was a special public holiday just for Peterhead! This rather surprised us. Even so, we did manage to obtain a new gas cylinder from the local garage and carry out some routine boat maintenance.

Roger:

Whilst in Peterhead there was ample opportunity to wander around the pontoons and it was on one of these walks that I noticed an interesting yacht with a deck saloon and great all-round visibility, a Sirius 35DS, built in Germany. I could not help but feel it would have been so much more comfortable against the north wind in a yacht like this! It set me thinking.

Sunday brought more bad weather and we were still not able to sail. We found a local caravan site with a laundry and made good use of it! Mike washed his towel which had blown into the sea and been rescued by Jan. We did a little shopping, cleaned the boat and scoured the weather forecasts for hopeful signs.

Because of the bad weather, delaying us at Arbroath and Peterhead, we were slipping behind the schedule that we had set ourselves. Diane and Madeline were supposed to join the crew in Inverness on Sunday. Now they would have to wait several days more before we could get there. They found accommodation in the city whilst awaiting our arrival, but they were as frustrated with the situation as we were. It turned out that this was the only occasion in the entire voyage that we were unable to meet new crew on time.

Our next passage would take us into the Moray Firth. It stretches in a south-westerly direction from Duncansby Head in the north to Inverness in the west, then back out eastwards to Fraserburgh. To enter the Firth we needed to pass around the headland at Rattray Head, and we would need reasonable weather for that.

Monday brought the improvement in the weather we were hoping for. After filling up with diesel we set a course for Whitehills on the southern coast of the Moray Firth. With two reefs in the main we motor-sailed north against some large waves left over from the storm. A few other boats were out, all of us striving to round Rattray Head. In the first four hours we had gone only 16 miles, but had worked our way sufficiently north to start altering course to the west and into the Firth. The town of Fraserburgh was now on our port side. We continued our steady turn to port until we were motoring along the coast towards Macduff and Banff. With this change of direction came a drop in the wind strength, plus a little sunshine. It cheered our spirits. The coast was attractive too: stunning rocky cliffs and picture-book villages around the coast against a panorama of green hills beyond. It was a joy to sail.

Roger:
Having developed a pilotage plan for entering Whitehills we understood that it would be tight. With fair weather conditions we identified the stone breakwater. The approach channel ran down the right-hand side of the harbour, with beacons marking its outer edge. At the end of the channel the entrance is reached via a sharp 90° turn to port. It needed some careful coaxing from the bow thruster to line us up and pass inside. We'd called ahead and spoken with the harbourmaster who kindly came down to the quayside to welcome us in and take a line. Immediately he saw our charity logos he offered free

berthing for the night and a few useful tips about where to eat out. The other impressive and distinctive feature of sailing into Whitehills was that the harbourmaster took photographs of our boat as we made our way down the approach channel, and these were made available to us on arrival. This was indeed a very hospitable welcome.

Inside the harbour, berthing pontoons lined the massive walls which towered above us. There wasn't a great deal of room to turn a boat, but after some nifty manoeuvring with the help of our bow thruster we managed to come alongside without a problem.

We had found the sharp turn, and the tight manoeuvring required, to be an interesting exercise, despite having three experienced crew on our 37-foot yacht. We were therefore all the more impressed when another yacht, of length circa 45-foot, arrived shortly after us. It was crewed by one man and a large old English sheepdog, the latter sitting on the foredeck! It glided effortlessly into the small vacant space on the pontoon.

Like most coastal settlements, Whitehills's economy was once based on the fishing industry. As fishing declined, the harbour was redeveloped. A marina with 47 pontoons and access at most states of tide was constructed. In the early 19th century, when a new parish church was planned, they purchased a disused church in nearby Banff, dismantled it and moved it stone by stone to its current location. The ultimate recycling!

The village itself has all that sailors need – post office, grocery, beauty salon (something we definitely needed) and a fish and chip restaurant. We chose to eat in the nearby Seafield Arms, a delightful pub. Local football supporters inside shared some choice words as they watched Scotland struggling to qualify for the 2016 Euro finals, but it was all in a good spirit.

The weather held, and after a very quiet and restful night we slipped our mooring on Tuesday at 0800 hours and set off towards Inverness. We had to motor the whole length of the Moray Firth in what was a windless day. More green hills, cliffs, rocky coves and beaches lined the coast, along with many small villages nestling between them. The cloudy day with milky-white sky developed into a very sunny day and we all took off layers of clothing and smeared ourselves with sunscreen.

By late afternoon the sun went away and our clothes were donned once more.

A strange 'clunking' sound developed, together with an occasional impact felt at the steering wheel. We noticed a looseness of the nut securing the top of the rudder post. Was the rudder about to fall off? That would be rather inconvenient to say the least! Roger got to work on the bathing platform at the stern and tightened the offending nut. That seemed to solve the problem. We kept a close eye on it for the remainder of our voyage.

By seven o'clock we were approaching the large, high road bridge over which the busy A9 leads to Inverness. Despite the height of the bridge it is still transfixing as you sit in the cockpit of a yacht passing underneath and wonder – did we get our calculations right? Will the mast fit under the bridge? Despite ample clearance, at least 29 metres between bridge and sea according to the almanac, it still seemed extremely tight from our viewpoint!

Once under the bridge a turn to the left took us into the River Ness and then almost immediately another left turn into the port. Inverness Marina, modern, and with excellent facilities, is situated a short car ride away from the city. We were tied up just in time to watch England's attempt to qualify for the football European Championship finals!

Diane and Madeline had been awaiting our arrival for several days. It was with some rejoicing that we were finally able to greet them and welcome them aboard. They would be joining the crew for the next stage of the voyage, the navigation of the Caledonian Canal.

***

Joke
Three sailors were shipwrecked on a desert island. They came across a strange bottle in the sand. On rubbing it, a genie appeared. 'I will grant you each one wish,' he said. One man wished to be back home with his wife. 'Poof!' He disappeared. A second man said he wished he was in his local pub downing a pint. 'Poof!' He was gone too. The genie turned to the third man. 'I'm lonely here now,' he said. 'I wish the other two were still here!'

***

Right: Merchant Navy Day ceremony at the Bell Tower Museum in Arbroath

Below: Roger on the helm as we head north towards Peterhead against a bitterly cold north wind

Above: Tied up at Whitehills

Left: Approaching the road bridge en route to Inverness – will we fit under?

9. Inverness to Corpach (The Caledonian Canal)

The skipper of the Mary Ann, a jolly chap is he,
With jaunty jest and merriment he gaily sails the sea.
He knows no navigation and he missed his course a mile,
But said, 'It doesn't matter, so long as I can smile.'
He ran against an island, and he almost sank the ship—
Well, never mind!' he brightly said, 'we'll have a cheerful trip.'

Amos Russel Wells, 'The Optimistic Skipper'

The 60-mile-long Caledonian Canal runs from Inverness, in the east, to Corpach, near Fort William, in the west. Strictly speaking, it is not all canal. It is comprised of four lochs, from east to west: Lochs Dochfour, Ness, Oich and Lochy, joined together by 22 miles of man-made canal sections. Constructed by Thomas Telford in the early 19th century its purpose was twofold.

Firstly, it eradicated the need for ships travelling from east to west, or vice-versa, to pass over the North of Scotland, which entailed navigating the treacherous Cape Wrath and the strong tidal area of the Pentland Firth between the Orkneys and the mainland. A canal would provide a safer, quicker route. This would be useful for both merchant and naval ships.

Secondly, it helped to provide badly needed employment. In fact, construction of the canal provided so much work that it could not all be done by the local workforce, and Irish navvies were used to provide additional labour.

The canal opened in 1822, having taken 12 years to construct at a cost of £910,000, far more than estimated. The original plan had foreseen ships of draught 20 feet being able to use the canal but this was reduced to 15 feet to cut costs. By the time the canal was completed, many ships were far larger, steam-powered and with iron hulls. They were too big to use the canal and were better able to tackle the route north of Scotland. Furthermore, Napoleon had been defeated, so the French threat to shipping no longer existed and the Royal Navy didn't need the canal.

The canal's main function became one of attracting people to the region. After a visit by Queen Victoria it became a magnet for tourists. It is now a Scheduled Ancient Monument and attracts over half a million visitors per year.

Wednesday, 9 September, we stocked up with food, filled the water tanks and motored round to the fuel berth to fill up, in readiness for our transit. Although there are stopping places on the canal, for most of its length opportunities to shop for supplies are limited. We were expecting the crossing to take about three days, although it can be done in less if one is determined! At the jetty two men were chatting …

Roger:

We struck up a conversation with two friendly American sailors, Bob and Steve, both 71. Their 40ft yacht, *Nora*, was on the hard for repairs. They told us they had come from Norway and were making their way back across the Atlantic to Maine. Approaching Scotland, they had sustained damage to their propeller, hence the lift out. We were in awe of their bold adventure and it made our round-GB sail look rather tame. We also felt sympathetic towards them, having endured bad luck in damaging their propeller.

Subsequent events told a different story about the intrepid duo. It transpired that the propeller damage was sustained as a consequence of running aground. The full story unfolded over the coming months and we began to wonder about their 'bad luck'.

The eventual sum of their 'misfortunes' were nine rescues! There were two by Norwegian and Danish teams, two off Scotland, one in Northern Ireland, one in the Republic of Ireland and three in Cornwall! The final call out was when the boat caught fire in Hayle having tipped over whilst against the quay. According to media reports the pair were not too concerned about these incidents. Bob, also labelled 'Captain Calamity' by the newspapers, commented, 'We're having great fun.' He went on to say how welcoming people were: 'Even if they think you are crazy and don't know how to sail.' It was even rumoured that they struck an oil rig and did not have the correct nautical charts on board!

The UK call outs were attended by the RNLI. With its strong ethos of rescuing people in distress, they attached no blame to the sailors. However, the legendary sailor Sir Robin Knox-Johnston described them as 'A catastrophe waiting to happen'!

With so many incidents, many advised them to call a halt to their sojourn, for their own safety. After the ninth emergency they took the advice and put the boat up for sale, abandoning their dream of sailing to America.

None of us knew what would unfold as we chatted on the quay that morning.

We motored out of the marina and turned to starboard, towards the mouth of the River Ness. The Moray Firth and A9 road bridge were on our right, but we turned left into the Beauly Firth. From here we could see the entry to the Caledonian Canal almost immediately to port at Clachnaharry. After radioing ahead, we received permission to enter the sea lock.

We waited for the lock gates to close and for the water level to rise. With *Blue Star* tied up we went to pay our canal transit fee. All locks on the canal are operated by Scottish Canals staff. The official at Clachnaharry took our payment and explained the procedure.

We were to put a crew member ashore before entering a lock so they could take our lines around a shore bollard and hand the free end back. Another crew member on deck would then pull in the excess line, if the water level was rising, or pay out extra line if the water level was falling. In practice we found the staff at most locks would do all the shore work for us, making it look very easy. The exception was at 'flights' of several locks all together, especially at Fort Augustus and at Banavie. At these flights the shore crew were required to 'walk' the boat into the lock ahead, the boat engine being turned off to avoid the build-up of fumes.

We would be passing through many locks in the next few days, and would develop our technique and competence. The locks represented something of a paradox. They caused delay, could be dangerous and required an element of skill and expertise. On the other hand, successful negotiation of the locks was most satisfying. They were an interesting feature of the canal and passage through them marked our progress.

The lock gates ahead of us opened and we motored out into a short section of canal leading to the first obstacle – a railway swing bridge. There are a number of road and rail swing bridges along the canal. You have to radio ahead and often it will open just as you arrive. Occasionally we had to moor up at a nearby pontoon and wait.

This time the bridge opened as we arrived, but beyond it was another lock. We passed through unscathed into a short, wide section of canal. On the left were pontoon berths for boats. This was Seaport Marina, a possible stopping point, but we weren't ready to stop. We motored on, past Muirtown, to the next swing bridge and a flight of four locks, all of which were negotiated without a hitch. A bridge at Tomnahurich and a lock at Dochgarroch saw us arrive at the first of the lochs.

Loch Dochfour is about one mile long and less than a quarter of a mile wide. By comparison with Loch Ness, it is very small. We were getting into 'God's own country' now, as rural Scotland is often called, and the scenery was really breathtaking! To port was rich green woodland and to starboard more woodland and grassland. Beyond that stood Dochfour House and gardens. A grand residence, it has been home to the Baillie family for over 500 years. The estate is not normally open to the public but is available for private hire. A series of green buoys, which we had to leave to port, marked the navigable route through the loch.

After another quarter of a mile of canal, a magnificent spectacle awaited: Loch Ness! Spanning nearly two miles at its widest, it stretched over 22 miles in front of us, with densely forested mountains on either side. It is Scotland's second-largest loch, measured by surface area, after Loch Lomond. Its maximum depth, 230 metres, makes it also the second deepest, after Loch Morar. It contains more fresh water than all the lakes of England and Wales combined!

The sun showed through the clouds and a gentle breeze blew from our starboard quarter – definitely time to raise some sail! With full main and genoa rigged, we started our journey towards Fort Augustus at the far end of the loch, our intended destination for the night. The water was flat, although as we worked our way along the loch the wind picked up, and waves developed.

We sailed past the anchorage at Dores and the harbour at Drumnadrochit. Nearby stood the ruin of Urquhart Castle which dates back to the 13th century. It played a role in the wars of Scottish independence and was partially destroyed in 1692 to prevent it being used by Jacobite forces. Further on was the anchorage and pier which serve Foyers Bay Country House.

Halfway along the loch the wind rose further and we were really shifting! What a feeling, sailing Loch Ness with full sail, sun and a fair old lick on. Diane and Madeline made sandwiches and tea, and all was well with the world. Towards the end of the loch the wind was still very strong and the boat was heeling over considerably. It became very choppy but we were almost there.

At the end of the loch, conditions improved miraculously. We took in the sails and motored towards Fort Augustus. It wasn't clear precisely where we were meant to steer – it was getting dark and there were entrances to Rivers Oich and Tarff as well as to the canal section. Eventually we found the red and green lateral marks, indicating the canal in the middle of the three routes. We motored on and tied up starboard side to, close to several other craft.

For our crew, as was often the case, the priority was to establish the whereabouts and condition of the facilities. Fortunately, they were only a short walk from where we had stopped and, using the key we'd been given at Clachnaharry, we opened the door to investigate. Shower and toilet, both fairly clean. The light inside was a little subdued, and the atmosphere humid, steamy even, but we were content.

The next priority was to locate the town. Rob went to investigate and returned with a tale to tell. We had been informed that yacht crews should be aware that many holidaymakers transit the canal in hired boats, and may be inexperienced. Rob had just witnessed a hire boat approaching the quayside without any fenders rigged, and at quite a pace. It smashed into the quayside, gouging a deep scratch into the boat's hull. Rob, ever helpful, mentioned to the skipper that he ought to have his fenders rigged when coming alongside. 'Yes,' says the skipper, 'I know that. I always just tie the boat up first and then put them out once I'm secure.' Completely mad!

The focus of the town was the road bridge crossing the canal a hundred yards ahead of where we were moored. There were a few shops beside the road. Beyond the bridge was a flight of five locks. We would tackle those tomorrow. At the sides of the locks were wide grass verges, beyond those more shops and cafés. Not many people about, now that it was getting late. We dined on board *Blue Star*, had a late evening walk ashore and turned in.

Thursday dawned, bright and sunny. After we'd showered and had breakfast a member of the canal staff walked along, chatting to each boat skipper to ascertain if they planned to pass through the flight of locks ahead. We confirmed it was our intention, and agreed a time to enter the first lock. We were reminded of the procedure explained to us at Clachnaharry. Having booked our passage for early afternoon we walked up into the town and bought groceries and newspapers. At a café next to the locks, we sat outside with coffee and cakes, relaxing in the sunshine. Once we'd returned and had lunch it was our appointed time to enter the locks. The road bridge swung open and we motored through into the first section, along with many other boats.

Mike:

It was very busy. There were numerous boats crammed in, all making the passage together – behind us a large commercial craft, with a vicious-looking steel bow that threatened to slice through us! I was on the helm, and Roger and Rob tended the bow and stern lines. The engine-off rule was troubling. I really needed it on tick-over, ready to give a little forward thrust if necessary to escape the blade behind!

Passage time through the flight of locks was estimated to be about two hours. Each successive lock had to fill and the crew had to walk the boat into the next lock. The shore crew had to climb a steep hill at the end of each lock and step round the lock-gate mechanism ahead, all the while tending the lines of the vessel.

We had deployed fender boards. These are suspended horizontally from the guard wires that form a 'fence' around the boat, the wires being held up by stanchion posts. The boards are positioned between a boat's fenders and the lock wall. They span at least two fenders, usually more, and prevent the fender being engulfed in any crevice lurking in the lock wall. At one point our fender board contributed to an incident.

The town was busy with crowds enjoying the sun, watching the boats rise through the flight of locks. The sluices in the gates ahead opened, allowing water to gush in. All the craft jostled and spun somewhat in response to the sudden torrent. The shore crew pulled the lines to try and gain control. Our boat was snatching this way and that. With the water level rising fast, our fender board became trapped in a cranny in the lock wall. It twisted at an awkward angle and the rope it hung from started to pull hard at the guard rails, stretching them to the limit. The boat started to lean to starboard and then one of our stanchions caught in the lock wall too. Pinned down hard on starboard, with the water still rising fast, the boat leaned over dramatically. Meanwhile the knife machine behind loomed menacingly!

The deck crew desperately tried to pull the fender board and stanchion clear and push us off the wall but it was impossible. All of a sudden, the stanchion gave up and bent, the guard wire stretched a little further, and with a 'twang' we were free again! Astern of us, the knife seemed to be smirking.

After that experience we didn't use our fender boards again. It was a lesson learnt. If they had been larger, longer boards the problem may not have occurred, but as it turned out we subsequently managed very well using fenders alone.

Roger:

Handling the mooring lines on the side of the locks seemed to attract a lot of curious onlookers. One lady followed us up a few locks and as she seemed so keen I asked if she wanted to help take a line – not that keen. She was in fact curious about the sponsors' logos on the yacht, particularly the one from Staffordshire University. It transpired she was a Professor of International Management at the University of Salzburg on holiday in Scotland. Salzburg had tentatively been in touch with Staffordshire University in the recent past. Having explained that I was not an academic we talked a little about my experience in the global energy business. By the time we reached the next lock we'd exchanged business cards and agreed that I would visit Austria to discuss becoming a guest lecturer! The relationship has led to me delivering a number of lectures at Salzburg over the last four years. You never know who you might meet!

After a few hours we were through the locks and making further progress. Afternoon tea was prepared and consumed on the go. The land on each side of the canal was flatter now. We passed the hamlet at Kytra and motored on to Cullochy where the next swing bridge halted our progress. We had travelled about six miles from Fort Augustus. We tied up at the waiting pontoon, and wandered over to the control point. We couldn't see anyone around. A sign on the door told us the bridge was now closed for the day. We would have to wait until morning.

An element of panic set in amongst the crew. Where were the facilities? There was a 'room' next to the bridge, but it really didn't pass muster. We just might have to use the somewhat cramped heads on board, but certain crew members didn't like that idea! We spotted what looked like holiday chalets on the other side of a field. Madeline set out to investigate. A few minutes later the whole crew were marching towards the collection of wooden buildings. After locating the camp restaurant, we explained our situation and were given permission to use the toilet. We must have looked very conspicuous, arriving in the dark from nowhere and forming a queue! Suitably relieved, we trooped back to *Blue Star*, had a late meal and got our heads down for the night.

Friday was a little overcast, but the bridge was up and running again. After a leisurely breakfast we got under way. Beyond the bridge was Loch Oich, four miles long and 47 metres deep. Despite being 300 metres wide, the navigable width is much less. We found ourselves passing very close to the trees on each side, many of which overhung the loch. Further along, the steep landscape towered above us on both sides. We had to take great care to ensure we remained in deep water, the navigable route being marked by a series of red and green buoys. We were now 32 metres above sea level, the highest point we would reach.

At the far end, the loch was wide enough to accommodate the small marina at Great Glen Water Park. We stopped and tied up on the pontoons. Lunch, and a chance to stretch our legs. We ate our sandwiches and chilled for an hour or two. Diane fed the swans and Madeline went for a long walk. After a pleasant break, we slipped our lines and headed off once more.

We negotiated another swing bridge to escape Loch Oich. Steep cliffs and vegetation on each side closed in around us, trying to shut out the sunlight. There were two more locks, at Laggan. This time we were descending, but the procedure for managing the lines was much the same.

Ahead of us was Loch Lochy, nine miles long and 0.6 miles wide. The land to each side, though hilly, stood well back from the loch, giving a more open feeling. The weather was a little overcast, but the scenery and sailing were an absolute joy!

It was five and a half miles from Loch Lochy to our intended destination at Banavie. We passed through Gairlochy, and a mile further on Moy, via two locks and bridges. We arrived late in the afternoon with a hint of rain in the air. Scotland's highest peak, Ben Nevis, was clearly visible to the south, overlooking both us and Fort William, four miles away. We tied up at the pontoon on starboard, just above the famous Neptune's Staircase. One of the longest flights of locks in Britain, eight locks in succession, it would allow us to descend 20 metres, but that was for later.

Tired of self-catering in cramped conditions, we decided to eat out. It would be a way of celebrating our passage through the canal. Unfortunately, there seemed nowhere available. Walking in the rain, beside Neptune's Staircase we found a hotel about halfway down the flight. We weren't able to eat there that evening, but we did visit for an after-dinner drink, having once more dined on board.

Saturday, 12 September saw new crew arrive. Jean-Francois and Joan Larrive, were a married couple. They were long-established friends of Roger and Judith, having met years ago when, in The Hague, Joan was teaching French to Judith. After walking into Fort William in the rain we spent the day exploring the town, visiting shops, a museum and cafés. Later in the evening we managed to get a table at the hotel by the locks. That night *Blue Star* accommodated all seven of us in relative comfort.

On Sunday, Rob, Madeline and Diane were to return home. At the bottom of Neptune's Staircase the main road runs south to Fort William crossing the canal. A neighbouring bridge allows the railway to cross the canal too. Banavie railway station lies just beyond it, a short walk from where *Blue Star* was tied up. We walked to the station and waited for the train. Our three departing crewmates were soon off to Glasgow. They were looking forward to travelling on what is perhaps one of the most scenic of rail routes in Britain! It did not disappoint!

With new crew now aboard, we had booked our time with the lock keeper for the descent through Neptune's Staircase in the afternoon. Less than a mile beyond lay the sea lock at Corpach. Come the appointed hour we slipped our lines at the top of the locks just as drizzly rain started to come down. It persisted for the remainder of our passage down. Despite the rain, many tourists strolled about, having arrived on local tour coaches. Neptune's Staircase attracts thousands of visitors every year. Some took a particular interest in our boat. *Blue Star* stood out with her sponsors' logos on the hull and the Cystic Fibrosis Trust banners attached to the guard rails. One group gave us a donation for the charity, which was gratifying. It took several hours to make the descent, await the opening of the two swing bridges beyond, and motor the short distance to Corpach. Here we tied up at the quayside for the night. In the morning we would be back at sea.

Navigating the canal had been an unforgettable, fantastic experience. It is the scenery which attracts many boat crews and we could understand why. But we had also enjoyed the challenge of the locks, visiting the settlements at the canal side and meeting the people.

***

Joke

I tried to visit the Caledonian Canal but it was all locked up!

***

Above: Roger helming on Loch Ness

Below: The staircase of locks at Fort Augustus

Above: Looking astern as we pass through Loch Oich

Above: Tied up at Banavie

10. Corpach to Greenock

I wanted freedom, open air, adventure. I found it on the sea.

Alain Gerbault

On Monday, 14 September we exited the sea lock at Corpach and entered Loch Linnhe. Free at last from the confines of the canal, we set out southwest down the loch on a 30-mile trip that would take us to the Firth of Lorne, but we would not get that far today. The West Coast of Scotland has a reputation for its natural beauty and sheltered waters giving some of the best sailing in the British Isles. We had not sailed here before and were expecting it to be one of the highlights of our venture.

It was downwind and we were under headsail alone. The sun shone but the following wind was cold. We were wrapped in jumpers, jackets and fleecy hats, downing hot drinks to keep warm. A picnic lunch was eaten in the cockpit as we passed Corran Narrows. On we sailed, south of Lismore, the long slim island that also points in a south-westerly direction. Here, in the Lynn of Lorne, we were amongst mountains, forests, green hills and remote villages. We were almost at the end of Loch Linnhe and could see the Isle of Mull out to the west. We turned into Ardmucknish Bay and to a vacant marina berth at Dunstaffnage, on the mainland. In spite of the chill in the wind it had been a pleasant if uneventful day. We dined out at the restaurant before turning in for the night.

Tuesday dawned. We had considered, when planning our voyage, that we might 'turn right' at the end of Loch Linnhe, to make further progress with our circumnavigation, with the intention of overwintering the boat in one of the northernmost ports. Recently we had reviewed this part of the plan. Our thoughts were that many of the northerly ports were relatively small and may not afford the best protection to a yacht on the hard over winter. The marina facilities at Greenock had been recommended to us. Greenock would also be easily accessible, by car or train, for visiting the boat during the winter. Now, having arrived at the end of Loch Linnhe, it was decision time – turn right or turn left? The clinching factor was the weather. We anticipated needing a reliable spell of good weather to round the northwest corner of Scotland, Cape Wrath. It was already late summer and the forecast for the time we might arrive there was not encouraging. We might need to press on further, past Cape Wrath and beyond Orkney before finding a suitable place to overwinter the boat. Neither of us wanted that – we were ready for a break. So, we decided to turn left and head for Greenock, near Glasgow, via the Crinan Canal. The whole crew saw a passage through the Crinan Canal as an added bonus! Our objective that day became to reach Crinan, where we could enter the canal.

We headed out from Dunstaffnage and followed the coast round, passing Oban, taking the route through Kerrera Sound, the narrow stretch of water separating the island of Kerrera from the Scottish mainland. It was a grey, dull and damp morning with a cold breeze. Long Johns were drafted into service. The sea was reasonably flat though and, once out of the bay, we unfurled the genoa and sailed, later raising the mainsail too.

Beyond Oban we were in the Firth of Lorne, still running southwest. We plotted a course through the Sound of Luing, leaving the islands of Seil and Luing to port, with Lunga and Scarba to starboard. We were definitely having the full Western Isles experience that we had looked forward to. The many islands create a sheltered area to sail in, giving some protection from the strong winds and making a flat sea more likely. Even if the weather was not top notch, the scenery was stunning! Rocky headlands and grassed hills, the odd remote dwelling here and there, and small villages on the seafronts. This was picture-postcard West Coast of Scotland at its best.

The Gulf of Corryvreckan lies between Scarba and the larger island of Jura to its south. It has a fearful reputation with intensely strong tides, and is notorious for its incredibly strong whirlpools. These are created when submerged rocks redirect the intense currents flowing past them. The gulf has the third-largest whirlpool in the world. Whilst the tide can reach speeds of eight knots, standing waves with a height of nine metres or more can be created, the resulting chaos heard up to ten miles away. Clearly, we didn't want to get caught in that! A similarly fierce tidal phenomenon between Lunga and Scarba is classified by the Royal Navy as 'unnavigable'.

We passed Craignish Point on the end of the isthmus stretching out southwest from the mainland, and stood well off the rocky islets to the west of the point. The charts showed large rocks lurking just beneath sea level in several areas. The pilot book warns that 'tidal streams in the area are as strong as any around Britain' and 'there are plenty of hidden dangers'. The tide was running strongly to the south. In order to retain control we turned on the engine. We were now at the north end of the Sound of Jura. We needed to make a turn to port into Loch Crinan, where we could enter the canal. Just outside the loch, without warning, we were suddenly caught up in a powerful whirlpool!

It was not the Corryvreckan – we were too far east for that to explain our predicament. As we surveyed the area we noted several mini whirlpools, flowing in tight circles for no apparent reason. We had been pushed to starboard and spun round, entirely beyond our control. We didn't panic. We resorted to full engine power, trying to force movement in the required direction, and we waited anxiously. Slowly, metre by metre, we started to make progress. With maximum throttle, our instruments showed we were travelling at eight knots through the water, but making progress over the earth's surface at barely one knot. Holding our nerve, painfully slowly, we clawed our way out. Maintaining full power, the Sound of Jura was eventually left behind and we were through into Loch Crinan. Scary stuff!

Black Rock, at two metres high, was north of the entrance to the canal. It's the main hazard once in the loch, but it was clearly visible and easily avoided. The sea lock itself was open, ready for vessels to enter. We rigged fenders and lines and motored into what seemed like the bottom of a deep, dark pit – there was clearly going to be a huge rise in water level as we passed through this lock. It was just as well that we had rigged some very long lines! A canal official was standing above us on the precipice, peering down. He took our lines, turning each of them around a bollard on the lock edge and throwing us the free end to pull in as the water level rose.

On the other side of the sea lock was the most picturesque canal basin – a small pool in which vessels can moor to the quayside. A large number were tied up, several of them beautifully maintained elderly craft, and some old commercial vessels, including a veteran 'Clyde Puffer' converted for holiday use. The basin was a focus for activity, attracting tourists as well as locals. As we exited the sea lock we noted a number of buildings – a hotel and a café amongst them. Beyond the basin, a car park with a toilet and shower block. Tied up in front of the café, we paid our transit fee and were briefed by the canal staff in their office. We exited the basin through another lock, and motored into the canal before tying up for the night, just beyond the lock gates.

We ate on board. Roger perfected a recipe for chicken in French onion and apricot sauce, along with potatoes and vegetables. This we had on other occasions too, and it always received approval. After dinner we walked around the canal basin and into the hotel bar to sample the beer.

The Crinan Canal can easily be traversed in one day, but we were not to be rushed. We started the next day with delicious bacon rolls at the café. A baker was delivering warm, fresh scones, baked in the nearby hotel. As he carried a tray of his wares past, Mike commented that they looked very good. The chap invited him to take one – for free. Naturally, we purchased three more for the rest of the crew. So delicious and enjoyable did we find them that we felt it essential to try to replicate the experience at all subsequent ports of call. Whenever the possibility arose, we dropped in on cafés and bakeries. We would compare the scones using the yardstick of the Crinan Canal Basin café. We never did find any that came up to that standard, although several came very close. We became expert samplers, with an extensive knowledge of the scone quality in various ports around the country. Once back home we were each inspired to bake our own scones!

It was sunny as we motored through the canal. At just over six metres wide, it is much narrower than the Caledonian Canal. The feeling was more akin to travelling on the inland waterways elsewhere in Britain. The *Skipper's Guide* to the Crinan Canal lists the depth as 2.7 metres, but there is a note to 'add 10 centimetres to your normal draught as craft sit lower in fresh water than in sea water'. It is also noted that the actual depth of the canal varies depending on rainfall and the availability of water from the seven reservoirs that supply it at the summit reach. The canal is nine miles long and runs from Crinan near the Sound of Jura to Ardrishaig on Loch Fyne, cutting across the head of the long peninsula of Kintyre. It was constructed to provide a quick link between Crinan and Ardrishaig, saving a journey of well over 110 miles if navigating all around the peninsula. Vessels reach a height of almost 20 metres above sea level at its summit. It was constructed under the supervision of John Rennie and opened in 1801, two years late, over budget and not properly finished. It always seems to be the way! Early problems with water levels, reservoirs and collapsing locks led to Thomas Telford being asked to redesign several sections in 1816. Further reconstruction saw the locks made deeper in the 1930s.

From Crinan the canal weaves its way through beautiful countryside, with wooded areas on each side, here and there branches overlapping the canal. There are stopping points at Bellanoch Bridge, Dunardry and Cairnbaan close to the flights of locks at each of these locations. The route then passes through the town of Lochgilphead before descending to Ardrishaig where it meets the sea. There is a small basin at Ardrishaig, as at Crinan, though perhaps not as pretty as it is set on the edge of the town. Still, there is a delightful view over Loch Fyne from the sea lock.

We'd been led to expect that, unlike on the Caledonian Canal, here on the Crinan we would have to manage all of the locks ourselves. It turned out that all were staffed. Even so, there were 15 locks and seven bridges to negotiate during the full length of the canal. By the time we reached the end of the transit the throwing and pulling on lines had tired us out.

Once back out at sea we found that the wind had disappeared completely, although the sun showed from behind the clouds from time to time. We motored south down Loch Fyne. We were now on the eastern side of the Kintyre peninsula, and headed for Tarbert, about ten miles away. There is a large marina at Tarbert and we were allocated a berth by the friendly staff. The town is spread out around the harbour where the marina is located, and after showering we walked the perimeter and found a restaurant in which to dine out to celebrate our arrival.

Early the next day a heavy mist hung in the harbour just above sea level. Climbing the gangway off the pontoons and onto dry land revealed a spectacular view! With just the tops of yacht masts projecting above the murk, the silent scene had a most ethereal atmosphere. By the time we had eaten breakfast, and everything was shipshape, the sun had burned off the mist, but there was still no wind. We motored slowly, pottering the three miles across to the other side of Loch Fyne to pay a visit to Portavadie for coffee!

The place has an interesting background. The harbour was first developed by the Scottish Office as a base where concrete platforms would be built, for use in the North Sea offshore oil industry. It was soon accepted, however, that steel platforms built elsewhere represented the way ahead and the development at Portavadie was discontinued. In the 1980s the harbour was used by a fish-farming company.

A brand-new marina with a five-star apartment complex was opened in 2010, with saunas, holiday cottages, conference rooms, restaurant and retail outlets. We marvelled at it. Definitely amongst the best marinas that we visited during our entire circumnavigation. Of course, we reviewed the toilet and shower rooms especially, and found that they scored very highly on our facility-rating scale. Naturally, we also inspected the coffee lounge, with its glass walls overlooking the boats, and the outside terrace where we sat in the sun to consume our coffee and scones (also very agreeable!). The place was almost deserted, save for a handful of visitors and the staff. Although there were many vessels in the marina we wondered how long it could survive without a higher footfall.

Portavadie lies towards the south of a peninsula, at the end of which is Ardlamont Point. Resuming our journey, we motored around the point to the eastern side. About a mile off the coast lies the island of Bute. Narrow waterways, the West and East Kyles of Bute, form a horseshoe shape around the island, joining together in the north. They have a reputation for their scenic setting. Mountains and countryside were visible from the sea, with the occasional town at the seafront. We were delighted by what we saw. We picked up a mooring buoy off Kames, a settlement on the west coast, and had a picnic lunch in the cockpit.

Slipping our mooring after lunch, we motored further north up the West Kyle and rounded the northernmost tip of Bute. The navigable water here is rather narrow and, although the deeper water is marked with buoys, we had to maintain our concentration. Heading southeast down the East Kyle we were again able to enjoy the countryside in the sunshine. A ferry service runs from Rhubodach on the island to Colintraive on the mainland, and we had to stand off while the ferry made its passage. For a short time the wind blew and we sailed, but soon after it was 'engine on' time again. We decided to put in to the marina at Port Bannatyne on Bute.

There had been some discussion about putting in to Rothesay, a little further along the coast of Bute, instead. Roger explained there were some unusual Victorian public toilets in the town which were well worth a look at! The crew scoffed at this idea, but on a subsequent TV programme featuring 'said toilets', they did indeed seem 'interesting'!

Having had such a tough day, with coffee, picnic and 'pootling' under the sun, we deserved to dine out. After walking the high street we selected the Port Inn. It just happened to be the night when live music was on, and we were keen to be entertained. Lots of locals had the same idea and the small dining room rapidly filled up. The last empty table, in the corner, was quickly taken by a sad-looking old chap, sitting down with his pint. A middle-aged woman joined him. It seemed that no one else could fit into the room, and yet more people were still arriving. Many had musical instruments; they were still squeezing in and were somehow, perhaps by magic, being accommodated. So far as we could make out, this was the night when anyone who could play anything, on any instrument, was invited to come along and entertain the punters. Electronic boxes, loudspeakers, guitars, and much more were soon crammed into the tiny room. It was getting rather hot with so many people crowding in. A couple of chaps started on their instruments and the woman from the corner table stood up and started to sing. The sad-looking chap didn't seem any happier. Next a couple of guitarists joined in the show and the woman began again. The people were friendly but the amateur performance was not 'easy on the ears' so we left, opting for a walk in the cool evening air, still astonished at how many people could fit into a small room!

Back at the marina we walked among the boats stored on the hard. One of them had us reeling in stitches of laughter. It was a small white hulled yacht with its name in large letters down each side of the hull – 'Baldrick's Cunning Plan'. Baldrick was a character, played by Tony Robinson, in the TV comedy *Black Adder*. Throughout the series his catchphrase was 'I have a cunning plan'. It was always so ridiculous that it was never accepted by his superior, played by Rowan Atkinson. Above the name on the boat was another line from the programme: 'As cunning as a fox what used to be Professor of Cunning at Oxford University but has moved on and is now working for the U.N. at the High Commission of International Cunning Planning'! We dissolved into hysterics, imagining the skipper using the VHF radio and having to announce the vessel's name.

The following day dawned another fine summer's day, albeit again no wind. We continued our passage down the East Kyle of Bute and turned into the Firth of Clyde. We passed Dunoon on the coast, once a favourite holiday destination for Glaswegians. The Firth takes a slightly west of north route before it turns to starboard after passing

Dunoon. Greenock, our planned destination for the end of the week, then lies on the Scottish mainland to starboard.

We had time to spare and opted to explore. Instead of turning to starboard we continued north into Loch Long. Very picturesque! Mountains all around us, much of it carpeted in sprawling forest, with vast expanses of bare rock. Five miles on and we came to Coulport, off to starboard. Nearby is the Royal Navy Armaments Depot where nuclear weapons are loaded aboard submarines and other vessels. The jetty at the seafront was fenced off by a substantial structure and several lookout towers guarded the perimeter. This was a place where visitors were not welcome! If we navigated too close we were likely to be marshalled by a navy vessel and escorted away. We didn't put this theory to the test.

Further on a turn to port took us into Loch Goil. The scenery here was equally stunning. A mile into the loch lies Carrick Castle, built on the rocky shore. Originally constructed in the 15th century, this was a stronghold of Clan Lamont. Its stone ruins magically enhanced the beautiful, surreal setting. We journeyed on another five miles to the end at Lochgoilhead and picked up a mooring buoy. This would be our stopping point for the night. The sea was as flat as a millpond and we took the dinghy ashore for a leg stretch and to sample an after-dinner drink at the nearby public house.

Saturday, 19 September saw us drop our mooring and motor towards Greenock. There was only a slight breeze and it was from dead ahead. Gliding once more past Carrick Castle, we enjoyed an on-board tea break. Off Coulport on Loch Long, an MOD patrol boat stood guard. We kept well to starboard to avoid any bother. It was blowing a very cold breeze but the sun shone and the sea was flat again. Several other yachts were out, trying to make the most of the conditions. Shortly after midday we arrived at Greenock.

In the marina we noticed a fine looking vessel tied up close to where we had berthed. It was the sailing yacht *Drum*. She has quite a history! Originally commissioned by Simon Le Bon of the pop group Duran Duran, *Drum* was built in order to compete in the 1985/86 Whitbread Round The World Yacht Race. To help prepare the crew and yacht for the race a 'warm up' exercise was undertaken – that of competing in the 1985 Fastnet Race. *Drum* was one of the favourites to win but off the Cornish coast its large, heavy keel fell off.

The boat 'turned turtle', trapping the crew inside. Heat treatment, required when welding the aluminium keel, had not been carried out. Fortunately, another boat nearby witnessed the disaster and was able to raise the alarm. Happily, all of the crew were rescued unharmed. There was only one month to get the boat repaired in time to compete in the Whitbread. This was achieved, and *Drum*, the only British maxi yacht in the race, attracted huge support and finished third in her class – a tremendous achievement given the disaster of the Fastnet Race!

Greenock was the end of the line for *Blue Star* as far as 2015 was concerned. She was to be lifted out and stored on the hard over the winter months. We took off the sails and swabbed the decks, and we removed the Cystic Fibrosis charity banners that were still attached to the guard rails. When we had left Hythe in May they were bright yellow; now they were bleached white by the sun!

Our log showed that since leaving Hythe on 17 May we had travelled 1,158 miles. It had been an incredible voyage so far and we were looking forward to resuming the challenge in 2016.

***

Joke

Sailor in café bar, complaining to manager: 'This coffee tastes like dirt!'
Manager: 'That's not surprising, it was ground this morning!'

***

Below: Passing through the sea loch into the Crinan Canal

Above: The yacht basin at Crinan

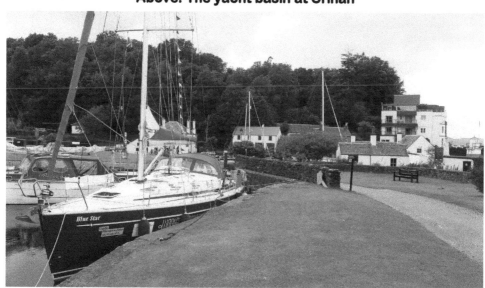

Above: Tied up at Crinan
Below: Roger helming in the Crinan Canal

Above: Early morning at Tarbert

Above: Port Bannatyne on the island of Bute
Below: *Baldrick's Cunning Plan*

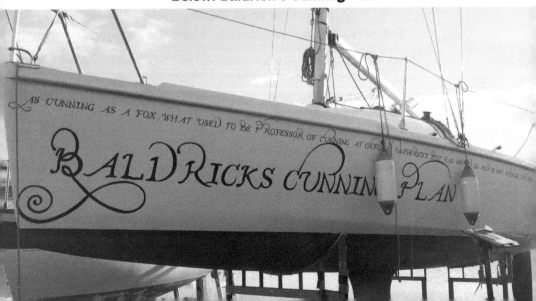

Right: On our mooring buoy at Lochgoilhead

Below: *Drum* at Greenock

11. Overwintering in Greenock

Home is the sailor, home from the sea,
Her far-borne canvas furled
The ship pours shining on the quay
The plunder of the world.

A.E. Housman, 'Home is the Sailor'

James Watt Marina is located in an old Greenock dock. Built between 1878 and 1886, it was constructed to compete with other shipping facilities in nearby Glasgow. It came into its heyday when vast quantities of sugar were shipped from the Caribbean to Scotland. At one time, up to 400 ships per year were landing their cargoes. To accommodate the imported sugar a large warehouse was built and is still known today as the 'Sugar Shed'. To support dock operations, a large 150-ton-capacity cantilever crane was built in 1917. This sits proudly on the quayside today and is protected as a listed structure.

Once we had arrived at the marina, a couple of days were spent cleaning the boat, removing perishable food, taking off all personal kit, emptying the fresh water and flushing out the holding tank.

We also made sure the diesel tank was full, a necessary precaution against 'diesel bug'. Water can form through condensation if air is present inside the tank. It supports the growth of microbes at the diesel-water interface. These 'bugs' can create a sludge that damages diesel engines, rapidly bringing them to a halt.

Roger took home all the ropes from on deck, for laundering. The build-up of salt renders them stiff and more difficult to handle. Once they had whizzed around the industrial washing machine at the home marina they were as good as new.

The rental life raft was taken off the boat and returned to the supplier. Various elements of deck gear (danbuoy, horseshoe lifebuoy, throwing line, etc.) were removed for cleaning and storing. The sails were packed away, and the boat looked skeleton-like on deck by the time we had finished.

The boat was lifted out using a mobile crane, different from the standard marina hoist seen in most ports. Suspended from the jib, *Blue*

Star looked vulnerable, but weighing nine tons, she was well within the machine's capacity.

The original programme for our round Britain adventure was based on breaking the voyage into short trips. We'd decided to sail only during the summers of 2015 and 2016. We were pleased with our progress, and were confident that our plan to finish the following year would come to fruition.

***

With the arrival of 2016 our thoughts turned to recommissioning *Blue Star* and continuing our voyage. For several months we had been looking forward to resuming the circumnavigation. We each visited *Blue Star* over the 'break' in proceedings to check that everything was safe and dry.

During one such visit Roger was able to meet Richard and Kim Pavey. They had posted a card on the noticeboard at Dunstaffnage Marina, asking for opportunities to crew on a sailing boat. Roger had followed this up for us and met with Richard and Kim on a cold spring day in Greenock. The two strangers waiting for him were most distinctive – Richard, well-built and boasting a long ponytail, and Kim with her American accent. They were friendly and helpful; we were to enjoy their company very much during our sailing. It was pleasing that they were so keen, helping with some of the boat cleaning and preparation for the coming summer. We scheduled them into our crew list for soon after we'd resumed sailing.

Roger:

On another occasion when Judith and I checked on the boat we met up with some former 'Shell' friends, Dave and Lilias, who keep their beautiful Nauticat 44 in the marina at Largs, just down the coast from the Clyde. They were impressed with our journey so far, and even more impressed that we were going north, over Cape Wrath and out to the Orkneys. As locals, they knew the waters around the West Coast of Scotland very well. Whilst we had seen and recognised what a magnificent sailing ground the coast of Scotland is, it has one drawback – the weather! Dave told us that the previous year he had been out less than ten days. During 2015 we had enjoyed some beautiful weather in Scotland. However, we were aware that it might be challenging in 2016 as we went further north. A quote from one of our crew members, Chris, hung darkly in the back of my mind, 'never sail anywhere north of latitude 53°' – a line approximately from the Wash to Anglesey. All would become clear in 2016.

Local technicians were contacted to carry out routine maintenance ready for the new season. The engine and saildrive were serviced, rigging checked and a fresh coat of anti-foul applied. The hull and superstructure were also given a polish before relaunching. During the visits we brought back car loads of equipment to reinstall on the boat prior to sailing, and we tested and reinstalled the boat's EPIRB.

Mike oversaw the relaunch of the boat, giving the hull a final polish before it went back into the water. The lift-in was done using the same mobile crane that had hauled her out several months earlier – there was no purpose-built boat lift at James Watt Marina and all lifting of vessels was done using this technique.

Mike:

On the day of the relaunch it was bitterly cold, snowing on and off. During a break in the snow the marina staff resolved to launch *Blue Star*, and I watched her dangle from the cable as the crane arm swung out over the water, praying that she would not be dropped accidentally! The staff had rigged lines from the bow and stern and used these to rotate the boat, so that she was more or less aligned to the pontoon when she was lowered down into the water. I hurried on board and looked around in the bilges to check for water ingress. All was well.

I was asked to motor the boat round to another berth in the marina, away from where the crane was to be used to launch the next boat. We were allocated a spot opposite the marina office, close to the shower facilities, convenient in snowy weather.

We'd arranged for professional riggers to scale the mast and check all of the standing rigging holding it up. At ten years old, it may not have many years of life left, but we hoped it would be OK to see us back to Hythe. Whilst I was down below, with the companionway hatch closed because of the cold, two riggers turned up and got on with the job, not realising that I was on board. To their surprise, I pulled back the hatch and made my presence known. I waited with bated breath for their report. A clean bill of health. No expensive re-rigging required!

Whilst aboard, the riggers also checked the mainsheet system and found a badly worn shackle; this was replaced. I thanked them for their work, gave them my address, and asked them to send their invoice. I'd spent some time talking to them about the *Blue Star* project and our efforts to raise funds for charity. We never did get a bill from the riggers, despite several reminders. We concluded that they'd decided to do the work for free, as a form of donation to our cause, which we really appreciated.

Back in the water, with all fittings and equipment reinstalled, we were ready to go again!

***

Joke
Q. What breakfast should a yacht crew be given on a cold day?
A. Frosties!

***

Below: *Blue Star* is lifted out of the water

12. Greenock to Mallaig

Fare thee well! The ship is ready,
And the breeze is fresh and steady.
Hands are fast the anchor weighing;
High in the air the streamer's playing.
Spread the sails – the waves are swelling
Proudly round thy buoyant dwelling,
Fare thee well! And when at sea,
Think of those, who sigh for thee.

Hannah Flagg Gould, 'The Ship is Ready'

By Wednesday, 4 May we were all set to depart from Greenock and resume our sailing adventure. It had been a long winter. We'd missed *Blue Star* and we were excited about resuming our voyage.

During the planning, Roger published an article in the company magazine, *Shell Pensioners Association News*, letting readers know of the *Blue Star* project and inviting anyone interested in sailing with us to contact him. The magazine is distributed to all past employees. Three people who responded to the article were to be our next crew.

Dave Twiney was a former Shell employee. His friend Graham Rennie, an architect, ran his own business in the Midlands. They had a third friend, Ingemar Hellgren, from Stockholm, a journalist and a PR officer who worked for Citroen and later Volkswagen. Ingemar's membership of the crew continued the international flavour of the project, with crew from New Zealand and from the United States having sailed with us during the preceding year.

We all met for the first time on Wednesday evening aboard the boat and introduced ourselves over a cuppa. There was friendly banter amongst the new crew; it was clear they would be fun to sail with. Dinner was prepared on board – stew, commonly known as 'crew pot'. We sat chatting about the week ahead, and bedded down early, ready for the next day – the continuation of our round Britain voyage!

Thursday dawned. Whenever we had new crew on board we always gave a thorough safety briefing, and we went through our normal routine. The sky was overcast, but a promising wind was blowing. After giving our thanks to the marina staff, we slipped our lines, bound once more for Portavadie.

A force 4 took us away from the marina and into the Firth of Clyde. Following the Clyde, we turned south. As our course changed we got the full strength of the wind in our faces. The single reef already in the mainsail was doubled up to two reefs, and more headsail was taken in on the furler. Still we struggled to make much progress against the onslaught of the strong wind, now gusting force 6, and the engine was switched on to give us a little more forward power. Motor-sailing proved effective but the going was still tough. We forced our way through many short but determined waves. It seemed they'd resolved to thwart our progress. We were close-hauled, under sail and engine, and the boat was leaning over seriously.

After a couple of hours' slog we reached the point where Loch Striven and the East Kyle of Bute join with the Firth of Clyde. We altered course to starboard and headed up the Kyle, retracing our path of 2015, albeit in the opposite direction. Now the wind was coming from our port side and we were on a beam reach. The engine was switched off and as we left the Firth of Clyde the sea state settled. We were now sailing in the lee of the island of Bute.

The Kyle was as strikingly beautiful as when we had sailed there the previous year. Once more we passed Rothesay and Port Bannatyne, this time without stopping for an evening concert! We cast an eye over Bute's coast and the little houses looking out to sea. Towards the north of Bute we again had to exercise caution so as not to impede the progress of the car ferry. The ferry there complements the busier service to Rothesay from Wemyss Bay, about six miles from Greenock. Beyond the ferry we followed the narrow, buoyed section of the Kyle, after which we turned to port and into the West Kyle.

The wind was once more on the nose so the iron horse was exercised to maintain forward progress. We sailed on, past Kames where we'd had a deck picnic on a mooring buoy seven months earlier. Reaching the southern end of the peninsula at Ardlamont Point, we needed to turn to starboard into Loch Fyne. We tried to unfurl the genoa to travel under sail alone but there was a problem. The furling mechanism at the top of the mast was suspected. Hmm! Somebody was going to have to go up there, someone else was going to have to winch them up. Still, that would have to be solved later. We continued under main and engine, and an hour and a half later we were tied up at Portavadie.

The marina was still as delightful as before, with a quiet, understated, relaxed atmosphere and five-star facilities. The retail outlets, holiday apartments, and extensive sun terrace seemed to belong somewhere in the Mediterranean rather than Scotland. Perhaps we had the wrong impression about the weather here? Naturally, we had to visit the restaurant once more, where we partook of pre-dinner drinks. After chilling for a while in the lounge we walked back to *Blue Star* and Ingemar cooked us all a splendid meal. There was bonhomie and chat over dinner, and we got our heads down after a final visit to the luxury facilities ashore. It felt great to be back in business!

We aimed to pass through the Crinan Canal again the following day, and finish in the yacht basin at the far end. A good place for scones, though that was not the only reason for wanting to take this course. This was the quickest way to progress north. So, no malingering! An 'early-ish' start was called for and we left port just after 0800 hours. Again, we were not charged for our stay, helping the fundraising.

We motored against the early morning breeze coming from the direction of Ardrishaig, where the entrance to the Crinan Canal lay. The water was flat and it was an easy passage. The sea lock opened a few minutes after we arrived.

We motored in and put crew ashore to organise the lines, and to pay our transit fee. The lock filled quickly and before long we were motoring out into the canal. It felt very familiar, and it was going to be a great experience! We were all looking forward to it.

There was an unwelcome surprise waiting for us though. During our 2015 passage, all locks had been staffed by Scottish Canals; many of the staff had been students doing summer vacation work; they had been a great help to us. We understood that staff would be available to provide the same support during this passage too, but as we worked our way through the locks during the morning there were no staff to be seen. We had to do all of the hard work ourselves! The crew took turns, cranking the sluices open and closed, and heaving the lock gates to and fro. Whilst the work proved tiring, we did find it rather satisfying.

After a few hours we stopped for a lunch break at Cairnbaan. This was the opportunity to fix our furling gear. We were concerned that the bearing at the top of the mast might need replacing. We had to investigate. It was decided, by lack of any other volunteers and by lack of protest from him, that Roger once more should be the one who would be winched up the mast to make a close quarters inspection. The rest of the crew felt that they had so much more to give with a winch handle in their hands.

Roger made himself acquainted with the bosun's chair, attached it to the main halyard and was duly raised by the rest of us. Whilst one crew member winched, another tailed, maintaining some tension on the free end of the line to help ensure it didn't slip. A second halyard was also attached to the bosun's chair as a safety measure, this line being fed to a different winch and the slack taken out of it as Roger ascended the mast. Once at the top, armed with a spray can of WD-40, he made short work of the problem. A generous squirt applied to the bearing, a little 'persuasion' to rotate applied by the deck crew, by grabbing hold of the forestay foil and turning it, a few threats and curses, and 'the job's a good 'un'! We decided that Roger was worth keeping as part of the crew and allowed him to gently descend the mast.

After a sandwich lunch, onwards! Still no canal staff to help us with the locks, but it was a lovely day and we were enjoying the exercise and scenery. By around 1600 hours we had Crinan firmly within our sights and were descending the flight of locks at Dunardry when, at the last lock in the flight, a member of canal staff appeared from nowhere, all innocent and jolly.

'I'll work this lock for you,' he says, ever helpful. 'But you do realise you can't get to Crinan tonight? It's home time for canal staff shortly, and you're not allowed to swing the bridges yourself.'

Well that certainly put paid to our ambition. There were two bridges between us and Crinan, so we weren't going to make it that evening. We were more than a little miffed at having our progress curtailed, unnecessarily as we saw it. After all we'd managed all the locks unaided. Could we really not be allowed to operate the bridges ourselves? It would have been an interesting exercise!

We motored on to Bellanoch Bridge, the first obstruction. Resigned to the delay, we tied up for the night. Dave prepared a sausage and mash dinner, and later that evening we walked the two miles to Crinan in order to 'support the hotel bar staff'. It was dark on our return, but *Blue Star* was waiting for us, as were our bunks. It was a lovely place to sleep aboard a boat and life still seemed grand!

The following morning, Saturday, 7 May, the canal staff were on duty by 8.30am sharp and the bridges were duly swung, enabling us to arrive at Crinan in a very short time. It wasn't the right moment to pass through the sea lock though, the tides would have been against us. The only option was to visit the café again and sample a few more scones. They did not disappoint!

By 11am the tides were in our favour and we were in the sea lock with another yacht, *Hesper*. To our delight, totally unprompted, her skipper handed us a £20 note and asked us to stick it in the on-board charity box. Our adventure led us to meet some lovely people!

Out at sea the aim was to get to Loch Aline by evening, around 35 miles away. It's a small loch on the Scottish mainland that opens out into the Sound of Mull, the seaway separating the Isle of Mull from the mainland. A picturesque place, it has a marina at Lochaline which would be our intended stopping point.

Once out of Loch Crinan we took care not to get caught up again in any whirlpools! Initially the sea state was smooth and we motor-sailed against the prevailing light breeze. Several other yachts were heading in the same direction, as though we were all one large fleet. We retraced more of our route from 2015, passing again through the Sound of Luing and into the Firth of Lorne. Then things got more serious.

The wind, blowing against the favourable tide, picked up some severe waves. With the engine working hard, we battled our way in a north-easterly direction, paying careful attention to the other yachts, to several motor cruisers and to a passenger ferry. It was a rough passage but slowly we clawed our way forward. After enduring it all for a couple of hours we were, at last, able to alter course to the northwest and into the Sound of Mull, where the sea state was smooth. We breathed a sigh of relief!

About four miles along the sound we turned into Loch Aline. The settlement of Lochaline is a short distance into the loch. A quick radio call and a member of the marina staff, Fiona, appeared on the pontoon to guide us to our overnight berth. There was a tricky wind to contend with while coming alongside the pontoon, but using the engine to counteract it, we crept gingerly into our allocated spot.

The marina there is modern and we found it suited our needs admirably. After relaxing and showering we walked into the nearby village for dinner.

Our target for Sunday was Tobermory, only about 13 miles to the northwest, on the Isle of Mull. It wasn't exactly an ambitious journey, but who could pass over the chance to visit this famous town! It was only a short distance to sail. An early start wasn't required, so we had time to shop for groceries. The general store didn't open until 11.30am, so first we walked into the village for coffee and scones (what else?) at the Lochaline Hotel. Mike had promised his speciality, baked salmon, but unfortunately the store didn't have salmon in stock. That particular dinner might have to wait.

After lunch we slipped our lines and motored out into the loch, raised full mainsail and unrolled the genoa. We soon passed out of Loch Aline into the Sound of Mull. It should have been a pleasant sail, but the breeze blew against us so we had to motor-sail to make good progress. Still, at least the sea was calm and it was a chance to sit back and appreciate the scenery. The mountains and hills on both sides of the sound, together with the greenery, somehow suited our relaxed frame of mind. There were a few other vessels in the sound too, but nothing to get in our way. The sun joined in on occasions, making a very pleasant afternoon. Three hours later we were safely berthed at Tobermory.

Despite it being a Sunday, there were still a few shops open, including a supermarket selling salmon! Visitors surveyed the beautiful harbour, the distinctive multi-coloured houses and the countryside beyond. We followed the tourists' town tour. We couldn't help but note the attractive entrance to Tobermory Distillery. Roger had his photograph taken outside, where he 'pretended' to be drunk, clutching frantically at the gates to hold himself up. Another very attractive feature of the town was the brown painted shop with white letters above, announcing 'Tobermory Handmade Chocolate'. We'd have liked to visit, but it was closed! Pity!

Monday brought us sunshine and a warm wind – perhaps the first warm wind since leaving Hythe the previous year! Our spirits were high as we slipped our lines shortly after ten o'clock and headed out into the sound once more, bound for Mallaig. We were heading northwest, needing to round the headland in order to set a course for our destination. The almanac warns that Ardnamurchan Point 'is an exposed headland onto which the ebb sets. With onshore winds very heavy seas extend two miles offshore and it should be given a wide berth.' Goodness! We wanted to sail close to the shore to best appreciate its beauty. Fortunately, the wind wasn't blowing onshore and we could still do that.

As we rounded the point the wind strengthened and we batted along at seven knots on starboard tack. It was a great sailing day! The sea state was slight, the sun blazed down on us from above and the scenery was magnificent. We passed the coloured rocky shoreline and, some distance ahead, were the islands of Muck, Eigg, Rum and Canna, with their green hills and rugged landscapes. Beautiful anchorages on the islands beckoned but we hadn't the time to linger. We had a passage of some 30 miles to make. Soon the wind died and we were under engine again. We crossed the Sound of Arisaig and the headland beyond at Rudh' Arisaig. Although motoring, we were enjoying the sun and scenery as we ate our sandwiches.

We arrived at Mallaig late afternoon. The port is geared up to support the fishing industry, and at first it wasn't obvious where the marina was located. We consulted the pilot book and motored on, having dropped the sails. Eventually all became clear, we found ourselves a berth at the visitors' pontoon and tied up. A very smart-looking marina building stood nearby on the shore and we entered to confirm our arrival and intentions.

It turned out to be a new construction, with excellent facilities. The only problem was, we were informed, it was only open from 9.00am to 5.00pm. The crew therefore had to make alternative arrangements – a meal ashore enabling us to use the restaurant's toilets. We were later informed – all too late for us – that the opening hours related to the office, not to the toilet and shower facilities! A breakdown in communication obviously, but we didn't see anyone else using the building outside the stated hours either.

Mallaig was a crew-change stop in our voyage. We were to say goodbye to Dave, Graham and Ingemar. They had been great company and we were sorry to see them go. Dave and Graham were met by their wives who came aboard *Blue Star* to say hello and take a look around. Before long we were all joined by the replacement crew.

Richard and Kim Pavey were a couple who lived near Aberdeen. They'd already met Roger at Greenock during the boat's overwintering. Having recently completed their RYA Day Skipper theory, they wanted to gain some practical experience. Richard was a metallurgist – a fact that resulted in some humour because he frequently referred to 'tin foil' used in the galley, and we debated at length, with plenty of ribbing, whether it was tin or aluminium!

David Shepherd, 'Shep' to his friends, was our other new crew member. He was a friend from Stafford Coastal Cruising Club. He ran his own engineering company before 'retiring' to focus on property development.

We sat on deck enjoying the sun and chatting over drinks. All too soon, the outgoing crew had to make their departure. It had been great to sail with them!

Ingemar:

I learnt a lot from you, not least how safety conscious you are. Always wear a lifejacket, never leave the cockpit without attaching to something. From now on I will always follow your rules when I am in a boat. From Mallaig I took a beautiful train ride to Glasgow and then Edinburgh. I will always remember our wonderful sailing trip to Mallaig.

***

<u>Joke</u>
Q. Where did the weather forecaster stop for a drink?
A. The local isoBAR!

***

Below: The marina at Portavadie

Above: Ingemar (left) and Roger work the lock gate on the Crinan Canal

Below: Entering the harbour at Tobermory

13. Mallaig to Kinlochbervie

The ship was cleared, the harbour cheered,
Merrily did we drop,
Below the kirk, below the hill,
Below the lighthouse top.

Samuel Taylor Coleridge, 'The Rime of the Ancient Mariner'

One of the joys of sailing is that you never know what will happen next. Occasionally it will be something that is a nuisance, or worse. Many times though, it will be something that inspires wonder – in nature, wildlife, history and in people. Or it will be something that brings great satisfaction in a passage well executed. The forthcoming week would bring all of these!

Mallaig lies at the southern end of the Sound of Sleat – the stretch of sea that separates the Isle of Skye from the mainland. It is a most beautiful part of the country and the next day, Tuesday, 10 May, was a treat indeed! After slipping our lines, luscious vegetation, forests and rocky shores slowly closed in on us, as we journeyed through the sound. Immediately north of Mallaig we passed Loch Nevis. Later, Loch Hourn and the smaller Loch na Dal were left behind. The Sound of Sleat then became narrower. It felt as though we were navigating a lake rather than the sea. We passed the small island at Sandaig and, five miles further on, the little bay at Glenelg.

The book and film *Ring of Bright Water*, set in this area, tell the true story of how Gavin Maxwell lived a simple life on the coast, caring for wild animals, especially otters. The tale also focuses on the beauty of the landscape and wildlife. We could certainly appreciate why Maxwell loved this area. The song that accompanies the film played in our heads, none of us daring to sing aloud and ruin the atmosphere. Inside, we were singing at full volume with the sheer joy of life!

Beyond Glenelg the sound becomes Kyle Rhea, a still narrower body of water, more akin to navigating a river. We took care not to impede the small car ferry crossing from the mainland to Skye, as we sailed on. Off to our left, on the island, lay an entrancing group of about a dozen seals. We couldn't help but stare at them as they lay basking in the sun. It didn't take too much imagination to envisage them on sun loungers with dark sunglasses, beach towels and drinks at their sides. They raised their heads slowly to give a nodding acknowledgement to the crew of *Blue Star*!

After a couple of miles, Kyle Rhea opens out into Loch Alsh, a wider stretch of water. Here we turned towards the seaboard end of the loch. Ahead of us the road bridge spanned the water, taking traffic to and from Skye. We weren't to navigate under the bridge today though. Our destination was Kyle of Lochalsh, a town on the mainland to starboard, a short distance before the bridge. It has a very small marina with a couple of legs off a single pontoon and an honesty box. This was a sign that we would soon be in the more remote parts of Scotland.

There were no marina facilities. We were directed to the public toilets in the town. We did test these out, but were dismayed to learn that a steel mesh gate would be drawn across them at 8.00pm and it would not reopen until the following morning!

At this point the resourcefulness of the officers of *Blue Star* were put to the test. It was suggested that some arrangement could be made with the nearby Lochalsh Hotel. The two of us would lead negotiations! We strode off purposefully.

At the hotel reception stood two young ladies, Ella and Caitlin. We explained our situation but they shook their heads; the hotel did not allow for any Tom, Dick or Harry (or Mike or Roger ...) to use a hotel bathroom. We pressed our charitable cause and they agreed to call the manager, Mr Macrae. Finally, a deal was struck. The crew of *Blue Star* could have free use of a hotel room, shower and toilet provided they did not use the bed or towels. To show our appreciation we would buy drinks and after-dinner desserts at the hotel. Result! We were delighted with the outcome, and also with the puddings that we ate later in the restaurant.

During our stay in Kyle of Lochalsh we were assisted by Hughie, the skipper of *Blue Migrant*, a motor cruiser moored immediately behind us on the pontoon. Hughie was quite a character. He lived aboard his boat with his dog, Wolfie, an Alsatian and Wolfhound cross. You would not want to mess with Wolfie!

We were running low on diesel and there was no fuel point at the marina. There was no guarantee that the ports we'd be stopping at in the coming days would have any either. If there was a chance to fill up now, we needed to take it. Hughie explained that he used the filling station in the town, loading up his car with jerry cans to transport diesel to his boat. We were not in possession of any cans. Hughie kindly drove us to his friends on the industrial estate, from whom we borrowed suitable plastic drums, then to the petrol station where the drums were filled with diesel. On returning to the marina we borrowed his funnel and strainer to pour the diesel into *Blue Star*'s tanks as Wolfie stood guard. With Hughie's help we also managed to replenish our gas supply, which was becoming a concern. We really appreciated all of his incredibly generous assistance.

To express our gratitude, we invited him to join us for dinner on board *Blue Star* that evening. Thai green curry, cooked by Kim, which was dee-licious! Hughie entertained us with tales of his interesting life, having once flown helicopters in the Antarctic for Greenpeace! Tired of life in Antarctica, he returned to Scotland where he started his business, Seadogs, aboard *Blue Migrant*. Clients book to survey wrecks under water, by piloting a remotely controlled underwater vehicle. They can then take a video disc home with them, showing their exploration!

Wednesday, 11 May. We decided the best way to start the day was with coffee at the Lochalsh Hotel. Shortly after, we slipped our lines and waved goodbye to Hughie and Wolfie. We were heading out under the Skye road bridge and into the inner Sound of Raasay, bound for Gairloch on the Scottish mainland, some 40 miles away. We had calculated that we would easily pass under the bridge, but still we all looked aloft to check on things. It looked awfully close! But then it always does.

Out in the Sound of Raasay, we left the Crowlin Islands to starboard and continued north, passing Applecross on the mainland, where Monty Halls based himself for his TV series about crofting.

The weather was just like the scenery – brilliant! Blazing sun warmed our passage. The sea was mostly flat but picked up a little as we cleared Skye and powered north. Out towards the Atlantic we could see the Outer Hebrides. A steady force 6 wind pushed us along on starboard tack. We took in two reefs and continued under double-reefed main only. *Blue Star* behaved impeccably, staying almost upright, as she ploughed on at a steady five knots, giving us a very enjoyable ride.

Shep prepared a Spanish omelette at lunchtime. We ate it in the cockpit, plates on knees, with knife and fork and a piece of buttered bread. Some sauce if you want it. There was a piece of David's special fruit cake for afters, washed down with a mug of hot tea, as we watched the land go by.

Shep was proving to be a dab hand in the galley, as well as bringing with him all his sailing experience. He entertained us with tales of racing across the English Channel in questionable conditions, having his boat, *Endora*, craned out of his garden at home, and trailing a new mast for her by road to the South of France where she was berthed.

As we approached Gairloch we wondered what access it had by land. It seemed so isolated. Situated in Loch Gairloch, it had a modest, though modern, marina, located at the end of the bay. Tall forested hills stood all around us, and in the background, many 'moonscape' mountains. There did prove to be land access to Gairloch – the A832 running through, what appeared to us, a small settlement.

The people we met were very friendly and the sun continued to shine. A large catamaran appeared in the bay and anchored. We watched the crew launch a small dinghy with an outboard to access the shore. Light became dark and we dined on board before going to bed.

The sun was still shining on Thursday, but the sea had taken a turn for the worse, with waves up to two metres. The wind wasn't so obliging, having opted to blow from the north. We left Gairloch under engine, bound for Lochinver, about 40 miles away. The pitching and rolling of the boat was unpleasant as we worked our way through the waves. We pressed on with the sprayhood raised to provide us with some shelter from the cold wind.

Kim shared the fore-cabin with Richard. She would often opt to chill there whilst we were under way. The rest of us were amazed at her fortitude since the fore-cabin probably experiences more bouncing up and down than any other part of the boat, so it must have been difficult to read or relax at times. Without fail, she would always emerge with a smile on her face, frequently ready to prepare a meal!

Richard had brought along his fishing rod and he planned to catch dinner. However, the practice did not adhere to the plan. The only thing he caught was a seagull, which had spotted his lure and tried to catch it for its own dinner. The seagull's feet became hooked on Richard's line and we ended up dragging it behind us. We tried hard to unhook it but it proved impossible. We ended up cutting the line, feeling very guilty for causing the bird so much distress.

As we approached Lochinver we spotted another yacht sailing nearby. It gave us the motivation to try sailing for the last few miles. Perhaps the wind had changed direction sufficiently. We unfurled the genoa and steered silently into Loch Inver. Behind the town we could see an endless barren mountain range and the especially strange shape of Suilven - a giant egg protruding above the rest of the landscape!

Lochinver is one of Scotland's largest fishing ports, the largest being Peterhead on the East Coast. At the time of our visit the port was used by fishing boats from Spain and France. In its heyday of the 1970s it was the busiest port on the West Coast of Scotland, with trawlers queueing to unload their catch. Now there are few Scottish trawlers; locals blame unfair EU quotas and rules governing the hiring of crew. Sadly, we didn't see any queueing fishing trawlers.

As we secured *Blue Star*'s lines the boat we had seen out in the bay entered the marina and tied up close by. The skipper explained that we'd need to walk to the office at the other end of a large fish warehouse to pay our marina fee. It was rather a hike to get there, but it gave us a chance to see the town, modest in size with many grey brick buildings.

Walking back to the boat we came upon a newly built sports centre and found that we were welcome to use the toilets and showers there for a small fee. Upstairs was a lounge and reading area where both a wi-fi signal and an excellent cup of coffee could be obtained!

The next day, Friday, we set ourselves the target of reaching Kinlochbervie, the northernmost port on the West Coast of Scotland. It would be the last stop before rounding Cape Wrath, the most north-westerly point of mainland Britain. Once again, the forecast was disappointing – a very cold wind blowing from the north. If Carol Kirkwood, our weather oracle, could not do better than this then ... well! In fact, we quite liked Carol, so perhaps she could just try again. We weren't impressed by what she had served up that day though. Even our favourite online sources offered no brighter future.

We filled the water tanks. At least we could have a hot cup of tea along the way. After moseying down to the sports centre and having a pleasant shower, we lingered with a cup of coffee, using the wi-fi to help plan our trip home from Kinlochbervie. We would be leaving the boat there for a few weeks. Ideally, we would have strolled to Kinlochbervie Grand Central Station or to KLB International Airport, but sadly neither of these places exist. The bus route seemed too time-consuming so it was going to have to be a taxi to Inverness and then train or plane. We arranged for a taxi to collect us at nine o'clock on Sunday morning.

The sail out of the bay was very pleasant – it was a flat sea and a slight breeze from starboard. We sailed past Soyea Island and arrived at the end of the loch to find ourselves confronting a strong headwind and two to three-metre waves, enough to halt our forward motion. We took in the headsail, put two reefs in the main and turned on the engine. Under this arrangement we were able to make some progress.

An hour later and we had managed to round the headland and the wind and waves decreased a little; forward motion was easier. This pattern continued as we rounded the next two headlands, the Point of Stoer and later Handa Island. We turned off the autopilot and steered by hand, concentrating hard on negotiating the waves. We fought to keep control, passing through the waves at the safest angle, one which gave least resistance.

Occasionally though, we smashed into a large wave head on and *Blue Star* would slam down as she went over the back of the crest, creating a dreadful sound. When this happens the downward pitching motion of the hull is stopped suddenly as the bow hits the water behind the wave. The mast does not stop quite so quickly though, the backstay stretching worryingly before bringing it to a halt. There is always a concern that the backstay might snap and the mast come down, but we tried not to think about that. We had 'bolt cutters' on board for such an eventuality; they would have allowed us to cut it free. However, we convinced ourselves that the conditions we were experiencing must have been allowed for in the design of the boat, and therefore the mast would stay up.

As the day wore on the conditions improved and we began to enjoy the passage. The rocky coastline and the mountains inland were spectacular. We had a sandwich lunch in the cockpit, which helped to revive us.

After passing Handa Island, Loch Laxford went by and we reached Loch Inchard. At the seaward end of the loch there are several small skerries, lying a short distance from the mainland; we kept well clear of them. Once past the skerries we could turn to enter the loch. It was narrow, and, half a mile in, a north cardinal buoy warned of where navigation was ill-advised. Another half mile and we reached Loch

Bervie. We dropped our sail and motored to a berth on the
pontoon at Kinlochbervie Marina. It was just a short way into the
on our port side. Once tied up, we made our arrival known to
harbourmaster, Davy.

It was a pity that the weather had changed. Had good wea
continued, we may have been tempted to round Cape Wrath the
day, but it wasn't to be. At least we had kept on schedule; we
pleased with that and were ready for a break.

Alongside the marina stands a large warehouse, intended to
with the fish from trawlers that land their catch there. The facility
constructed with a significant investment from the European Union,
we gained the impression that it was substantially underused.
harbour, like that at Lochinver, was past its heyday. Even so, we
see a handful of refrigerated, articulated lorries arrive to take the
to market.

At the far end of the fish-processing warehouse were the toilets a
showers. Whilst preferable to the cramped heads on board *Blue St*
the facilities were definitely 'used'. A waft of fish odour hung in the a
One of the wooden partitions was partly held in place by a short leng
of string tied to a point on the ceiling, and flapped to and fro if touch
accidentally whilst showering. This was not the five-star facility we ha
enjoyed at Portavadie! It was, though, all part of the adventure. A ho
meal was cooked on board and we relaxed before retiring to bed.

Before returning home we spent a day cleaning the boat and taking
the chance to appreciate the delights of the village. The settlement had
little to offer – not surprising considering its rather isolated location in
the far Northwest of the country. Walking along what passed as the
main road, one almost expected to see tumbleweed blowing in the
breeze. We didn't see tumbleweed, but we did see a great many sheep;
they appeared to have free run of the port and surrounding hills.
Kinlochbervie was clearly a place for farming as well as fishing.

Further on we found a SPAR shop and were able to buy a few
groceries. A few other dirt-covered, former shops close by were
boarded up. The area was rather depressed, but even so, it still attracts
tourists.

We spotted a hotel as we continued along the main road out of town.
A path took us over a stile, and into a field. Here we scaled a steep

rassy hill, weaving our way around sheep and heaps of manure, arriving finally at the Kinlochbervie Hotel.

Ordering coffees and teacakes, as scones were not available, we settled at a window seat to admire the view. Mountains all around us, rocky coves down by the sea and, in the distance, the port and marina.

During our walkabout we met Barry Pearson who ran the Container Gallery – an art gallery arranged inside an old steel shipping container. We had paused to admire the Stag yacht that he was refurbishing on the hard next to his gallery. He invited us in to see his workshop, pointing out a nesting dove in the roof. Barry also had some of his own marvellous watercolours on display.

Other locals chatted with us too. They were all very friendly and welcoming, taking an interest in our circumnavigation project. It was clearly a small community where most people knew each other.

We got in touch with the harbourmaster, reminding him of our intention to leave our boat for a few weeks. He directed us to leave it rafted up alongside *Aeron Lass*, a large old wooden motor yacht, on the inside of the pontoon. Just as we were securing our lines, a rather angry lady arrived to remonstrate with us, having watched our activities from her house on the other side of the loch. She informed us, in no uncertain terms, that she owned the boat that we were rafted against and it was not acceptable to her. She declared her intention to paint the boat whilst we were away, pointing out that we wouldn't want paint splashed onto our boat, would we? She also told us that she planned to go out sailing soon. After further consultation with Davy we returned *Blue Star* to her original position on the outside of the pontoon and everyone was satisfied.

The next day our taxi arrived on time, at nine o'clock. The journey to Inverness was over two hours by car, a considerable excursion itself! The road trip did, however, give us the opportunity to enjoy the spectacular scenery at close quarters – mountains, lochs, lakes, heathers, forests and fields. We passed through several small villages and towns before arriving at Inverness from where we each continued our own journey home.

***

Joke
Q. What do you call a sheep covered in chocolate?
A. A chocolate baa!
***

Above: The marina at Kyle of Lochalsh. *Blue Star* is on the far side of the pontoon, *Blue Migrant* moored astern of her.

Below: Afternoon tea at Gairloch (left to right – Kim, Richard, David, Roger)

Above: Suilven dominates the landscape at Lochinver

Below: Tied up at Kinlochbervie Marina (photo courtesy of Richard Pavey)

14. Kinlochbervie to Inverness

A life on the ocean wave,
A home on the rolling deep,
Where scattered waters rave,
And the winds their revels keep!

Epes Sargent, 'A Life on the Ocean Wave'

Friday, 3 June. After a couple of weeks' 'home leave' the *Blue Star* project got under way again with a new crew. Richard Pavey had enjoyed the previous leg with us, enough to sign on again, this time as part of the team that would be rounding Cape Wrath and ending the week at Inverness. It was good to have Richard on board once more. We met Richard and Kim at Inverness airport from where Kim drove us to Kinlochbervie.

A man was walking past the fish warehouse and along the deserted, dusty road to the marina as our car pulled up. It was Robert Langford, who was also joining the crew for the next leg. Roger had met him at Lymington Town Sailing Club, where a note had been placed to see if any of the members wanted to join us on our voyage. Robert studied engineering at university before joining the Parachute Regiment, later going into business. Robert and Richard were brave and daring enough, or foolish enough, to face the demands of what might be our toughest leg yet!

Robert:
Joining *Blue Star* in the far North of Scotland was the first challenge. Thanks to Flybe, I found myself at Inverness by coffee time, after a brief stop at Manchester en route. I took a bus journey into the town, where I put my sailing bag in a shopping trolley, stopped for a bite of lunch and found a shop for some mosquito repellent. A train journey around the Moray Firth, evidently a 'parking lot' for oil-drilling platforms, took me to Lairg station. No taxi to be seen but some kind people gave me a lift to the Highland Hotel, where a minibus was due to leave for Kinlochbervie just after 7.00pm. I was the only passenger on the single-track road across the mountains. The lady driver obviously knew the road well, timing her arrival at passing places

whenever an oncoming vehicle approached. It was 2015 hours when we reached the harbour at Kinlochbervie. There was no need to ask where *Blue Star* was moored – there were no other yachts in sight. I took refuge in the cockpit, awaiting the rest of the crew. I was taking a stroll when they arrived by car a little later on.

We loaded our gear on board, relaxed for a while, cooked a hot dinner and talked about rounding Cape Wrath. Frankly, we didn't like the sound of Cape Wrath – why did it have to be called that? It sounded like some angry beast waiting to trap and consume innocent yachtsmen like us!

The plan was to wait until conditions were ideal before setting out from Kinlochbervie, bound for Scrabster – the mainland port close to the Orkney Islands. A wind from the south or west would be ideal to blow us around the Cape, and the forecast sea state had to be acceptable. The prevailing wind is from the southwest, and the direction of our route around Britain had been chosen so that it might aid our passage at this critical and potentially perilous stage of the voyage.

The day after our return we spoke to a local skipper who advised, in the most colourful language, that it would 'not be a good idea' to sail to Scrabster that day. This confirmed our own thinking. We had already seen the forecast, force 6 and moderate to rough seas, and decided not to sail. Towards the end of the day we saw the same skipper again when he told us it hadn't been as bad as prophesised! The prediction for the next day held some promise, however.

Davy, the harbourmaster, arranged for diesel to be delivered to us in jerry cans. There was a diesel pump in the port but, intended for commercial fishing vessels, it was not on a quay suitable for yachts to tie up at. We topped up our food supplies at the SPAR shop, and went again to the Kinlochbervie Hotel. After elevenses, retracing our steps down the field and over the stile onto the road, we passed a roadside pigsty, with happy, muddy, grunting occupants.

Mike:

In the afternoon the rest of the crew were ashore when another yacht appeared in the marina, *Calobra*, a French-flagged aluminium-hulled vessel. Standing in the saloon of *Blue Star* I could see the boat manoeuvring, preparing to come alongside the pontoon. I was

146

concerned because it didn't have any fenders out, save for a couple at the stern ... and it did appear to be getting VERY close! I was about to offer assistance when suddenly ... BANG! Then a graunching screech. The boat collided with *Blue Star*.

Rushing up on deck I saw that the French boat, with a crew of just a man and a woman, was now alongside the pontoon, their lines being made fast. The skipper made light of the 'coming together', but I insisted on recompense for the damage. We'd sustained several scratches to our hull. After he asked how much I thought the repair would cost I suggested that instead of paying us he should make a donation to our charity, which he did. We could have done without the aggravation but the damage was only cosmetic and something we fixed ourselves later.

We spoke again to the French skipper and asked him about his experience at sea that day. He said that his forecast had suggested 15 knots of wind but that he'd found 22 knots. Were the forecasts for this area to be relied upon we wondered?

In the evening Richard cooked us a traditional Scottish meal – haggis. We didn't like to think of what went into it, but we couldn't visit Scotland and not try the national dish. After dinner we studied the forecast for the next day.

During the night, waves slapped against the side of *Blue Star*'s hull and kept us awake. The noise finally abated at 6.30am, perhaps heralding a change in the weather? By late morning the sun was up and the forecast wind was force 5, but from the east! We decided to wait another day.

We walked what was now one of our favourite walks – to the Kinlochbervie Hotel; there we enjoyed our usual coffee and teacakes, saying hello to the pigs as we passed by and receiving a grunt in reply.

After coffee we walked to the bay at Oldshoremore, about two miles away. It was a route which took us out of the village and through the surrounding countryside. We passed several buildings and up on the heath we met a shepherd, Michael Otter. With the help of his two dogs, he was rounding up his sheep and moving them to a field across the road, one that had drinking water for the animals.

It was at this point that Roger informed us that he'd once completed a one-day 'shepherd's course' in rounding up sheep. The thought occurred to us that he might 'have a go' at rounding up Michael Otter's sheep for him, thereby providing us with entertainment. As it was, Michael managed perfectly well without Roger, but we did what we could to help.

We strode on through a caravan site before finally descending from the hills onto the beach at Oldshoremore. And wow! What a beach! White sand stretched into the distance around an almost deserted bay of turquoise sea, in a scene that surely belonged in the Caribbean. The sun burned down on us to complete the picture. We strolled onto the beach and down towards the sea in the gentle breeze. Like little boys, we took off our shoes and socks to paddle. For a short while we were lads having fun on the beach. Roger added a finishing touch of a knotted handkerchief over his head. The water was crystal clear, though rather cold. It was a wonderful place. Later we learnt that the Northwest of Scotland was enjoying the best weather in the country. Some good fortune at last.

Monday was 6 June and we decided to go! We noted that it was the anniversary of D-Day. 'D' for Daring, Do or Die?

This was potentially our most hazardous passage so far. A mark of the respect with which we approached it was that Roger contacted the coastguard before we set out, to brief them of our intentions. It turned out to be the only time we logged our plan with the coastguard during the whole circumnavigation.

There was little wind forecast, and the predicted sea state was 'slight'. The French yacht, *Calobra*, left at around 6.30am. Another Bavaria yacht, *Wizard*, had rafted up to us over night and, like us, their crew planned to sail for Scrabster that day.

Wizard headed out to sea, and soon afterwards we did the same. It was 0700 hours. The sun glinted on the surface of the flat, glassy water. Rocky shorelines gave way to several bays with deserted white sandy beaches, including Oldshoremore. A rock stack stood alone, away from the seafront, a sentinel perhaps, warning of the dangers ahead. Elsewhere, crags from the shore formed arches, dipping into the sea.

We were under engine and mainsail and moving at a pace towards Cape Wrath; after 30 minutes we had overtaken *Wizard*. In the calm sea we continued to make good progress.

The cliffs around Cape Wrath rise over 110 metres above sea level and are some of the highest sea cliffs on mainland Britain. At the top of the cliff stood the lighthouse, a white column 20 metres tall, flashing its warning with four flashes every 30 seconds. Just off the Cape is Clo Kearvaig, a 40-metre high rock stack with two pinnacles, for which it is nicknamed the 'cathedral stack'.

The name Cape Wrath is derived from the old Norse 'hvarf', meaning turning point. It is believed that Vikings used the Cape as a navigation aid where they would turn. Things certainly turned for us as we rounded the Cape!

It had been our plan to navigate between the Cape and the stack, which seemed feasible from the chart. However, on our arrival it was soon evident that with a strong tide flowing it was not advisable. The tide by now was moving very quickly indeed! It dictated that we shouldn't pass between the stack and the Cape; perhaps that was just as well. We had a hasty rethink and decided to stop fighting against the current, focusing instead on keeping well clear of the stack. Any mistake here was likely to be serious if not deadly.

A rock in a river causes turbulence and disturbed white water downstream. Here, Cape Wrath was one giant obstruction to the torrent flowing around it. The tidal stream swept us on our way as total chaos was unleashed!

Giant waves from all directions confronted us. From dead ahead, then starboard, then on port beam. Another from starboard quarter and now dead ahead again. With every wave we turned the wheel to stop it striking the boat head on. We were rushed through the 'rapids' of Cape Wrath, turning the boat this way and that, altering our heading over and over, minute by minute to deal with the mass of waves coming at us from so many directions.

It was essential to prevent the hull slamming down on the back of the wave crests as the boat rode over them. Neither could we allow a wave to approach dead on the beam, for that risked rolling the boat.

We estimated the waves to be between two and three metres in height, and very steep. Watching them approach we felt sure they would break over us and swamp the boat's cockpit. Incredibly, as they arrived, *Blue Star* lifted herself up and each wave passed miraculously underneath us!

We had experienced conditions similar to this when navigating past The Needles stacks off the Isle of Wight, on Britain's South Coast. There, such conditions last only a matter of minutes, and we anticipated a similar duration here. How wrong could we be! After about half an hour we had clearly rounded the Cape, but the raging waters had barely subsided.

We looked behind us to see how *Wizard* was coping with the conditions. There was no sign of her. Either she had turned around or she had sunk.

After battling for about two hours the sea state became a little more tolerable. We were still dealing with some turbulence but, desperate for a much-deserved drink, we were able to brew up. It was a great relief to have come through. A real achievement and a baptism of fire for rookie crewmate Richard. By this time we were exhausted and looking forward to getting into port.

Along the North Coast we had passed Loch Eriboll and later the Kyle of Tongue. We had considered exploring them. Now, we could see that entry through the off-lying skerries required calm conditions. There is no harbour inside either inlet, only the beauty of a scenic anchorage. It would have been a marvellous opportunity to be close to the wild nature of the north, but now wasn't the time to stop.

Scrabster is about 50 miles from Cape Wrath and it was not until early evening that we arrived. By that time the sea was almost flat and it was once more a pleasure to be out on a sailboat. After letting the coastguard know of our arrival, there was the usual search for the facilities, in another fish-processing warehouse, before we settled down to a hot dinner.

Looking out across the Pentland Firth we could see the Orkney Islands, our intended destination the following day. Later we discovered that *Wizard* had also made it to the marina in Scrabster. The crew had watched *Blue Star* brave the seas off Cape Wrath and had decided to turn about and make a much wider sweep around the Cape. The French yacht, *Calobra*, had also gone further out around the Cape, standing off several miles.

We visited a small grocery store the following morning. Back on board, we reviewed our plan for making the short crossing to the Orkney Islands. We were aiming for Stromness on the islands' mainland, but to get there we needed to cross the potentially dangerous Pentland Firth.

Around the coast of the United Kingdom each country has its own most challenging stretch of water. For England it might be the Portland Race off the South Coast, for Wales the Swellies in the Menai Straits,

Northern Ireland has the Rathlin Island channel and for Scotland it's probably the Pentland Firth. The potentially dangerous waters around the UK coast are highly influenced by the topography and environmental factors. This is as true for the Portland Race in the south as for the Pentland Firth in the north.

As with all our passages, the weather and forecast conditions were closely watched. This was especially important for the potentially more hazardous legs like the Pentland Firth. Extreme care needs to be taken when crossing this water as the tides are some of the strongest in the UK, reaching speeds of up to seven knots. The almanac warns that 'a good engine is required'!

To help prepare for crossing the Firth we downloaded a 'Yachtsman's Guide' and consulted with the local coastguard and harbour staff. There could be no mistakes here!

Once across the Firth we would have to leave Hoy Island to starboard and enter Hoy Sound, which separates it from the Orkney mainland. In the sound lies the smaller island of Graemsay which we also had to leave to starboard.

We departed Scrabster at 1500 hours, in the sun. Our timing enabled us to cross to the Sound of Hoy whilst also avoiding the strong overfalls that develop at some periods of the tide cycle. Overfalls occur when strong tides rush over submerged rocks and undulations, and are forced upwards, creating confused seas.

Initially we were under sail but after a short while we put the engine on, the wind being from almost directly ahead. The crew drank tea and snacked on Mars bars and all was well with the world until ... suddenly, a thick fog came down. We could barely see beyond the bow of the boat, and here we were in the middle of the Pentland Firth!

Fortunately, we had invested in a new radar system on the boat; now was the time it was needed. We also had an electronic chart plotter giving us a visual representation of our position relative to the land, to cross reference with the information obtained from our radar. Our electronic systems included AIS too. This placed an electronic symbol on our chart plotter 'map' wherever there was another vessel nearby that also had AIS. All was in hand, but we were now navigating by electronics rather than by sight.

We continued on our way to Stromness with a tense and serious mood in the cockpit. We had to maintain concentration but we remained calm.

About halfway across, the electronics warned of another vessel coming our way from Stromness. It looked like we were on a collision course. We were able to identify the vessel using our AIS and call them up on the VHF radio. The subsequent conversation confirmed that they had 'seen' us on their electronic systems and that we should maintain our course. They would alter course to avoid the risk of a collision with us. The vessel slipped past us in the fog, and we saw nothing and heard nothing. Later, we spotted the same vessel back in Stromness. It was a huge ferry. Just as well we made sure there was no collision.

As we approached the coast of Hoy, we were starting to be concerned with precisely how far into the marina we could navigate using electronics, given the density of the fog. At that very moment we suddenly emerged into brilliant sunshine! There in front of us stood the 'Old Man of Hoy', a well-known rock stack, on the shoreline. Splendid it looked too, as did the rest of the Orkney Islands – yet more spectacular rock formations and luscious green fields! The 'Old Man', 137 metres high, had been front-page news a few years earlier when Sir Chris Bonington climbed it aged 80.

'Mr Sun' continued to oblige us and we easily found our way to the marina at Stromness, located close to the ferry terminal. We can also report that the facilities were of a favourable standard.

At the end of most passages we would lift the floorboards in the saloon to check for water ingress into the bilge. It was usually bone dry. We checked again once into Stromness and got a shock. Water lapping just below the floorboards! Had we holed the boat during the intensity of the last few days? Fortunately, the water level didn't seem to be rising, and our panic receded a little. Roger tasted the water and declared it to be fresh water, mixed with an element of who knows what. The problem was finally tracked down to a faulty pump delivering water to the galley and heads. After scooping the mucky fluid out of the bilge, we mopped up and decided that we could cope by regular sponging. We would buy a replacement pump when we next returned home.

That night we found it hard to sleep. We were as far north as our voyage would take us and there were now very few hours of 'darkness' during the 'night hours'. There was just a reduction in visibility, but not pitch black. It was incredibly cold and every blanket was employed.

We decided to spend a day exploring Stromness and finding out more about the islands. We visited the local museum which has a magnificent exhibition detailing the history of the area.

General Kitchener led the British forces during the First World War, featuring prominently on the 'Your Country Needs You' recruitment poster. On a mission to meet the Russians he departed from the Orkneys aboard HMS *Hampshire* on 5 June 1916. The ship struck a German mine a mile and a half west of Stromness and he was among the 737 people on board who perished.

Another major incident occurred a year later on 7 July 1917. A St Vincent-class dreadnought battleship, HMS *Vanguard*, exploded, killing 843 of the crew instantly. The blast was so great that a 12-inch gun turret, weighing more than 400 tons, was found on the island of Flotta, about a mile away! A Navy Board of Enquiry could not confirm the cause of the explosion but thought it most probably linked to degraded cordite in the main magazine.

The Orkney Islands are grouped around what is one of the largest natural harbours in Britain – Scapa Flow. Understandably, it has been of major importance in naval history. At the end of the First World War the German High Seas Fleet was interned there as part of the armistice agreement. Fearing that the Allies would seize the fleet, Admiral Ludwig von Reuter decided, on 21 June 1919, to scuttle the ships. Of the 74 interned vessels, 52 were sunk.

In view of its remoteness from Germany, Scapa Flow was the northern base for the Royal Navy in the Second World War. Despite the perceived safety, on 14 October 1939 U-47 penetrated the anti-submarine nets and sank HMS *Royal Oak*, with the loss of 833 men from the ship's complement of 1,400. After an unexpected air raid a few days later, the Allies reinforced the defences to counter further attacks from the air or sea.

It was another bitterly cold but light night. Difficult to sleep again.

In the morning, with all the history fresh in our minds, we slipped lines early and got under way just after 0600 hours. Our course would take us through Scapa Flow, then out into the Firth once more, and on to Wick on the Scottish mainland.

Scapa Flow was incredibly quiet, with calm waters and a westerly wind of ten knots. It was extremely cold again – hard to believe it was summer! The stillness and the absence of other craft in the rising mist and the distant outline of the coast created a surreal and eerie atmosphere. It was particularly noticeable that the chilly air and silence somehow reflected the dark history of this graveyard of so many ships and men. We felt very sombre, thinking of all who had lost their lives.

It was a morning for several layers of clothing – fleecy hats, gloves, hoods and high collars. Hot cups of tea were handed round to the crew. They had to be drunk quickly if they were to be drunk warm. We swapped helms frequently, giving crew the chance to warm up again after standing at the wheel in the wind.

Once through, we headed towards the Pentland Firth. As with all the other challenging passages, fine attention to detail of the tides, weather and charts was paramount. Our timing proved to be accurate and, as we entered the Firth proper, we benefitted from the east-going stream, making an average speed of seven knots. As we rounded Duncansby Head on the mainland the wind was set fair for a pleasant beam reach down to Wick.

On arrival in Wick there was some discussion, shouted instructions we could not understand, as to which berth we should take. Eventually all was made clear and we tied up in time for lunch. The afternoon afforded the opportunity to explore this Northeast Scottish fishing town and its Viking heritage. It had a rich history of herring fishing and was renowned for once landing 24 million herring in one day! A lot of fish in anyone's language! The fish were gutted by a workforce of 3,000 people, mostly women. Catches such as this cemented the town's fame, in the 19th century, for being the busiest herring port in Europe. Today there is more tourism than fishing.

With the weather fair the next day, after a leisurely breakfast we set sail towards Lossiemouth, across the Moray Firth. By good fortune the wind turned out to be ideal for this trip and we had the luxury of sailing for about six hours of the eight-hour passage. Our course deviated only slightly to enable us to dodge round an oil rig, mid-Firth.

Approaching Lossiemouth, we knew we would be on a falling tide. If for any reason we were to run aground we would probably not get free. We calculated that we would be fine. It was in fact a tight squeeze to enter, with less water than we'd calculated. The pilot book informs that berths are dredged to give adequate depth but it looked like the dredger had not been out in the approach channel!

Large waves tried to push us off course as we approached the narrow harbour entrance, but we powered through them. With Mike doing a sterling job on the helm and the Volvo engine working hard we passed through into the harbour without incident.

We were not yet out of the woods though. The harbour was small and compact inside, with little room to manoeuvre. The wind had picked up during the last hour and was now blowing strongly even inside the harbour. We looked around quickly for a free pontoon, wanting to tie up before we lost control. Luckily, we spotted a free finger berth, not really big enough for us but it would have to do. We needed to tie up as quickly as possible, with the force 6+ trying to crash us against the other moored boats. With all fenders out, we came against the vacant berth, rather forcefully in the blow. Once secured we could relax.

The marina was very quiet and it took a while to find out how to register and obtain the keys for the facilities. We were pointed in the direction of a pub on the sea wall, where the key was held and could be borrowed overnight for a small deposit. Roger volunteered to go – having lived in Aberdeen, he felt quite at home in this part of the world.

Roger:

On approaching the pub it sounded as though a pitched battle was in full flow with raised voices, ungentlemanly language and a general air of hostility. On opening the door, all fell deathly quiet as 30 pairs of eyes followed me to the bar. Having paid the deposit and secured the key I quickly left – the 'riot' starting up again immediately on my exit. Perhaps some of the Vikings who founded Wick had come south for a wee dram? We did pluck up courage to go back en masse in the evening, to a small restaurant near the pub, for a meal which turned out to be excellent. Large bowls of Cullen skink all round!

It rained hard overnight, and the following morning the remnants of the wet weather were still with us. The tide was higher than the previous night and we had no problem exiting the marina along the narrow channel. With a gentle but variable wind we tried to set sails a few times but were making little progress so resorted to motor-sailing.

Travelling west along the Moray Firth we could see the low headlands of the Culbin Sands and forests. Our next landmark was Fort George at the narrows leading to Inverness; this is claimed to be the mightiest artillery fortification in Great Britain. Built to control the Scottish

Highlands in the aftermath of the Jacobite uprising in 1745, the current fortress has never actually been attacked. It's been an active garrison ever since it was built. It is alleged that in 2016 the Ministry of Defence announced that the garrison would close in 2032 because the Highland rebellions are over. History may prove otherwise given the growing support for Scottish independence!

As we motored on past Chanonry Point we could see a large number of people on the northern shore. Slowing down to investigate, we watched a pod of dolphins leaping and playing in the water. It was a spectacular sight and became one of those moments which helped make the voyage so memorable.

We motored into Inverness Marina by mid-afternoon for some food and a crew change. Richard and Robert were to leave us here. Having conquered Cape Wrath and the Pentland Firth with us, they had proved themselves worthy crew members. Replacing them was Bob Hillyer, a retired air traffic controller and Lymington Town Sailing Club friend of Roger's and, returning for another stint with us, David 'Shep' Shepherd.

***

Joke
Q. Why did the candle not get any rest?
A. There is no rest for the WICKed!

***

Below: The beach at Oldshoremore

Above: *Blue Star* en route to Cape Wrath (Photo taken from on board the yacht *Wizard*, courtesy of Chris Mason)

Above: The fog lifts as we approach Stromness and we are greeted by the 'Old Man of Hoy'.

15. Inverness to Dunstaffnage

On a day when the wind is perfect,
the sail just needs to open and the world is full of beauty.

Rumi

Richard's wife, Kim, came to collect him from the marina at Inverness in their posh 'Mini'. It was amazing what a great deal of kit could be crammed into the vehicle, but after some careful stowing all was loaded inside. We bid farewell to Robert too. They were each travelling home to opposite ends of the United Kingdom.

Bob and David joined us on the boat on the evening of Saturday, 11 June. With the new crew assembled, we chatted about the forthcoming transit of the canal.

Breakfast on *Blue Star* was usually cereal, often followed by toast. Our secret weapon was concealed in a hidden location, behind the cushion of the starboard saloon seat. Our microwave cooker! Excellent for cooking morning porridge, a favourite for both of us! The visiting crew also came to enjoy the benefits of the secreted appliance.

With slick timing, we dropped lines at 0930 hours on the Sunday and headed for the eastern entrance of the Caledonian Canal for the second time.

Our passage through the canal in 2015 had given us some experience and knowledge about what lay ahead. We had some great memories from the first transit and were looking forward to a repeat performance. After handing over what we felt was an extortionate sum of money to the canal staff, we were once more given a guidebook and a set of keys for the facilities.

Once past the Clachnaharry Lock we were into the canal proper and then through the small Loch Dochfour and on to Loch Ness. At 23 miles long and 230 metres deep, it's known world-wide for the alleged cryptozoological monster! The loch is the largest single source of fresh water in the British Isles.

The plan for the day was to rendezvous with Diane, her cousin Angela, and Angela's husband, Keith (Woolcool executives). We were to meet them at a private quay at the eastern end of the loch, close to where they had rented a cottage on the Aldourie Estate. We had kindly been given permission to use the estate's quay by the owners, who assured us that there would be adequate depth.

Keith:

Mid-June 2016 and Angie and I were very much looking forward to meeting *Blue Star* and her crew at the Aldourie Estate on the northern tip of Loch Ness. We had rented a holiday cottage there and been assured that the estate pier could easily accommodate *Blue Star*. Mike's wife, Diane, had joined us for a few days, and it was with great excitement that we all kept a look out for *Blue Star* to appear on the horizon. There she was! Making stately and graceful progress towards her private mooring at the foot of Aldourie Castle grounds. What style!

As we approached the landing point it became obvious that whilst the jetty was suitable for a small sailing dinghy it was far from suitable for a yacht of *Blue Star*'s size, with her draught of 1.7 metres. Our first attempt to come alongside had to be rapidly aborted before we ran aground. We edged in again, very slowly, with full attention on the depth gauge. There was sufficient depth only on the very corner of the pier, but not on either side. We weren't able to bring the boat in and moor up.

We knew that lunch awaited us ashore, and we certainly didn't want to miss that. Neither did we want to disappoint our would-be hosts. A solution had to be found.

Eventually, after much head scratching, with amazing ingenuity and physical exertion, Bob saved the day. He led us in fashioning a 'bridge' out of a small dilapidated dinghy moored nearby. With *Blue Star* perched precariously on the corner of the pier, at a very awkward-looking angle, we tied her lines. We weren't quite sure how Bob used to position planes in the air, but if it was anything like the way he positioned our boat on the pier it must have been 'interesting'!

Our berthing arrangement certainly looked very unseamanlike, but our vessel was finally secure. We justified it all to ourselves on the basis that we were not at sea and we were hungry! Angela and Keith were the best of hosts and gave the whole crew an excellent meal.

Without so much as a siesta, we set sail, keen to make our next mooring before it got dark – no boating is permitted on the canal at night. We just about stayed legal, arriving at Fort Augustus around dusk at 2000 hours. That evening, meeting up once more with the group from the cottage, the whole crew were taken to dinner at a nearby restaurant, all at Woolcool's expense! It would be difficult to have found a more supportive sponsor and we were very appreciative.

Rowena Cass arrived for dinner in the nick of time. A lively character, she was joining the crew for the rest of the week. Another member of Stafford Coastal Cruising Club, she was a retired school teacher who had her own yacht berthed in Southern Spain, where it was used as a holiday base. Her boat had not left the marina for some considerable time, so Rowena was looking forward to getting out on the water again.

The following day was a 'corporate' day to entertain our Woolcool executive friends, and it was a great pleasure to welcome Keith on board the boat. We took him for a sail on Loch Ness. There wasn't a lot of wind, but enough to get a taste of the *Blue Star* sailing experience before we returned to Fort Augustus. So impressed was Keith that he promptly signed on as crew for a week, later in the year.

We all posed for photographs in the cockpit, each of us wearing our navy-blue polo shirts. It felt very satisfying to be part of a team engaged in an adventurous challenge whilst raising funds for a worthwhile cause.

Sailing on Loch Ness had been a special experience for us all. Bob took a 'selfie' with the loch in the background and, feeling pleased with his achievement, sent the photo to his son. A few moments later the photo was returned to him with the question, 'Yes, but what's that in the background?' – behind Bob, on the returned photo, was a green snake-like 'Nessie' monster, quickly added by his son!

What is living in Loch Ness...
This ancient animal of lore?
A sinuous serpent?
A giant humped creature?
A prehistoric plesiosaur?
Is this fabled monster really
Lurking in the lake,
Gliding through its chilly waters
Leaving legend in its wake?

Elaine Magliaro, 'Nessie'

We wandered around an interesting old Gothic building beside the canal. It was originally constructed as an English fortification in 1729. The fort was seized by Jacobite forces in 1746 during the Scottish rebellion but handed back to English forces two months later when the Jacobites had been defeated. In 1880 it was turned into St Benedict's Abbey. Now self-catering apartments, the property stands in 20 acres of landscaped grounds.

In the evening we watched a succession of charter boats come alongside on our pontoon. We looked out for the technique that had been witnessed by Rob during our first transit of the canal – that of running hard into the pontoon, tying up and then getting the fenders out! We didn't spot anyone adopting this technique. Charter vessels were common on the canal – the lock keepers tended to put them in the lock together, and as far away as possible from the private yachts!

Whilst berthed in Fort Augustus we were sitting in the cockpit enjoying the sun when we heard a voice on the VHF radio. 'This is the warship, Archer,' proclaimed the voice. A warship? How could they possibly fit through the Caledonian Canal? The canal had been built originally with the navy in mind, but that was two centuries ago. The size of warships has moved on since then! Turning around, we espied, in battleship grey, three large, high-bridged Royal Navy patrol boats. Each was crewed by new recruits who were being put through their paces as part of their training. Later, we were able to chat with some of the young crew who were enjoying both their passage through the canal and the training they were receiving.

Tuesday, 14 June. We slipped our lines at Fort Augustus and started working our way up the flight of locks around which the town was built.

Whenever boats pass through a lock it always seems to attract bystanders who like to watch the process. A flight of locks such as those at Fort Augustus seems to be even more attractive than a single lock, and so it was that we had quite a crowd watching *Blue Star* as she ascended the lock staircase. It was a sunny day and observers were intrigued by the sponsors' logos on the hull, several of them asking questions and donating to the charity. It was gratifying to have such interest shown.

We had set the best part of the morning aside to allow for ascending the locks; by the time we exited the upper stage lunch was beckoning.

It arrived in the form of a sandwich picnic, taken in the sun as we motored onwards through the canal.

Meals on board came to signify a number of things during the voyage. Of course, they satisfied our hunger, but they also marked our progress, both through the day and around the coast. They were something to look forward to, with most crew joining in the preparation. They became a focus of interest, of competition even. Some crew members were most adept in the galley, others not so but willing to 'have a go'. The two of us developed our own particular specialities – Mike with his baked salmon and Roger his apricot chicken. A meal always raised our spirits. Often, when negotiating a particularly testing passage, an 'extra' bacon sandwich snack would be inserted in the day.

Ahead of us in the canal was HMS *Archer*, and the two other navy patrol boats. Behind us in the locks had been an interesting vessel. The orange-hulled *Teisten* had been a former Danish forces patrol vessel, a large boat by our standards. We spoke with her crew whilst in the locks together. They were a father, son and a family friend, all of whom lived in Greenland, where the best way of getting about is by sea. The crew had seen *Teisten* advertised for sale and had travelled to Denmark to buy her. They were now delivering her back home to Greenland, via a holiday in Scotland. She was to be the new family 'run-around'. A robust vessel such as *Teisten* was considered a standard requirement for navigating the coasts of Greenland.

And so it was that we became part of a convoy of vessels transiting the canal together, led by the three navy vessels, then *Blue Star* followed by *Teisten*.

As we relaxed with our cockpit picnic we observed one of the 'training routines' being implemented on board *Archer*. On passing through a lock, a crew member would be put ashore. They would be required to run whatever distance was necessary to the next lock, and to get there before the ship. The speed limit for craft on the canal is five knots and so they would have to go faster to outperform the boat. Their mission included warning the lock-keeper of *Archer*'s imminent arrival so that the gates could be positioned ready to receive her. Often lock-keepers could be contacted by VHF radio from transiting vessels too. The weary crew member would then be permitted to re-board and the next 'lucky' victim would take over.

We chatted with the odd trainee and understood there to be a competitive nature to the operation; the young crew were actually enjoying the exercise. There was some discussion amongst the officers of *Blue Star* as to whether a similar training regime would benefit our crew. Disappointingly, the proposal was not well supported by the crew who seemed more interested in cups of tea, sandwiches and cakes.

We had planned to moor overnight in Laggan Marina at the eastern end of Loch Lochy, but on inspection it proved unsuitable. It was exposed to a strong wind that was blowing. We pushed on to Gairlochy, at the western end of the loch, putting in to the small marina there. Here, we were well positioned for a relaxed journey the next day to Banavie and 'Neptune's Staircase'.

The morning was grey, wet and windy. Once at Banavie we had no appetite for pressing on further and negotiating a multi-lock staircase under those conditions. Even so, it was still as impressive as before, the series of eight lock drops and the massive lock gates, all in such a picturesque setting. The snow-covered peak of Ben Nevis dominated the horizon, set among a range of lower mountain tops.

We were close, once more, to the nearby town of Fort William. The town dates back to the 17th century when a fort was built as a base for English troops to control Clan Cameron. It was named originally after William of Orange, and later after Prince William, the youngest son of King George II. The prince was also the Duke of Cumberland, and known as 'Butcher Cumberland' to the Scots who he defeated at Culloden. Understandably, some Scots even today are not well disposed to the name of the town and there are moves to change it. We found it both interesting and sobering to reflect on the turbulent times of centuries ago, when so much fighting took place. We, on the other hand, had only to enjoy the scenery and sail our boat! It reminded us of how lucky we were. We appreciated the regular history lessons that came with our travels.

In the morning the weather was still changeable but we made our way down the locks. The road and rail bridges at the bottom of the staircase were swung, allowing us to proceed into the final section of the canal, leading to Corpach and the sea lock. We chose not to press on immediately, opting instead to come alongside on a pontoon just beyond the two bridges. Here we stayed for the night. We were unsure about the room available for us at Corpach and we were keen to stroll into the village close by, to dine out. We found a convivial atmosphere in a pub showing the Wales v England Euro 2016 football match and there was much excitement among those watching, England winning by two goals to one.

On returning to *Blue Star* that evening we could not help admiring an impressive vessel tied up just ahead of us. *Woolfi's Toy* was a striking blue and white Open 50 racing monohull, similar to the type used in single-handed non-stop, round-the-world racing!

Friday dawned dry but cloudy, and with a little wind. The sea lock at Corpach began operations at 0800 hours and we hoped to be in the first group of boats to pass through. On our arrival there were a large number of boats in the basin, many of them vessels competing in the Three Peaks Race. This is the event in which yachts must navigate close to each of the highest mountains in England, Scotland and Wales, and two crew from each yacht must run to the top of the mountain!

Once through the sea lock, we raised some sail and the sun came to brighten our day. Two other boats had come through the lock with us. A monohull, *Monkey Business*, motored past us, and a catamaran, *Sail Mhor*, set its spinnaker for a downwind run. The sea was flat in the protected waters of Loch Linnhe and it was a splendid sail as we drank in, once more, the fantastic scenery! We passed the narrows at Ardgour, avoiding the ferry crossing to Corran, and reached the wider part of the loch. Mountains and forests surrounded us, and small settlements nestled on the shore. A road traced the coast on our port side. The blue sky allowed the sun to light our way. This was what sailing should always be like!

Onward we sailed, leaving Shuna Island to port and Lismore to starboard. We were in the Lynne of Lorne. This is a narrow channel with a number of marks identifying isolated dangerous rocks under the water. We had to keep our wits about us to ensure we came to no harm. Here the hammerhead-shaped piece of land penetrated the sea on our left. We navigated past and turned behind it into Ardmucknish Bay. Over to the right was Dunstaffnage Marina where we planned to stay. The entrance was straightforward with a clear but unmarked channel between the island, Eilean Mor, left to port, and Rubha Garbh, on starboard. We arrived mid-afternoon after a passage of 28 miles.

Just as we were coming alongside, a man on the pontoon grabbed a tripod-mounted camera and filmed our manoeuvres. We suddenly felt the pressure to get our mooring technique right! It was not a simple operation as the wind was trying to blow us off, and to cap it all there was limited room. We did manage to get the manoeuvre right though, the cameraman congratulating Mike on his boat handling. Afterwards we chatted with him. He turned out to be Dylan Winter whose website, 'Keep Turning Left', we were familiar with. Dylan, too, was circumnavigating Britain, albeit at a much slower pace than us. He was exploring many of the rivers and inlets that pressure of time forced us to bypass. Dylan produced excellent films of his experiences, making them available on his website.

The next morning we had some repair work to organise. When sailing we had noticed some wear in our mainsail. Like many mainsails, the aft edge, or leech, of ours had three long horizontal pockets stitched into it, these being spaced roughly equidistant up the edge of the sail. Into the pockets were inserted battens – lengths of rigid plastic which help the sail to maintain its correct shape. We'd discovered that the stitching around one of the pockets had come apart and the batten lost. Our plan was to leave *Blue Star* in Dunstaffnage for a few weeks while we returned home. We wanted the sail repaired whilst we were away.

The representative from the nearby sail loft was visiting the marina any minute, so a desperate panic set in. We had to remove the sail and bag it up, ready for the agent. We just made it in time. Any later, the sail would not have been ready in time for us to resume our voyage.

Having set in motion the repair of the sail and briefed the marina on our plans, we took a taxi to nearby Oban and boarded a train to take us home. We'd had yet another marvellous fortnight, enjoyed great company and had a fascinating insight into life centuries ago!

Rowena:

I did enjoy being aboard a sailing vessel again, one that was going somewhere other than the yard and back! I loved living aboard. The leg that I sailed in *Blue Star* offered the opportunity to support the two of you, to take part in a worthwhile venture, to revive some of my nautical knowhow which has not been exercised since 2009, to be one of a crew, to be in the company of experienced sailors and to see again from the sea the beauty of Scotland where I had sailed before. *Blue Star* was modern and comfortable and I felt privileged to have the forepeak to myself. I'd certainly sail with you again!

Bob:

I had worked in Scotland in the 1970s, flown over Arran and the Mull of Kintyre, driven through the Scottish borders, but since then had never been back. When the chance arose to transit the Highlands via the Caledonian Canal, with some convivial company, in a good cause, I was keen to sign up.

My abiding memory of the trip was that from the moment we set out into the Moray Firth I was reminded of what fantastic scenery Scotland has to offer. I knew, but I'd forgotten somehow. This was the most wonderful reminder and I enjoyed every second, a sailing boat being the perfect way to do it. I think it's the pace of travel, the engagement, slipping along in the elements whilst enjoying the scenery, chatting with a cup of tea and mince pie.

Best memory. Difficult. But sailing Loch Ness, the most famous stretch of Scottish water was special. At lunchtime we tied up at a remote mooring and were taken to eat, at an idyllic cottage, courtesy of one of the trip's sponsors, Woolcool. Stayed the night at Fort Augustus, but didn't see Nessie!

***

Joke

The sailor stayed up all night to see where the sun went.
Then it dawned on him.

***

**Left: Bob's selfie is returned to him with Nessie in the background!
(Photo courtesy of Bob Hillyer)**

Above: Bob works out a way for us to berth at the quay without grounding the boat

Above: The three Royal Navy patrol boats at Fort Augustus

Below: In the lock with HMS *Archer* and *Teisten*

Above: In a convoy, following HMS *Archer*

Above: Out of the Caledonian Canal and into Loch Linnhe with the catamaran *Sail Mhor*

16. Dunstaffnage to Douglas

I'm on the sea, I'm on the sea!
I am where I would ever be,
With the blue above, and the blue below,
And silence whereso'er I go

Barry Cornwall, 'The Sea'

Saturday, 2 July saw us meet up once more in Oban. Robert Langford was back for another week of sailing with us, as was David Shepherd. A fifth, new crew member, Peter Williamson also joined us. He had trained as a control engineer and later moved into logistics. His membership of the team came about in an unusual fashion, to say the least.

Roger:
Judith and I had taken a short break reconnoitring the ports on the East Coast, prior to our sailing there. As part of our holiday we travelled by vintage steam train from Pickering in North Yorkshire as far as Goathland, where the TV series *Heartbeat* was filmed. At one of the in-between stations, in the middle of nowhere, we were sitting on a bench in the sun, waiting for our steam train, and fell into conversation with a very pleasant couple. When we explained why we were in the area Peter enthusiastically told us he was a keen sailor. Within minutes details had been exchanged and he promised to join us on *Blue Star*, all completed in the nick of time just before our train arrived!

Not quite a case of wandering into the street and coercing the first person we came across, but not far off. It was through the generosity and sense of adventure of friends and acquaintances that we always had crew and did not need to resort to press-ganging as in the days of yore!

After meeting up in an Oban teashop the five of us arranged to share taxis to take us all to the boat.

Dunstaffnage Marina is one of few that have no outer wall to give added protection; its location in Ardmucknish Bay provides shelter. The pontoons spread out from the shore, the preferred route in and out from sea being marked by red and green buoys.

Our taxi stopped at the main building on the hill that overlooks the boats. We paid the driver and walked around and onto the pontoons, each dragging our wheeled baggage behind us. Unsurprisingly, *Blue Star* was exactly where we had left her a few weeks beforehand. It felt good to be back with her.

Roger had brought with him a new fresh-water pump to replace the one found leaking in Stromness. Having deposited his bag, he soon got to work, removing the mattress from his bunk in the port aft cabin, and lifting the plywood cover to the storage space below, where the electric pump was located. The replacement went very smoothly and we were soon able to use the taps in the galley and heads again without fear of flooding the bilge.

The next morning we expected to collect our repaired mainsail, but would it be ready? We walked to the building and scaled the external steel stairs leading to the small veranda and the marina office. Holding our breath, we asked for the return of our sail.

'Mmm, no, I don't know anything about that,' said the duty receptionist. Our hearts sank. Without the return of our mainsail we couldn't continue our voyage. 'Oh wait a minute what is this?' continued the receptionist. A receipt was found which indicated that the sail might be in the storeroom. Fortunately, it was. We were back in business!

We reinstalled the sail, carefully inserting the slides on the leading edge into the slot that runs up the back of the mast. One of the things that particularly pleased us on *Blue Star* were the low friction slides attaching the sail to the mast. Whenever we wanted to drop the mainsail it was just a matter of releasing the halyard from the cockpit and ensuring that it could run freely. The sail then whistled down the mast, falling quickly to the boom where it was caught by the lazyjacks. This was particularly useful when we needed to drop the sail whilst out on a rough stretch of sea. It made it unnecessary to run the risk of sending a crew member to the mast to help haul the sail down.

Once the slides were located in the mast, we attached the ropes that control the sail – the clew outhaul and the reefing lines. We were ready to go.

After filling up with diesel we set a course for Crinan. We weren't going through the canal but we aimed to tie up in the yacht basin there for the night. Leaving the harbour and keeping clear of the fish farms, we steered first for Oban, keeping a good look out for the large ferries which serve the Western Isles.

With little wind, we motored along, enjoying the scenery. To add to the air of relaxation we activated the autopilot. A conundrum appeared. The course being driven by the autopilot did not match that of the binnacle compass. A quick check round and the culprit was found. Mike's laptop was stored too near the autopilot's fluxgate compass. Once moved, we had full navigational accuracy. It is so easy to place a ferrous or magnetic object too close to one of the ship's compasses and not realise the effect it has.

It was a cloudy day with light showers. The wind was directly against us, as usual, and so we continued under engine in a rather lively sea. We left Maiden Island to port and continued into Oban Bay. There was shelter in the lee of the island, Kerrera, and the sea state improved.

Lunch of soup and sandwiches, prepared by Peter, was gratefully received, raising morale. From here we headed southwest down the Sound of Kerrera and into the Firth of Lorne. The picturesque Isle of Mull was to starboard. Here, with a change of wind direction, on a flat sea, we turned off the engine and enjoyed a marvellous sail. Retracing our earlier steps we sailed into Loch Crinan, avoiding the whirlpools that had grabbed at us previously.

Before long we were entering the yacht basin at Crinan via the sea lock once more. Lots of spectators lined the walls of the lock as the waters rose and lifted us up. We showered at the modern facility near the car park, ate on board and made a social visit to the bar of the Crinan Hotel.

US Independence Day, 4 July 2016 dawned. It was overcast and there was moisture in the air. We needed something to brighten our mood. We had learnt from our earlier stops at Crinan that the nearby shop sold some of the finest scones we had tasted on our travels. We visited once more, hoping to buy some fresh warm produce, to help us on our way. Alas, they had none available! Disappointing!

We locked out of the basin and back out to sea at 0930 hours. Under low clouds, we set out on a 40-mile passage to Port Ellen on the southern tip of Islay. With insufficient wind to sail, we motored in a southerly direction with the Isle of Jura on our starboard side. Making optimum use of the tides we kept up a good average speed, seeing more than seven knots over the ground for some considerable time. Shep resolved to temper our disappointment about the absence of scones by making pancakes. Immediately our spirits were lifted as he disappeared into the galley. Strangely though, it was not pancakes that emerged a short while later but a Spanish omelette! Even so, it was very tasty.

We were now in the Sound of Jura on a flat, glassy sea. It remained a windless, misty, grey day. Occasionally another vessel would be seen in the gloom. It was reassuring to have our electronic systems on board, making us aware of their presence even when we couldn't see them.

The mountains on either side of us, when we caught a glimpse of them, were magnificent and commanding. Jura was to starboard. To port were several lochs leading off from the sound: Loch Sween, Loch Caolisport and Loch Tarbert. Once again there was no time to explore.

Presently, as the southern tip of Jura came into view, we picked up the first glimpse of Islay. The island's main harbour, Port Ellen, has a series of rocks running southwest out to sea. Using the green buoys and the east cardinal we piloted a passage through to the small marina. We were accompanied by a couple of other yachts. Like us, they wanted to escape the threatened wet weather. A heavy shower greeted us as we approached the pontoons, and it was a relief to take our wet gear off and dry out down below once the lines were secured.

The town is named after the wife of Frederick Campbell of Islay. Built around Leodamais Bay, it is the main deep-water harbour for the island and the second-largest town. Large inter-island ferries provide freight and passenger services. Up until 1983 Scotch whisky was produced here.

The plan that evening was to freshen up and find somewhere to eat out. We took turns at 30-minute intervals to visit the one decent shower. Later we found a lively pub in town and enjoyed a hearty meal and the opportunity to sample the local whiskies and ales!

Leaving early the following morning to pick up the south-going tide, we set the mainsail with one reef, in case the wind strengthened. It died instead, and so we motor-sailed, still with one reef and ready for a blow should one arrive, heading south towards Northern Ireland.

The peninsula, Kintyre, was over to our left. After a few hours we passed its tip, the Mull of Kintyre. Was this really the place that Paul McCartney sang about? It looked so very grey and foreboding as we gazed at it through the damp air, a tall chunk of mountainous land stamping its presence on the surrounding sea.

Our course then took a turn to starboard as we headed out towards Northern Ireland, crossing at right angles to the 'Traffic Separation Scheme'. This may be likened to a nautical dual carriageway in which large ships navigate in defined lanes and at speed. Yachts are required to cross on a heading at 90 degrees to the scheme. Whilst crossing, we were being swept sideways by a very strong tide.

We were east of Rathlin Island which lies to the northeast of Northern Ireland. There is a narrow channel between the island and the mainland with turbulent water, very fast tides, dangerous overfalls and whirlpools. Purely under sail, we passed Rathlin at over ten knots, speed over the ground! Tidal flows of 4.5 knots at spring tides are charted for this area.

The wind finally picked up a little and we shook out the reef and began to enjoy ourselves as the sun came out. Working the tide, we continued south down the coast of County Antrim towards the small harbour of Glenarm. With the help of the tide it had all happened very quickly and we found ourselves a short distance from the marina before lunchtime! We decided to take an early lunch whilst still at sea, Shep once more demonstrating his culinary skills. After a short visit down below, he appeared back on deck with bacon and egg sandwiches for all!

We were tied up at the marina by 1300 hours and walked into town in the afternoon, visiting a local tearoom. Returning for dinner of spaghetti Bolognese, prepared by Peter, rounded off a brilliant day.

Roger:

In memory of our son who lost his life following the Asian tsunami in 2004, Judith and I developed a close link with the RNLI and, at their request, sponsored an inshore lifeboat at Red Bay near Cushendall, just north of Glenarm. The lifeboat, an Atlantic 85, was named *Geoffrey Charles*. Since it came on station in 2007 we'd built up a good relationship with the crew and therefore could not pass this part of the coast without making a social visit.

The following morning we left Glenarm and motored back up the coast, against a determined wind, to Red Bay where we picked up a mooring buoy just offshore from the lifeboat station. The station Coxswain, Paddy, came out to meet us in a large powerful rib and whisked us ashore. After a tour of the station we headed into the village and had an excellent lunch at Harry's, Paddy's hotel. A few of the other lifeboat crew joined us and it was wonderful to catch up on the latest launches and life in general at the station.

Before returning to *Blue Star* we were taken on a whirlwind tour of Red Bay Boats, the factory owned by Paddy's brother which builds RIBs for a variety of commercial and recreational uses, and which exports to many countries.

Afterwards we were boarding the RIB to go back to the yacht when Paddy pointed out a small rowing boat complete with outboard, which was manoeuvring near the lifeboat station slipway. He told us that these casual fishermen, who were not local, had caused them to launch many times due to their lack of knowledge of the dangers of this coast, and their disregard for safe nautical practice. Paddy was to have us back on *Blue Star* in minutes but, just as we started back, sure enough, on the very boat he'd been talking about, the engine failed. The men on board were being swept onto the rocks, having travelled only about 100 metres offshore. Another mission for the *Geoffrey Charles*!

Once we had dropped our mooring off the RNLI station we set sail for Bangor, just south of Belfast Lough. Again, the wind was fickle and we motored on, past Glenarm and onwards for about six hours, under engine for most of the way. The sea state was rather 'lumpy' initially but flattened out later as dusk fell.

Shep was doing a sterling job in the galley. Whilst in Red Bay he had taken the opportunity to nip into the village butchers to buy some steak. The excellent stew which he prepared whilst under way turned out to be a highlight of this passage. On a different day Shep produced a similar stew, but we all found it very tough to eat. We concluded that on that occasion the butcher must have misheard Shep's order and served him chewing-steak instead of stewing-steak!

In the dark, with our navigation lights on, we crossed the entrance to Belfast Lough, keeping a vigilant eye open for ships entering and leaving. Once across, we were soon tied up at Bangor.

The marina was of the highest quality, with excellent facilities and very helpful staff. There was some 'entertainment' during our overnight stay too. A large motorboat set out with some gusto from its berth. Unfortunately, the crew had inadvertently forgotten to unplug the shore power cable! The result, as they roared out from the pontoon, was that they ripped the electric power tower from its mountings on the pontoon! As far as we know they just continued on their journey, with internal combustion engine roaring away and a trail of destruction behind.

At a civilised hour the following morning we set sail for Douglas, Isle of Man, a crossing of some 66 miles. The weather was fair with a gentle wind from the southeast; however, we did need to supplement it with the engine for a few hours. We headed east and then passed inside Copeland Islands and through Donaghadee Sound. The coast here was low-lying, with little activity on either side of us. We could see the lighthouse over to port on Mew Island. Apart from the lighthouse, the islands appeared to be rather bleak and featureless, other than rough grass, bracken and rocks. The last of the population departed in 1946. The islands have been responsible for many a shipwreck, especially when vessels were in rough seas with poor visibility.

Fortunately, we had good conditions and we were enjoying the day. Several other yachts left Bangor with us, taking advantage of the favourable tidal stream. Were they coming with us? Apparently not. As we headed out to the Isle of Man the other yachts seemed to follow suit initially but then took a turn to starboard and followed the Irish coast southwards.

From the southern end of Donaghadee we set a course of 150°, which we would follow for about 40 miles – approximately seven hours at our average speed. As with many of the longer legs, there was a pattern of dedicated crew on watch, those taking it easy and always someone ready to make a cup of tea. Some sailors relish long open water passages, often out of sight of land. We preferred the excitement of coastal cruising, seeing the ever-changing landscape, and always preparing for a new harbour and port.

By midday we could make out the profile of the Isle of Man on the horizon and for the next few hours spent a relaxing time sailing on the headsail.

It continued to be a sunny day, with a fair wind and a 'slight' sea state. We were to sail between the Isle of Man and the Calf of Man, a small island to the south, passing through Calf Sound. This is a narrow channel between rocky headlands. The passage through was spectacular, with off-lying cliffs and rocks, and green hills beyond.

As we left the sound and turned east we passed Langness Point before shaping up for a north-easterly route along the mainland coast to Douglas. We had experienced a pleasant passage. Birds and the occasional seal had kept us company, and with music playing in the cockpit there had been a relaxed atmosphere.

Roger:

We were looking forward to sailing in the last of the evening sun towards Douglas. However, when we were about ten miles out a thick fog rolled in from the east. We watched it approach, but were powerless to avoid it. Immediately the atmosphere became more serious. On went the AIS, radar and navigation lights. All other poor visibility measures were initiated too – air horn on deck, reduced speed and extra lookouts. Everyone was already wearing lifejackets, standard procedure on *Blue Star,* from slipping lines to mooring up.

Mike was on the helm and I was in the cockpit, focused on looking astern and to port. With the fog swirling around us, I was conscious of a large paddle-wheeled ship sliding up our port side, slowly overtaking us before disappearing from view. It was clearly a leisure boat of some kind, although no passengers were visible among the empty rows of seats. There was no noise and the outline was indistinct – however, it was definitely another vessel, we all saw it. Mike and I both checked the chart plotter – nothing shown on AIS and nothing on radar. There was no trace of the vessel. Was it a ghost ship?

The final few miles into Douglas were navigated with a thick stew of murk all around us. We were concerned not to enter the harbour without permission, for fear of being rammed by any large commercial vessel that might be leaving. We radioed port control to take advice. Several other vessels could be heard taking the same action. There was a tense atmosphere as we peered through the dark and the fog looking out for other craft. Our instrumentation told us that the harbour was only a short distance away on our port side when, right on cue, the walls reared up beside us and the entrance became visible! Phew!

Douglas is a busy commercial port. At night, the recommended route is indicated by leading lights, two lights which must be made to line up by vessels entering the harbour, that guide vessels in. We had not followed that route but had instead hogged the coast until the entrance showed up. Once inside the harbour we tied up on the waiting pontoon at Battery Pier. Here, small craft wait for the lifting bridge to open, and for the correct tide to enable them to pass over the flap gate into the marina beyond.

On went the kettle and we began to relax. Lighting around the harbour penetrated the fog and made the surrounding scene rather spooky. Gazing about, we could make out the harbour entrance through which we had come. None of the other vessels in the harbour fitted the description of the mysterious boat we had seen earlier.

After a few hours we were able to pass into the marina where we found a berth. The Isle of Man has a reputation for being a tax haven and a strong financial centre. We expected top-notch facilities and a huge number of very expensive boats. What a let-down! The shower block was dismal and there were many very poorly maintained vessels, giving a general run-down feel to the place.

We had planned to sail on from Douglas towards Wales, but the weather forecast for the forthcoming few days was not encouraging. We decided to leave *Blue Star* in Douglas whilst we returned home for a short while. We all booked our tickets to travel on the ferry to Liverpool. There, we boarded trains to take us home. Before leaving for the ferry, however, we could not help but smile at Shep as he dumped his 'oilies' into the marina dustbin, muttering something about how useless they had become! Even so, knowing Shep, we suspect he had definitely got his money's worth out them.

***

<u>Joke</u>
Q. What goes 'croak, croak' in the mist?
A. A froghorn!

***

Below: The marina at Glenarm

Above: Visiting the lifeboat station at Red Bay,
(left to right: Roger, David, Liam, Robert, Paddy, Peter and Mike;
Liam and Paddy are lifeboat station crew)

Below: Passing through Calf Sound (left to right: Robert, Roger and David)

Above: The fog starts to clear in Douglas Harbour

Below: Shep decides to dispose of his 'oilies'

17. Douglas to Milford Haven

No literature is richer than that of the sea. No story is more enthralling, no tradition is more secure.

Felix Riesenberg

Roger:
Mike was unable to join the boat for the leg from Douglas to North Wales. His son, Daniel, suffering with cystic fibrosis, was particularly unwell. We had got crew arranged, though, and didn't want to let them down or fall behind schedule. Layton (Lenny) Quinton, a university finance worker from Manchester, had won a charity competition to sail with us on *Blue Star*. The prize was for two people, so he arranged for his father, Len, to join us too. Jamie, an engineer from Bedfordshire, I had known since he was a boy and I knew he had a keen sense of adventure. I arrived back in Douglas the day before the crew to prepare the boat.

The crew arrived the following day, Saturday, 23 July, and we set to, getting to know each other and the boat. Len senior had sailing experience, his son a little too, and Jamie a passing acquaintance. I called on Jamie's skills as a chartered engineer to double-check some of my passage plan calculations. Although he was not familiar with the mechanics of tides and so forth, he made sure there were no mistakes in lifting dates or reading times from the almanac.

The plan was to head towards Holyhead on Anglesey, making maximum use of the currents as we approached North Wales. Over dinner we discussed a host of potential safety issues and how we would handle them. The next day the weather forecast was poor so we delayed our departure by 24 hours.

The extra day to prepare was a bonus. We warped *Blue Star* around on her berth, to ensure she pointed in the right direction for exiting the marina. It was the only way to turn the boat, given that there was so little space.

We had to synchronise our departure with both the lifting bridge, which opened on the half hour, and a lock. The crew were briefed the night before and I recommended an early night as we had to leave at 0445 hours.

At 0400 hours on Monday I came out of my cabin to find the crew around the saloon table having breakfast and all kitted up, complete with lifejackets! Len made me a cup of tea and I ate a bowl of porridge. After stowing everything away we were ready to drop lines on time and we passed out smoothly through the lifting bridge and lock, past the waiting pontoon where we had stopped for a short while before entering Douglas. It was a calm morning, slightly overcast and with a wind of ten knots, and the sea was smooth which was ideal. After motoring out past Battery Pier we set a southerly course for Holyhead.

Within an hour we had the mainsail and headsail flying and were enjoying the steady wind, gusting 15 knots from the southeast, but backing to the east. This provided excellent sailing conditions and we were consistently doing six knots over the ground.

Jamie:

Having only previously messed around in dinghies, the *Blue Star* trip would be my first real yacht experience. With duffel bag over my shoulder I set off from Bedford for Douglas via train and ferry. As expected, Roger was a no-nonsense skipper and I quickly needed to learn the ropes; it wasn't long before I was grateful to recall my knots from Scouts many years earlier.

From Douglas we set forth at dawn in a stiff breeze with a reef in. Taking the gamble of not taking a seasickness tablet soon proved a mistake, so I missed a couple of hours sleeping through part of the passage.

Roger:

By the time we were about halfway to our destination, young Lenny was not feeling too well either and he joined Jamie below. Len and I discussed the situation; he was feeling fit and well and good to carry on.

As I plotted the hourly position it became clear that we were ahead of the planned position which I had conservatively calculated on an average speed of five knots over the ground. The consequence of this was that we would reach the North Wales coast early, just before the tide turned west. Given the depleted crew and excellent progress, I changed the destination to Conwy which was a slightly shorter distance, would work the tide better and get the crew into harbour sooner. With Len and myself doing half an hour about on the helm I was able to minister to the sick, do the plotting, make a new pilotage plan, prepare food and all the other usual shipboard duties.

About ten miles out from Conwy the wind dropped slightly and the sea state improved. Not surprisingly people started appearing from down below to sample the joys of a sunny North Wales coast! Shortly afterwards we stowed the sails and put on the engine, ready to motor towards Conwy Marina. As I double-checked my new passage plan I realised that we had sailed for about 45 miles of what was to be a 57-mile passage, mostly exceeding 5.5 knots.

The buoyed channel up the River Conwy is clearly marked; amongst flat sandy dunes it was easy to follow, especially with the help of Len who had sailed it many times previously. The charts and chart plotter were also a big help. I was glad of the experience from a previous trip with Mike where we had explored North Wales and Anglesey.

A cockpit briefing with the now fully functioning crew discussed the need for quick, but not rushed, preparations for entering the marina, now that the tide was ebbing. The crew set about their duties, preparing mooring warps and putting out fenders. As we approached the marina entrance I noticed all three crew members on the starboard foredeck having an animated discussion – clearly not ready to enter the marina yet. This delay in preparation meant I had to balance the boat against the now increasingly strong ebb tide and stay away from the shallows whilst enquiring what the issue was. To my surprise it was about the correct way to tie a clove hitch! I promptly advised them, in my best Michael Caine impression, 'Just tie on the b****y fenders'! With fenders secured we motored into the marina and berthed the boat in one smooth motion. Now we could discuss how to tie a clove hitch!

A light lunch was followed by a session cleaning up the boat; later we went for an early dinner at the marina restaurant and then back to discussing what the following day would entail. Having made a slight change of plan I telephoned Mike and we agreed that rather than sail for Holyhead I would bring the boat to Port Dinorwic through the Menai Straits, separating Anglesey from the Welsh mainland. It is a picturesque small harbour, south of the Menai Bridge which spans the Straits.

Another early start to catch the tide saw us setting off at 0530 hours and heading west towards Puffin Island. We would be passing through the Swellies, an area with the potential to be very dangerous and where careful preparation is needed to avoid mishaps. Tidal streams run at up to eight knots and the navigable channel is bordered by rocks that lie in wait to trap the unwary skipper. Even local skippers have been caught out.

Our passage needed to be at the right time. We picked up a mooring buoy northeast of the Menai Suspension Bridge, just before the Swellies, and had lunch. At the appointed hour we dropped the buoy and headed through the notorious, narrow and often fast-flowing waterway at the optimum state of tide – approximately high water slack.

The timing was good and we safely navigated through and, after entering through lock gates, tied up in Port Dinorwic at around 1430 hours. The following day Mike was able to join the crew.

Port Dinorwic, Y Felinheli in Welsh, is a former Welsh slate export harbour and was a pleasant place to spend the day whilst we waited for the right height of tide to pass out through the lock. The port had once flourished when a narrow-gauge tramway was built in 1824 to bring the slate from the inland quarry to the coast. The marina is small and not very wide. A swing bridge spans the full width and allows access to the inner harbour for craft planning to stay longer. We had berthed in the outer section, between the lock and the bridge. As with Douglas we warped the yacht round during the morning, ready for a smooth exit later.

During the day we chatted with John and Avril Eardley, owners of the motor cruiser *Bliss*, moored nearby. The home port for their boat was Pwllheli which was, by coincidence, our next port of call. We mentioned to them that Jamie would be leaving us in Pwllheli to go and take part in a charity cycle ride. Good fortune smiling on us, John said that he would like to join us for the subsequent leg from Pwllheli to Milford Haven.

At around 1500 hours on Wednesday we locked out and headed in a south-westerly direction down the Straits towards the town of Caernarfon. Leaving the town and its castle to port we motored through the narrows past Abermenai Point and worked our way out of the Straits on an ebbing tide into Caernarfon Bay. The route out was through a well-buoyed channel over the bar, towards the red and white safe-water mark. Years before, Mike had chartered in this area, providing us with useful experience of the shifting sands and narrow channel to be negotiated.

We now headed southwest down the Lleyn Peninsula. It was very scenic, with green hills and mountains sloping down to us. There were many interesting rock formations at sea level. Higher up, mountains dominated the skyline. We passed the village of Trefor which once served the workers at the nearby quarry from which granite-like stone was extracted and loaded onto ships. The wooden quay still stands there today. Nowadays Trefor is a base for diving, angling and holidaymakers.

Further on was Porthdinllaen which had once been proposed as the main port from which ships would depart for Ireland. It never came to pass however. When the railway to Anglesey was constructed and terminated at Holyhead, that is where the major port developed. Today Porthdinllaen boasts a quiet harbour with several holiday cottages and a well-known, popular pub, The Ty Coch Inn, on the beach.

Darkness had fallen by the time we had reached the tip of the Lleyn Peninsula and were passing the off-lying Bardsey Island. The island, one mile long and 0.6 miles wide, used to be a centre for pilgrimage and once had a monastery. King Henry VIII ordered its dissolution and the demolition of the buildings. The island is now a bird sanctuary and an area that attracts dolphins and seals. It also supports a sheep farm that is run by the National Trust.

Unsurprisingly, strong tidal currents flow in the two-mile channel between Bardsey and the mainland, and passage has to be made with care. We had managed to sail for a few hours but the wind was dying. It was motor-sailing for the remainder of the trip, approximately 17 miles to Pwllheli from Bardsey. We would be arriving in darkness.

We had switched on the navigation and steaming lights as darkness fell when we passed Bardsey, and motoring on past Aberdaron we could see the lights of the village off our port side. Through the dark, our way was lit only by the moon and stars and the small amount of light from the shore. The sky was a series of silhouettes, half-lit clouds blocking some of the available light. These, together with a few stars, broke the pitch black of the night. The rhythmic motion of the boat and the repeated 'sshhh' against the hull told of the waves that we were brushing aside as we forced our way forward. Behind us, green-tinted phosphorescence in the disturbed water helped illuminate the scene. It is such a completely different experience to sail by night, and under the right conditions – a flat sea and a following, warm summer wind – it is an absolute delight!

Some days earlier Mike had found a mysterious package on his doorstep. It turned out to be a delicious-looking fruit cake, baked by David Shepherd. When Mike thanked him, David explained that he 'always felt that it was really nice to have a hot cup of tea and a piece of cake when on night watch' and that it was for the crew of *Blue Star*, for just such an occasion. How very thoughtful!

It was at this point in the passage that we remembered Shep's cake. Mike took a visit down below to pop on the kettle. Ten minutes later, shortly after passing Bardsey, with the lights of Aberdaron abeam and in the near-pitch black of night, we all enjoyed a hot cup of tea and a piece of 'Shepcake'!

The next headland was that off Abersoch. Care is needed here to pass the two small St Tudwal's Islands that lie a short distance off the mainland. The choice is to go either between the islands and the mainland or to take a wider sweep outside them. We opted for the latter, taking care to miss the rocks that lie just below the surface a little distance off.

About an hour and a half later we were lining ourselves up to enter the marina at Pwllheli.

Roger:
I really enjoyed the transition from dusk to darkness, and the lights of our destination coming into view. Gradually my eyes adapted to the low light conditions; the cockpit instruments were all dimmed and it felt comfortable helming. The entrance channel is well buoyed, a series of five starboard greens to follow into the harbour. By now it was 0145 hours, and to help the pilotage we brought our large searchlight up to the cockpit. Powered from the cigarette lighter below, the cable would just about stretch to the cockpit. Once turned on, there was a dazzling brightness and reflected glare from the white coach roof and foredeck. For what felt like an age I was completely blind from the aura of brilliant, white light and we were still making a few knots in confined conditions! As the beam was redirected, my vision partially returned. Fortunately, we were still well positioned in the channel and heading for

the mooring pontoons. A valuable lesson; in future we would find a way to take the searchlight to the bow!

The next day was shore leave. We decided to have a leisurely shower and walk into Pwllheli for coffee and supplies. We prepared for our passage on Friday to Milford Haven, telephoning John Eardley to let him know of the early departure time.

Friday dawned bright but with some grey-white clouds, and a fair wind. As John joined the boat, Avril very kindly provided a large box of homemade Florentines for a treat along the way towards our next stop. Jamie departed, with our best wishes and thanks.

Jamie:
It had been a great first experience sailing a yacht. The night passage and the need to understand all the flashing lights from lighthouses and navigation buoys made a particular impression on me. I learnt a lot in a short time from Roger and Mike. Suitably inspired I followed it up by doing my Day Skipper qualification. I have subsequently taken the family on our first yachting holiday around the somewhat warmer Greek Ionian islands, and we loved it! I will always be grateful to Roger and Mike for having the opportunity to be part of their charity fundraising venture.

We had examined the options for stopping earlier than Milford Haven but none of the other ports on the West Coast of Wales were really suitable. Only Aberystwyth offered walk-ashore facilities but access was dependent on the tide. Milford Haven had excellent shelter and a locked marina. The estimated distance was 90 miles and with our normal average speed the passage should take approximately 18 hours – we actually made it in 17 hours.

We exited the marina and harbour with no problems; it is surprising how different things look in full daylight! Initially it was unpleasant; we were close-hauled on starboard tack, making way in a moderate sea. After a while the sea flattened and the wind direction was more from the beam, giving us an easier ride. We were out of sight of land for much of the passage, under a grey sky on a black-green sea. Very soon the engine was employed in order to arrive at slack water for our passage through Ramsey Sound, the narrow stretch of water between

St David's Head and Ramsey Island. The majority of the journey across Cardigan Bay was uneventful and spent motor-sailing.

Approaching the sound, a fishing boat trawling a short distance off was on a collision course with us. To avoid any doubt, we made a distinct change of course so as to not impede its path. The trawler immediately changed its course and was then once again heading for us. We changed tack once more, back to our original heading, and the trawler did the same. We decided that there was nothing we could do if the fishing boat's skipper was hell-bent on a collision. We stuck to our guns this time. He continued coming closer but at the last minute turned away before things became too hairy. We concluded that, having noted *Blue Star*, with her multi-coloured logos and banners, the skipper was simply inquisitive enough to want a closer look. Perhaps it was a boring day towing a fishing net off St David's?

With the sun setting we entered Ramsey Sound around 2000 hours and started our passage between the island and mainland. There were multiple small rocks to be avoided as we progressed through. Arriving at slack water avoided the risk of losing control in strong tides and overfalls. Ramsey Island has a population of just two wardens from the Royal Society for the Protection of Birds. It is a nature reserve and an area where grey seals breed.

We passed through into St Brides Bay. About seven miles wide, it's a part of the Pembrokeshire Coast National Park and of the Heritage Coast. The authorities aim to conserve its outstanding natural beauty and to improve access for visitors.

As we motored slowly into the bay we were suddenly aware of the extensive flocks of sea birds, both on the wing and on the water, a magical sight, and we were completely absorbed by it. We'd been playing music in the cockpit and at that moment Take That sang out 'the world comes alive ...' which seemed incredibly apt. It was an amazing experience, navigating amongst so very many birds. All the crew felt it imperative to film what we were witnessing, such was our total enchantment.

At the southern end of the bay are two islands, Skomer and Skokholm, both nature reserves, with rocky coasts. Half the world's population of Manx Shearwaters nest on Skomer! It is also home for grey seals, toads and slow worms.

With darkness falling, we passed between the islands and shaped a course for the nearby headland, St Ann's Head, around which lay Milford

Haven. The passage across St Brides Bay had been a wonderful, tranquil and almost ethereal experience. As we lined up for the large industrial port, the vista and the atmosphere changed dramatically. There was a huge amount of background light associated with the gas and petroleum complexes!

With the decline of the fishing industry in the 1950s, the government decided to create an industrial complex, centred around the oil industry, in Milford Haven. In 1960 Esso opened a refinery, followed by BP, Gulf and Amoco. By the early 1980s the Esso refinery was the second-largest in the United Kingdom. The supply of oil to the refinery by ships was not without its risks, exemplified by the disastrous grounding and break-up of the BP chartered vessel *Torrey Canyon* in 1967. It was estimated that between 25 and 36 million gallons of oil were discharged into the sea when the super tanker, fully laden with crude oil, ran aground on rocks west of Land's End. We would soon be sailing in this area ourselves. In more recent times two large liquefied natural gas terminals have been constructed at Milford Haven. Gas from primarily the Middle East is cooled down to -160°C whereupon it becomes liquid and is then transported in specially constructed ships.

There are two clearly buoyed channels into the harbour, and leaving St Ann's Head to port we kept out of the main channel, and headed initially towards the Dale Roads anchorage. From here a turn to starboard took us past loading jetties on our port side before Milford Marina was in view. It was an easy entrance, with the leading lights on a bearing of 348° beckoning us towards the lock, the way in illuminated by three port-side channel markers flashing red. After a short stay on the waiting pontoon, preparing fenders and lines, we passed through the lock, found our designated pontoon berth and tied up on the stroke of midnight.

Having had a hot meal along the way, all we wanted to do was get into our bunks. We intended to leave *Blue Star* at Milford Haven for a few weeks and to reacquaint ourselves with our families. The following morning, after cleaning up the boat and talking with the marina office staff, we tested the produce of the marina café. Soon it was time to walk to the railway station, baggage in tow, to start the journey home.

The train towards Cardiff was 'local' and made numerous stops at small stations to pick up passengers. We were crowded in with a wild group of people off to party in the city. They had started drinking and getting in the mood early. We were relieved to reach Cardiff where we went our separate ways back home.

John:
What a fantastic experience I had joining the crew, with great company! I'll never forget sailing at night into Milford Haven beside those huge tankers!

***

Joke
A young sailor had never been on a yacht before. He was now thinking it was the stupidest thing he'd done in his life. Who would have believed that seasickness could be so awful? With every pitch and roll he wondered how he was going to survive the remaining two hours of the passage. After a while the captain came to reassure him.

'Don't worry, young fella. Nobody ever died of seasickness.'

'Oh, no!' said the sailor, 'That was my last hope of relief!'

***

Above: Leaving Douglas early in the morning

Above: Passing through the Menai Straits (photo courtesy of Jamie Riach)

Above: Locking into Milford Haven at midnight

18. Milford Haven to Falmouth

The rocky ledge runs far out to sea,
And on its outer point, some miles away,
The lighthouse lifts its massive masonry,
A pillar of fire by night, of cloud by day.

Henry Wadsworth Longfellow, 'The Lighthouse'

Saturday, 13 August. New crew, Rob Hollins and Bob Costello, both members of Stafford Coastal Cruising Club, assembled on Platform 4 at Stafford railway station for the journey to Milford Haven with Mike. Rob was a town planning engineer specialising in roads and transport. His wife, Val, had come to see him off. Bob, a larger-than-life character, was CEO of his own civil engineering consultancy, and had been dropped off by his wife, Jenny.

Mike:
Remembering the riotous train journey from Milford Haven back home, it was with some trepidation that we set out to travel back. The train journey was as tedious as expected. The carriages were old and full, and the journey over six hours long, with changes of train. At least there were no drunken passengers. We were glad when the carriages pulled up at the rail terminus at Milford Haven. After a short walk to *Blue Star*, we were able to relax with a cup of tea.

There was a puzzle though. A mysterious box had been left on the sliding hatch that covers the companionway of the boat. The package had been sent by post, and delivered by marina staff to the boat. But what was it? It turned out to have come from Avril Eardley. It was a gift of more of her homemade Florentine cookies. What a lovely surprise!

Sunday was spent provisioning the boat and planning the next leg. We would be crossing the Bristol Channel to the North Coast of Cornwall. A Tesco supermarket trolley, loaded to the gunwales, was pushed onto the pontoon beside the boat where we formed a human chain to pass the contents, one to the other and down below, until the trolley was empty. Bob said that he would take care of the empty trolley – we assume he returned it to the supermarket.

Roger returned to the boat in the evening, after dropping off his hire car at the local agent. The intention was to depart for Padstow shortly after midnight, and so, after an early dinner on board, we all got a few hours' sleep. Our destination was about 75 miles and 15 hours sailing away.

We departed just after midnight. There was enough light in the marina to easily find our way into the sea lock, and to manage the lines as the water descended.

Out in the Haven things were a little different. We were surrounded by lights – on buoys, on the quays where oil tankers were unloading, and on the ships themselves. It was not immediately obvious what all of the lights were, but we had a pilotage plan to get us out to sea and we carefully followed the prescribed compass course, aimed for the next navigation light, checked our progress via the chart plotter and correlated it all with depth readings. Large ships were navigating in the harbour and we had to keep clear of them as they did not have the manoeuvrability that we had.

Milford Haven is a large harbour and about one hour after setting out we were still within its shelter, now at the western end, where we raised our mainsail. Turning to a more southerly course to exit the harbour we worked our way out, picking a path between more red and green flashing lights that told us the way. We paid careful attention to the white flashing cardinal mark that guarded the mid-channel rocks. Best not to hit them!

Out at sea, in the dark, we could only hear and feel the waves. Conditions were no worse than expected, and under engine and mainsail we were making over five knots.

Mike:

Here we implemented a watch system. Bob and I on until 0330 hours and Roger and Rob providing the relief. It was pitch black except for the light of the moon and the stars. Occasionally the lights of another vessel were seen, and we would correlate its position with the AIS. We couldn't see the waves, but we knew they were there by the rhythmic motion of the boat, by a regular 'sshhh' and occasional spray on our decks.

After a while Bob went down below and prepared a cup of tea and we made use of the ship's biscuit box to help it go down.

194

As we did during daylight, every hour we would make an entry in the logbook and place a mark on the chart, checking our progress. At night, yachtsmen often use a red light to illuminate the chart table – it detracts less from one's night vision on returning to the cockpit. A white light is much easier though, despite it taking a while to regain full night vision. It is less of an issue when there is another crew member maintaining their night vision and helping to keep a lookout.

Onwards, through the dark and the occasional twinkling navigation light. Sometimes a small course adjustment to starboard, sometimes to port. Always, the sound of wave after wave breaking against *Blue Star*'s hull.

Ten minutes before the end of the watch the kettle went on again so that a hot drink might welcome the others. After a five-minute handover Bob and I went down below to visit the heads and to catch up on some sleep. The boat's motion often makes visiting the heads a tricky job, but it was not too bad on this occasion. Finding one handhold after another, we each worked our way to our bunks.

For me it was hard work simply to take off my lifejacket and waterproofs, the yacht's angle making balance in a small cabin difficult. I lay on my bunk, too tired to undress and, in any case, I might be needed on deck at short notice. And then a fitful sleep. The throbbing of the engine forbade anything more restful.

Roger:

Crawling into my bunk after leaving Milford Haven, with images of the massive terminals fresh in my mind, I reflected on the advances of technology which had brought natural gas from 3,000 metres below the Persian Gulf to the UK. In the early 1970s, as a young Drilling Supervisor, working offshore Qatar, I participated in the drilling of some of the first exploration wells on what became one of the world's largest offshore gas fields. We worked 12 hours a day, nine offshore and two rest days onshore. Working the night shift, commencing at midnight avoided the crippling heat of the afternoon sun, had the bonus of the sunrise over Iran in the far distance and the pleasure of a large hearty breakfast at 0530 hours. Soon I would look forward to another sunrise, this time in the Bristol Channel.

I came up on deck at around 0330 hours refreshed, and with a cup of tea prepared by Bob. After a watch handover Rob and I checked the charts and looked forward to dawn. Just over an hour later it was beginning to break in the east; as the wind had dropped it was only the gentle sound of the Volvo which accompanied us through to full daylight.

Many a well-known vessel has sailed down these waters from Bristol, including SS *Great Britain* which was constructed there. After being rescued from a potentially watery grave in the Falkland Islands, these days she is back in the dry dock where she was originally built, having been restored to her former glory.

As anyone who has sailed at night time will know, the arrival of dawn at sea is somehow different from being on land. From a world of darkness we could now see the horizon. The bonus for this beautiful morning, with pinks and reds colouring the sky, was the sudden appearance of dolphins playing around the boat. Not only a magnificent dawn but also incredible creatures. Amazing!

The dolphins continued playing, diving under our bows and leaping into the air alongside us for 20 minutes or more.

By 0930 hours we had covered more than 50 miles, and with a gentle breeze springing up we were able to set full sail, turn off the engine and enjoy the warm sunshine. Even the 'off watch' crew opted to remain on deck.

Our course for Padstow took us past the island of Lundy, 12 miles off the Cornish mainland. Owned by the National Trust, it is said to be where the Atlantic meets the Bristol Channel. A granite outcrop, it is three miles long and half a mile wide. The majority of day trippers are brought from the mainland on MS *Oldenburg*. The island is famous for its bird life; many 'twitchers' come to observe migratory flocks. We didn't stop at Lundy as the main anchorage is exposed to waves and swell. A *Yachting Monthly* article describes it as being 'lumpy'.

After Lundy we continued to sail until a few miles off the North Cornwall coast. Soon Padstow Bay was in sight.

The entrance into Padstow Bay is guarded by a series of rocks just offshore. Leaving the most westerly of these, Rayner Rocks, to port, we lined up for our entrance into the River Camel. Many UK pubs sell a popular beer of Cornish origin called Doom Bar. It was the large sandbank of this same name which started to appear on our starboard side as we approached the entrance. In the days of sailing vessels many were swept onto the Doom Bar. It led to a large winch being built on the opposite bank which could be used to pull them off the sands.

The timing had worked out well – we had arrived close to high water, necessary for sufficient depth in the river. Also, the marina lock gates open only for around a couple of hours either side of high water. It is just over 1.5 miles from the mouth of the river to the harbour. The pilot book emphasised the shifting sands in the narrow river and the need for careful navigation, the safe route being marked by red and green buoys.

We passed the first two marks without a hitch, first a red left to port and then a green left to starboard. The chart showed another red close to the marina, but where was it? The pilot book showed the deep channel to be well over to the right-hand side of the river; slowly and carefully we worked our way across, but still we couldn't see the buoy. We dropped our speed down to barely more than half a knot as our depth gauge showed only half a metre under the keel. Still we couldn't see the next red mark. Just as the depth was reducing further we had an incoming call from the marina on the VHF radio. We had called ahead to let them know that our arrival was imminent, but what did they want now? We needed everyone on deck to search for the red buoy so we didn't respond to the call – one wrong move now and we would be aground! Suddenly we spotted the red buoy. It had been hidden behind a yacht on a nearby mooring. We could see now that the channel was even further to the right than we had reckoned.

Roger went below to reply to the VHF call – the harbourmaster had been watching us approach and had wanted to warn us that we were in danger of running aground!

It was good that he had been looking out for us but we had made it to the lock gates. We lingered close to them and after ten minutes they opened and allowed us in. There were no free spaces on the pontoons so we tied up, as instructed, against the stone harbour wall. From there, access to the quay was via a vertical steel ladder. It had been a really good passage.

It is thought that there was a settlement at Padstow from as early as 2500 BC. In the Middle Ages it increased in importance as a port trading in copper, tin and lead ores as well as pilchards and agricultural produce. The first stone pier was built in the 16th century and the inner harbour wall completed in 1989. More recently the town has become known for its Rick Stein restaurant. Apparently, some people actually call Padstow 'Padstein'!

What remained of Monday gave us all a chance to catch up on sleep. Night passages are something else. Sailing under the stars and the moon, or even in pitch black, is such a completely different experience. On the right night, with a warm wind, a flat sea and a beam reach, it is exhilarating. But on the down side it invariably interferes with the crews' sleep pattern, leaving them feeling jetlagged.

Rejuvenated after a rest, we set out to walk around the town. First stop – check out the Rick Stein restaurant. It did indeed have an exotic menu, priced to match, and we felt rather underdressed to book a table. We did, however, go up onto the roof terrace for a pint of Doom Bar just before sunset. Dinner for us that evening was fish and chips in one of the quayside restaurants.

The weather forecast determined that Tuesday would be a port day. It gave us the chance to clean the boat and carry out a few maintenance tasks. Despite the forecast, in our corner of the harbour there was little wind and it was baking hot on deck and below.

We decided to tackle the slightly loose grab handle on the top of the binnacle, just forward of the wheel. This was well positioned for moving safely about the cockpit and needed to be secure. Whilst tightening the two holding screws was straightforward, it did entail removing the chart plotter to access it. It turned out to be one of those 30-minute jobs that took the whole morning to complete! Still, we were in no rush and it kept us entertained. Through a great team effort, with Mike the Procurement Manager, Rob the Senior Shipwright and Roger the Chief Artificer, the chart plotter was removed, the new nuts mounted and the plotter reinstalled and sealed – job done! Whilst doing this we watched a continuous procession of pleasure craft taking tourists up the river.

For Wednesday, 17 August the forecast looked reasonable and we aimed to set sail for Newlyn on Cornwall's South Coast. There were several considerations to take into account. The latest time that we could exit Padstow in the morning was soon after high water at 0520 hours – it would be barely light at that time. Having travelled down the river and out to sea, if we did not like the conditions, there would be no getting back; the lock gates would not be opening again until late afternoon! Our only option would be to seek shelter at anchor somewhere in the river mouth. Another issue was the challenge of rounding Land's End, the most westerly part of the English mainland. It is a major headland with strong tidal streams and, nearby, the rocky skerries and islets of Longships to be safely dealt with. There was no other port on the North Coast of Cornwall that could accommodate a boat with *Blue Star*'s draught, so no port of refuge. Once leaving Padstow we really did have to make it round to Newlyn.

We rose at 0500 hours and had breakfast. Should we go? Had the bad weather passed over? In the harbour, boats were jostling, jerking to and fro in the wind, each trying to escape their lines. If it was like this here what would it be like out at sea? We checked the latest weather forecast. Gusts of force 6 from the northwest and a moderate sea state. Force 6 can give some unpleasant conditions, but from the northwest it just might be a good sail for us, heading southwest. We decided to go.

After a quick visit to the shoreside facilities and a speedy breakfast we were ready to slip lines and enter the lock. Another yacht, *Tiger Moth*, was leaving with us. It was reassuring that, with the forecast, another skipper had also decided it was safe to put to sea.

Out in the river we raised the mainsail with two reefs, and unfurled a little headsail. *Tiger Moth* was similarly rigged. We must have it right then! Away we went down the river, too late to turn back now. At the river mouth *Tiger Moth* turned right and we turned left. We were on our own.

Travelling down the river had been easy, but out at sea the waves made life uncomfortable. Even with our reefed sails *Blue Star* was heeled well over to port. Whenever there was a gust the boat tried to round up into the wind. We couldn't go on like this. We had no third reef so the mainsail was dropped completely and we proceeded under reefed headsail alone, and this made the boat far more stable.

We headed a few miles offshore to give ourselves some sea room, away from the danger of the rocky coast. Then the wind died and we had to motor, past a distant Newquay and St Ives. With 26 miles on the log we were off Cape Cornwall, adjusting our course to port to run south towards Land's End. As with all the headlands around the UK, planning for the optimum tides was the key to a quick and smooth passage.

It was at this point that a thick fog descended. There had been no mention of this in the forecast. Visibility was down to little more than a few boat lengths. We found it an inconvenience rather than a concern, for we had experienced these conditions earlier on in the voyage, and we had excellent electronic systems to guide us. And, of course, we had a compass! The sea state levelled out considerably with the arrival of the fog. Under these conditions we sailed on, not that we had much choice. We hoped that the fog would go soon as it hadn't been forecast, but it didn't.

At 1600 hours our electronics told us we were approaching Longships Lighthouse, marking the dangerous rocks offshore, close to Land's End. We kept well away. The fog lifted momentarily, enough for us to just make out the light atop its stone column, built on the treacherous rocks below.

We had been looking forward to sailing around Land's End, a major turning point in our journey and such a well-known headland. It would have been a memorable experience to view it from the sea. But we were to be denied, the fog persisting. We were all very disappointed.

As we turned from the Atlantic into the English Channel it felt like a significant moment. After more than 2,000 miles and having sailed the waters of England, Scotland, Northern Ireland and Wales, we were now on an easterly track for the Solent and the completion of our circumnavigation.

Still in the murk, we continued following a track a few miles off the coast. Now on the South Coast of England, there remained little wind and we were in the lee of the land.

Off Mousehole we altered course to head inland, towards Newlyn, still in thick fog. Our passage through the harbour entrance, according to the electronics, was imminent when, as if by magic, the lights on the harbour wall were suddenly visible and we could actually see!

Ten minutes later we were tied up in the marina, rafted against a much larger Bavaria yacht. The skipper of the other yacht proclaimed their intention to depart at 0500 hours the next day. 'Fine,' we said, 'in that case we will leave then too, so as not to impede you.' And so all was well.

Newlyn has an important role in cartography. It was chosen as the principal location for determining the Mean Sea Level (MSL) due to the tide arriving unimpeded from the Atlantic and its stable granite foundation close to the continental shelf. Automatic measurements of sea level were made between 1915 and 1921 that fixed the value of MSL. Heights on Ordnance Survey Maps for mainland Britain are referenced to Ordnance Datum Newlyn, marked by a brass bolt placed in the floor of the observatory, 4.75 metres above MSL.

A few of us took a rather long walk on the pontoons, up the ramp and along the shore to the marina facilities. We were aware that Newlyn majors in catering to the needs of fishing trawlers and their crew, although more recently it has tried to appeal to yachtsmen too. We found the facilities to be extremely basic. A visit to the 'gents' involved dodging around several buildings and passage through into a large area with urinals, a hosepipe lying on the bare concrete floor. We weren't quite sure what we were supposed to do with the hosepipe and we left it alone. We definitely preferred what was, in comparison, five-star luxury on board *Blue Star*.

Over a hot meal on the boat we chatted about our experiences that day and then retired early to bed.

At 0500 hours the next day we were all on deck, engine running and ready to slip our lines. Strangely, there was not a sound from our neighbours and we wondered whether we should tap on their coach roof with a winch handle and remind them of the time. As very polite sailors, we decided to let them sleep – who knows, perhaps they had no intention of leaving.

We were ready and so we left, bound for Falmouth about 35 miles away. The fog of the previous day was still present as we motored out across Mount's Bay towards Lizard Point, the most southerly headland in Britain. There was the occasional lit navigation buoy to guide us, flashing its colour and light sequence; the visibility was slightly better, but we were principally using our electronic systems once more. Fortunately, like yesterday, the sea state was smooth.

We stood two miles off the land as we rounded 'The Lizard'. We wanted to avoid the worst of the waves, generated as the tidal stream rushes round the peninsula. Even two miles off, there were large rollers that caused *Blue Star* to roll repeatedly from port to starboard and back again.

Once past, we altered course to the northeast. The boat's motion steadied and we were able to surf down some of the rollers. To improve matters further the fog lifted so that we could finally make out the finger of land that we had just rounded. And then the sun came out to cheer us on our way. A cup of tea and a piece of cake made life even better!

We noted that on our left were the hills of Goonhilly Downs which host a famous satellite tracking station. It was one of only three earth stations involved in the first transatlantic TV transmission, via the satellite Telstar, in 1962. In 1969, it beamed the first moon landing to viewers in the UK. As well as these astonishing technical firsts,

Goonhilly was significant in the development of international telephone, TV and data network services.

The remainder of the journey to Falmouth was uneventful. Compared to previous legs, this was a short hop and in no time we found ourselves setting up to enter the River Fal.

The entrance was straightforward – with due recognition to the single hazard, Black Rock, with its isolated danger mark, between Pendennis Point and Shag Rock. In the lower part of the river, Carrick Roads, we were careful to watch out for pleasure boats and small ferries running between Falmouth on the west bank and the picturesque village of St Mawes on the eastern side.

Once in the river we radioed ahead to the marina to book a berth. Every other yacht in the area must have been planning to stay there too because it was crammed full so we had to raft up. We concluded that the governing factor was probably the gales forecast for the next day!

After spending the afternoon cleaning up the boat we headed into town. Although it was busy with holidaymakers we found a convenient place to eat, overlooking the harbour.

With poor weather forecast for the next few days we decided to call a temporary halt to our voyage and return home for a short while. The following day we towed our bags to Falmouth railway station and made the journey home.

It had been a tough and testing week of sailing, but immensely satisfying.

Rob:

This was my first experience of being in Milford Haven and crewing on a night sail. I watched the sun set with a mixture of excitement and trepidation about the planned midnight departure – next time the sun appeared we would be in the middle of the Bristol Channel. Its appearance at dawn was spectacular; the burnished copper tone of the sky brightening until the sun slowly emerged above the horizon. It turned out to be a sparkling day and in the early afternoon, with the coastline of North Devon coming into view, we were escorted by a pod of dolphins. After a short time they disappeared as suddenly and silently as they had appeared. Magical!

Above: *Blue Star* **in the harbour at Padstow**
Below: Our view of Land's End

19. Falmouth to Brixham

To reach a port we must set sail –
Sail, not tie at anchor,
Sail, not drift.

Franklin D. Roosevelt

Mike:
Blue Star had a two-week stopover in Falmouth prior to continuing her voyage and in that time I visited the boat with Diane. It was rainy when we arrived but a lovely rainbow soon gave way to lots of sunny weather. Angela and Keith joined us for the day and we explored the River Fal, tacking under sail, in sun and light winds, as far upriver as the depth of water would allow. Later, Cliff and his partner, Ash, came to stay with us and we sailed across the Fal Estuary to St Mawes and to the Helford River, a short distance further west. The delightful scenery bordering both the Fal and the Helford makes you want to return. In all too short a time the others had to leave, and I awaited Roger's return with new crew to continue our circumnavigation. The finish line was now getting close!

Roger arrived back on 3 September together with Chris and Jean-Francois. Both had crewed in *Blue Star* earlier in the voyage; it was good to have them on board once more. As they all lived in the Dorset area they had hired a car to drive together to Falmouth – more convenient than the train. Keith, who had last joined us on the Caledonian Canal, also rejoined the crew, bringing with him some excellent weather!

During the stopover in Falmouth, Mike had noticed a small amount of water in the bilges again. After some detective work the leak was tracked down to the water heater. We thought it was the original unit, and so it had perhaps done well for ten years. As the leak was minor, we decided to press on and postpone a repair until the voyage was completed, Roger volunteering to change the whole unit once we were back in the Solent. Jean-Francois helped identify a small leak at the foot of the mast where a cable passed through. A swift exercise with some self-amalgamating tape and the leak was fixed.

We were now back in familiar waters on the South Coast of England.

Our next few weeks of sailing would need to work the tides and weather to ensure that we arrived back in Hythe in good time for the already-scheduled celebration party.

From Falmouth it was a short sail of 23 miles to Fowey, our next stop. Leaving the harbour and the River Fal we headed approximately northeast towards Dodman Point. After rounding it we passed the quaint port of Mevagissey. A ten-knot wind had helped in the beginning but it didn't last long and we were soon back to motoring. With each hour of motoring we needed to sponge out the bilge because of the leaking heat exchanger, but we handled the problem well enough.

It was cloudy, but the rain held off and, as expected, the scenery, hills and rocky cliffs once more reminded us why we enjoyed coastal sailing. There were a few other yachts on passage, some headed east with us and others going west.

Off to port, tucked into the coastline just south of St Austell, is Charlestown. Originally a port from which Cornish clay was exported, it is now a private harbour. Here, training is offered on square-rigged vessels, some having appeared on TV programmes such as *Poldark* and *The Onedin Line*. It has to be one of the most charming harbours along this stretch of coast. Visits by sea can be declined, but it is certainly a tourist attraction and worth a visit by land.

The estuary of the River Fowey was then almost upon us. Entry to the river is between St Catherine's Point to the west and Punch Cross Rocks to the east. Together with a sectored light at Whitehouse Point, they guide sailors safely in.

We intended stopping in the small marina at Penmarlam in Mixtow Pill, a short distance up the river from the town and directly opposite Fowey docks. The docks are primarily for the export of clay from the region and if you are unlucky it can be quite noisy when they are loading. About 450,000 tons of clay are exported each year. In more recent times small cruise liners have used the harbour too. Irrespective of these commercial activities, for the majority of the time the harbour is a beautiful and serene setting. We motored slowly into Penmarlam Marina and were fortunate enough to find a vacant section of the pontoon where we tied up.

The town of Fowey has been in existence since well before the Norman invasion, with the local church first established around the 7th century. The estuary of the river forms a natural harbour which enabled an important trading centre to develop. The *Domesday Book* records two manors and a priory in the area. Piracy was also prevalent. One group of privateers, the Fowey Gallants, were given licence to seize French ships during the Hundred Years' War. The town was attacked by the French in 1457 and by the Dutch in 1667, both attacks being repulsed. Nowadays tourism is the main activity and is said to account for half of the jobs in the town.

Mike and Jean-Francois walked to the local pub at the upper Dart ferry crossing and watched England's Euro 2016 football game against Slovakia, England winning 1-0. Roger, who was both first mate and chef of the day, prepared his delicious chicken and apricot dinner. Throughout the whole adventure we encouraged all crew to cook a meal on board. Whilst not being too pedantic, putting the porridge in the microwave at breakfast time did not count! We were, of course, fortunate to have regular crew members such as Rob and Shep whose culinary skills were legendary. We were also indebted to Woolcool for their delivery of prepared meals and to Kim and Margaret for their homemade cooking. There were a couple of crew for whom the galley was a complete mystery and who needed coaching to prepare even simple offerings.

One special seating place in the saloon of *Blue Star* is perhaps worthy of mention. It was light-heartedly referred to as 'Skipper's Corner', although it was not occupied solely by the skipper. If seated in this corner it was invariably 'difficult' to get out to help with on-board jobs without disturbing everyone else. The rest of the crew would then feel obliged to volunteer for the washing, drying, coffee making and so on. Result, for whoever was sitting in Skipper's Corner and ended up being waited on!

Whilst we could have spent several days in the idyllic harbour and surrounds of Fowey, the schedule demanded that we headed out to sea the following day, Monday, for another short hop eastwards towards Plymouth. There was a damp, heavy mist in the air and we decided that first we would visit Fowey town, hoping the visibility would improve. We left Penmarlam at 0900 hours and motored downriver a short distance to the lifeboat pontoon. The harbourmaster gave us permission to stay for a short while.

We found a café that looked out over the river where we monitored the visibility. Sailing out to the Eddystone Lighthouse on our way to

Plymouth had been a consideration, but because of the mist we chose to linger with warm drinks and pastries. The trip to Eddystone would have to wait until another time.

A local shop selling Cornish pasties beckoned and we felt we should support local industry prior to leaving Cornwall. We wondered whether we would come across border guards off the Cornwall-Devon coast, checking for illegal exports of pasties! More depression descended after a phone call from the Bavaria agent about the cost of a new hot-water tank. A reminder of the expression 'BOAT', meaning 'Break Out Another Thousand'.

Despite the gloomy atmosphere we got under way, convincing ourselves that the mist was lifting and would soon be burnt off by the sun. After an enthusiastic start, with both sails hoisted, the wind let us down and we motored the majority of the 23 miles to Plymouth. Heading almost due east we passed the holiday town of Looe on our port side, keeping well away from the off-lying Looe Island. Scanning the horizon, we spotted warships. Silhouetted far in the distance we glimpsed the Eddystone Lighthouse. Soon we were lining up for Penlee Point on the western side of Plymouth Sound.

Motoring past the large breakwater, 1,600 metres long and built in 1812, the full vista of Plymouth Sound opened up, several islets, Plymouth Hoe and the city beyond. There are a number of secure harbours and marinas there; we chose Sutton Harbour which lies immediately north of Queen Anne's Battery. Although it has to be accessed via a lock, it is convenient for walking into town and is protected from any sea swell. It also has excellent facilities!

Plymouth has always been associated with the naval exploits of Sir Francis Drake. Legend has it he casually played bowls on the Hoe before going out to give the Spanish a good run for their money! He had what today we might call a 'colourful lifestyle', having been a sea captain, a privateer, slave trader and naval officer. Knighted by Queen Elizabeth I in 1581, it was some seven years later that he commanded the English fleet that saw off the Spanish Armada. His deeds are celebrated in the name of the island which guards the western side of the sound, leading to the Royal Navy Devonport base. Drake's Island is separated from the mainland by a shallow channel that can be navigated by most yachts towards high water. Protection of the harbour is provided by a wide variety of fortifications, namely Picklecombe Fort, Cawsand Fort, the Breakwater Fort, Fort Bovisand, Staddon and Stamford Forts. Many were built to protect the Devonport base, which has been operational since 1691. It is a vast military site.

The following morning, Tuesday, we had to wait until lunchtime for a favourable tide heading east. It gave us ample time to explore the surroundings, including a stroll on the Hoe. Of course, we just had to sample more scones and coffee in a café overlooking the panorama of the sound – the verdict: very good.

Back on the boat we slipped lines around 1300 hours and set sail for Salcombe. We left Plymouth Sound via the eastern side then headed out for the Great Mew Stone which we left to port, before crossing Bigbury Bay. Once again fair winds had deserted us and we had to motor. By late afternoon we had identified Bolt Head on our port side and were ready to go into Salcombe. There is a sand bar across the entrance but with sufficient height of tide this is not a problem. Although on the chart the coast and geography look like an estuary it is in fact more of a drowned valley; there is no river. As we entered the harbour we lined up the leading marks – red and white beacons on the shore – that keep inbound vessels away from the shallower part of the bar. They also kept us off Bass Rock, a threat towards the left of the entrance.

In front of us were high cliffs on which part of the town is built. It is a rocky shoreline. Once past Bass Rock the route takes a turn to starboard and the town quay pontoon is then on port after a further half mile or so. Opposite the town quay, across the harbour and over to our right, was a small, sandy beach served by a passenger ferry linking it to the town.

There isn't a great deal of room on the town quay. Vessels must expect either to raft up against another boat, pick up a mooring buoy or anchor off. We were fortunate to be able to tie up on the pontoon near the harbourmaster's office which meant that we could walk ashore. At the end of the gangway a car park had a well-used public toilet and shower next to it. Beyond that stood a beckoning restaurant. Woolcool, represented by Keith, bought dinner out in the restaurant for everyone, which was incredibly kind.

Although there were facilities on the quayside, they were cramped and rather grubby. With this in mind we walked up the hill and found Salcombe Yacht Club, with its commanding position overlooking the entrance to the harbour from high up on the cliff. We bought drinks and enquired about using the club's facilities. Permission granted, we had a quick look around and found them to be much more salubrious than those in the public car park. It was explained to us that for 'out-of-hours' use we would need to walk up the path at the side of the building to find the one door at the back that could be opened by way of a security code. Having made a note of the code, we strolled back to the boat and bedded down.

Mike:

Early the following morning I was completing a few tasks when the rest of the crew said they were off to the yacht club to use the shower. I said to go without me and I would catch them up shortly. Ten minutes later I found the secret door, past the bins at the side and towards the back of the yacht club, as instructed. I fully expected to see the rest of the *Blue Star* crew enjoying the showers and warming one up for me, but no – they were nowhere to be seen! Perhaps I had passed them whilst I was making my way to the club? No matter, I had a shower, shave, etc. and returned to the boat, but the crew were not there either! Where could they be? I put the kettle on and awaited their return, hoping that all would become clear.

Roger:

The following morning early, most of the crew elected to walk up the hill and have a pleasant shower at the yacht club. The night before we had been given instructions on entering 'out-of-hours', which all seemed straightforward. However, we found it difficult to locate the one open door to the clubhouse. After some searching we gained entrance and discovered that everywhere was in darkness. How difficult could it be to find a light switch? We spent about ten minutes looking everywhere but to no avail. Eventually, by the light of our mobile phones, we discovered that the ladies' changing rooms were open and, although meant for 'Ladies who Launch', we felt the risk was worth it. The light from our mobile phones provided sufficient visibility to have a quick shower and shave. Ablutions complete, we left the yacht club and headed back to the boat. Having entered and used the club under somewhat clandestine conditions we became convinced that somewhere in the gloom there was a low-light intensity surveillance camera which would have recorded our every move. We fully expected to be the subject of a local news item but fortunately our presence must have passed unnoticed.

When, finally, we all reconvened on board *Blue Star* it became clear that the two sorties ashore had each scored a hit on finding a door, Mike being the only one to find the 'Gents'. It was not official *Blue Star* policy to misuse facilities in the way exercised by one of the shore parties, but sometimes you just can't get the crew!

The sky had brightened in Salcombe so we resolved to leave. A good job too, bearing in mind the shower debacle! As we motored clear of the estuary we set a course towards Start Point, en route for Dartmouth. We passed the National Coastwatch Institution lookout point high up on the cliffside at Gammon Head. It seemed it would be a lovely sunny day but once out at sea another heavy mist descended.

Visibility was reduced to about 300 yards so electronic navigation became the order of the day, including lights and radar. We had to stand several miles out from Start Point as there were strong overfalls, causing large waves closer in. Even at our distance the boat's motion was very erratic. Slowly, we inched our way past Start Point, although we couldn't see it. We had several 'engagements' with other vessels, fishing boats, yachts and motorboats that we 'saw' on AIS and radar. We manoeuvred to avoid them, catching the odd real glimpse of them in the mist as they passed by. Half a mile out of Dartmouth the fog lifted and suddenly we were experiencing a hot sunny day again! This may have only been a passage of 17 miles but it had plenty to keep us on our toes.

The entrance to Dartmouth is not very obvious from seaward, but once identified it is well buoyed and has deep water. At night there is a very helpful sectored light to guide craft safely into the river. We aimed for the Castle Ledge starboard-hand channel marker and then gradually, with a little turn to port, we were in the River Dart. Dartmouth was on the left-hand riverbank. We put in to Darthaven Marina, on the opposite side of the river, close to Kingswear.

The following day the forecast was for the wind to strengthen so we decided to leave as soon as was convenient in order to make our passage before the worst of the weather. Fortunately, this was only a short trip of about 12 miles. Before leaving, we motored up the river towards Dittisham, proudly showing our huge 'Woolcool' proclamation on our hoisted mainsail.

Later, motoring out of the river, the wind died to almost nothing, then out in the bay it suddenly rose to force 6! We immediately put two reefs in the mainsail and rolled away some of the headsail to wrest back control of the boat, which was rolling and yawing wildly. That task completed, things were under control, but we still romped away out to sea on a broad reach.

Keith:

I will always remember leaving Dartmouth. Lulled into a state of over-confidence by the calm conditions in the river, what a shock was in store for this poor unsuspecting novice. Emerging into the bay, *Blue Star* was suddenly struck without warning by gale-force winds. (Actually force 6.) Pandemonium! Crew in all directions. Ropes flying. Winches spinning. Images of shipwreck and disaster flashed before my eyes as cries of 'Two reefs' were heard. I need not have worried; Roger and Mike soon had the situation in hand and *Blue Star* was positively zooming out to sea. Sheer exhilaration! This was my Damascene moment, a precious insight revealed, and I was completely converted to the joys of sailing.

The waves were two to three metres high, and we had to concentrate hard to ensure no mishaps occurred. After a while we gybed the sails and headed for Berry Head, just off Brixham. The sun shone, and it was exhilarating sailing. After rounding the Head we hardened up to a close reach, taking us towards Brixham. Tacking brought us a little nearer, before we dropped the sails and motored in.

Protected by the Victoria Breakwater, Brixham Marina was to our left as we entered the port. It is a very sheltered stopping point. To starboard was the commercial fishing quay and behind that the old inner harbour, which dries at low water.

Once in the marina we were visited by a film crew who were making publicity material to appear on the marina website. They filmed *Blue Star* on a 360-degree-view film which would be accessible online, where we were told they would put a link to *Blue Star*'s website. They were very impressed by all our sponsors' stickers.

We needed reasonable weather for our next leg, some 50 miles from Brixham to Weymouth, and the forecast wasn't too bright. Knowing that we had a few days in hand we decided to delay our departure. Chris and Keith had to leave us, as they had other commitments.

We explored the town the following day. There was a food and music 'Festival of the Sea' next to the harbour. We took a quick look but then opted to make the bus and ferry journey to Dittisham, beside the River Dart. It is one of the most picturesque riverside villages, and we had some knowledge of it from a previous visit. Once off the bus we boarded the ferry and on the other side of the river we found ourselves being drawn to the Ferry Boat Inn. There we got chatting with a group of sailors on the table next to us. They were very impressed to hear of our, shortly to be completed, circumnavigation of GB and asked how they could make a donation to our cause, which was very kind.

Later back at Brixham we walked into the town and, whilst admiring the boats in the inner harbour, fell into a conversation with Charlie who was refitting his large, old, engineless, wooden sailing boat, *Iris*.

'How do you get her out of the harbour?' we asked.

'I drop an anchor over there,' Charlie said, pointing to a position just out from the harbour wall, 'and haul her off the quay, then just raise the sails.'

Hmm. Easy then. 'What about bringing her back in to the harbour, you must need some help for that?' we enquired.

'Well I just sail in and run her onto the mud, then let the sea do the rest as the tide comes in,' he answered!

We discovered that *Iris* was a Looe Lugger built in 1921. She was 44 foot on deck and stretched to an impressive 95 foot overall with her spars out; the objective was to make her suitable for carrying cargo under sail and preserving the old seafaring traditions. We got ourselves invited aboard to view things from deck level. She looked very smart indeed, with an attractive sky-blue paint job on the hull but we saw that there was still much work to do down below.

We retired for coffee and scones at the shop just across from this classic lugger and debated the relaxed simplicity of the 'old days' – no fin keels to worry about, no bow thrusters, no engine!

After, we walked to Berry Head and looked out from the clifftops, over the sea where we'd sailed from Dartmouth. Berry Head had been fortified since Iron Age times. In the late 1700s defences were updated to protect against a possible invasion attempt by Napoleon. It was also a defence post in both World War One and World War Two and hosts a lighthouse and radio beacon to assist modern-day sailors.

The forecast for the next day, Sunday, looked promising, and we started to plan our departure. We had enjoyed the company of Keith and Chris, but it would be just the three of us remaining who would make the long trip, out of sight of land, across Lyme Bay to Weymouth.

***

Joke
Never leave broken pencils at the chart table. They're pointless.

***

Above: Sunrise at Salcombe, *Blue Star* is tied up at the pontoon

Above: The harbour at Brixham

Above: Charlie's lugger, *Iris*

20. Brixham to Hythe

O Captain! My Captain! Our fearful trip is done;
The ship has weathered every rack, the prize we sought is won;
The port is near, the bells I hear, the people all exulting ...

Walt Whitman, 'Captain! My Captain!'

As the sun was rising in the east we slipped lines at Brixham around 0600 hours and motored out past the breakwater to a glorious morning. With dawn breaking, there were other vessels, identifiable by their navigation lights, also starting out on passage. With this being a longish leg, some 50 miles, we needed reasonable weather and the correct timing to reach the potentially treacherous waters off Portland Bill. The bright sun and calm sea were very welcome, but we would have appreciated a little breeze to allow us to sail. It was four hours later that a few breaths of wind came and we were able to raise the sails, shut down the engine and enjoy the peace. The real bonus that morning was, once more, having dolphins around the boat, a magical sight! Perhaps they were leading us home? Soon the wind filled the sails and we simply powered along, at six knots plus, on a flattish sea. It was just a wonderful sail! Such an exhilarating feeling, the sea state and wind combining to generate the perfect conditions. It was good to be alive!

About 16 miles away on our port side the holiday towns of Sidmouth, Lyme Regis and Bridport occupied the shoreline, not visible to us – in fact, this leg took us out of sight of land completely, such is the expanse of Lyme Bay. The Jurassic Coast, England's only natural World Heritage Site, was designated thus by UNESCO in 2001 for its outstanding fossils, rocks and landforms. In total it is 95 miles long, from Exmouth to Old Harry Rocks near Swanage. This unique piece of coastline represents 185 million years of geological history with Triassic, Jurassic and Cretaceous periods clearly visible. At various times, the area has been desert, shallow tropical sea and marsh. The fossilised remains of the various creatures that lived there have been preserved in the rocks and attract both amateur and professional palaeontologists. Whilst we could see very little of the coast on this leg, the next leg from Weymouth to Poole would give us a much better view.

Eventually we could see the Portland headland, albeit some miles away. From a distance it looks like an island but it is, in fact, connected to the mainland by an isthmus. The southern tip, Portland Bill, juts out into the English Channel, giving rise to very strong tides and turbulence as the tides fight their way around it.

Tom Cunliffe, in his book, *The Shell Channel Pilot*, describes the Portland Race as 'the most dangerous extended area of broken water in the English Channel'. Having already successfully negotiated the Pentland Firth in Scotland, Rathlin Island in Northern Ireland and the Swellies in Wales we now had the chance to complete a clean sweep of challenging stretches of water around the UK!

The topography of the area causes massive overfalls at both the flood and the ebb, with south-going tides roaring down either side of the headland meeting east/west tides off the point. It was essential to get the timing right, passing close to slack water before turning to port and heading for Weymouth. There is an option of taking the inside channel close under the cliffs. Mike was once advised that if you take the inside route you need to sail close enough to toss over a sandwich to someone on the shore! That does seem mighty close! Perhaps exaggeration?

On this occasion we elected to stand off and pass about two miles south of the headland. Just after lunch we were through the race, which was surprisingly calm, and soon thereafter took the sails down for our approach to Weymouth, passing the historic naval station of Portland. We'd had a fantastic sail, for almost six hours in glorious weather. This was why we love sailing!

As we approached, we had to wait outside the harbour whilst the historic paddle steamer, *Waverley*, prepared to leave. Built in 1946, she is the last sea-going paddle steamer in the world. She is beautifully restored, with distinctive twin funnels and a colourful profile in black, white and red. Roger immediately recognised her, having once taken a daytrip on her himself. Her departure is controlled by port signals recognised internationally (International Port Traffic Signals or IPTS). A few other boats didn't bother to follow the signals and wait – they were promptly radioed by the authorities.

Weymouth is one of few British ports with a deep-water harbour in the centre of the town. Yachts tie up in the old port or pass through a lifting bridge into the marina. We opted for the old town quay which has a charming character, with brightly coloured Georgian houses and shops bordering the river and old railway lines on the quay. Once tied up we needed to register at the Harbour Office. Mike volunteered to do this.

Mike:

There was obviously some kind of event taking place in the town with crowds of people, blaring public address systems and a general air of fun. What was it? I strode up the ramp from the pontoon to make my way to the office. Suddenly people were yelling at me to run. I looked around and found myself in the midst of the running stage of a triathlon. Why on earth was the track across the top of the gangway? Several runners, with numbers pinned to their vests, were about to collide with me. Luckily, I put on a sprint of my own, and quickly got to the other side of the road, out of the way.

Mike returned to the boat somewhat perplexed, disappointed that he had not been given a medal for his part in the triathlon. Roger made a mental note and decided he would ensure there would be a medal at a later date. To ease the shock of the trip to the office, and being so central in the town, we decided to find a restaurant for dinner and to enjoy the holiday atmosphere.

In the morning, Jean-Francois's wife, Joan, joined the crew again. We had a relaxed breakfast then dropped our lines, bound for Poole, our final port of call on the Dorset coast. Outside the protection of the harbour it was rather choppy. The wind was on the nose and so we motored. We had to avoid the army firing range, where we might otherwise have a shell put through our hull or rigging. Hazardous preoccupation this sailing business! The yacht's motion was most unpleasant, but once past the southern limits of the firing range we were able to turn east. We could then set some sail and the motion improved slightly.

During this passage we had a worrying encounter with a motor vessel which led us a merry dance. We were on a collision course with the other craft, but we were under sail – a reefed main and genoa. This made us the 'stand on' vessel, and the other boat the 'give way' vessel. As they continued to get closer it was starting to look like a collision was a distinct possibility, and we were starting to sweat. What should we do? Stand on or give way anyway? We bore away to port. The International Regulations for Preventing Collisions at Sea (IRPCS) require of us to take action if it seems an accident is otherwise unavoidable. Blow me! The motorboat changed course to put us back on a collision path. We hardened up and headed more to starboard again, on our original course. The motorboat changed course again. There was really nothing more we could do. As it neared us it finally slowed right down to have a good look at us. A large sign on its side read 'Sea Cadets'. They really should have known better. Then away it zoomed. We gave them an icy stare as they sped off. This had happened before. We think, again, they just wanted to have a closer look at the yacht with all our sponsors' names, but even so, it was extremely annoying.

Before we reached St Albans Head we saw in the distance the geological features of Durdle Door and Lulworth Cove, wonders of the Jurassic Coast. Once around St Alban's Head and then Anvil Point the sea settled and we were able to eat lunch in comfort. Tea, sandwiches and Joan's favourite – Cherry Bakewells! 'Exceedingly good cakes!'

The shallow ledges around these and other headlands make it ideal for local fishermen to put out their lobster pots, each tied to a 'marker' on the surface. The pots can potentially be very hazardous should their line become entwined around a boat's propeller. A debate about how such pots ought to be marked has raged for several years. Some fishermen use brightly coloured floats, often with a flag attached. These can generally be easily seen in daylight. Others, not so obliging, might use a black 'float' and a length of rope from the pot that does not quite allow it to properly break the surface. A strong tide will tend to drag it just below the water. A boat becoming caught by its propeller in a lobster-pot rope is effectively anchored. Waves might swamp or even sink the vessel. A boat can be freed by a crew member diving overboard with a sharp knife, but this action can be very risky. Once the boat is free, the propeller may still be fouled, and the vessel then drift, out of control.

We kept a keen lookout for lobster-pot markers, then passed Swanage and Old Harry and his wife, chalk stacks, just off the coast. The nudist beach at Studland Bay was next on our port side. No, we didn't look! Ok, we did, but we couldn't see any. Adjacent to Studland Bay, red and green lateral marks that guide boats into Poole were visible and they kept us in the deep water. Poole has a large natural harbour protected by a narrow entrance; once inside, it is a tranquil area with many islands and wildlife habitats. There are no harbour walls, just a spit of land on either side protecting the massive inner waterway.

The spit to starboard is known as Sandbanks, where some of the most expensive houses on the planet can be found! We cast them a swift glance but then looked quickly back at the activity in the harbour entrance. To port was Studland, from where a chain ferry was about to depart, its yellow flashing light indicating that it was getting under way. It was important to keep clear of the ferry and of the massive chains coming up from the sea bed, allowing it to haul itself along. Close to the ferry, the chains may not be far below the water surface.

Many other yachts and powerboats were entering and leaving the harbour. We concentrated on navigating in the correct part of the channel whilst avoiding other craft. Inside the harbour the deep-water channel turns first to starboard before arcing slowly to port. We followed the channel for over two miles before arriving at the Town Quay Marina, completing the 29-mile passage in about six hours.

Whilst moored in Poole we spoke with a young couple, Lucie and Jake, who had arrived from Alderney in their small open-decked Tiki 28 sailing catamaran, *A Roamer of Alderney*. They helped run 'barefootboatbums' which markets sailing merchandise. Jake had attended a meeting in London and now they were going to set out for the return trip to Alderney. *Roamer* had reached speeds of 15 knots and they had dealt with some difficult seas whilst on their way to Poole. They hoped to fly their repaired spinnaker to get even faster speeds on the return leg. In comparison, *Blue Star* cruised at five knots. But then our boat weighed nine tons. Too many scones, biscuits and Cherry Bakewells perhaps.

The following day, Tuesday, 13 September, we had visitors. Diane's friend Hilary, her husband Duncan, and Archie the dog came aboard in glorious sunshine. They had made a generous donation to the charity. It seemed like the ideal opportunity to give them a short sailing experience. We sailed past Sandbanks and out to sea, noting some dark clouds on the horizon. We turned around rapidly when lightning flashed and the heavens opened! With our guests safely down below in the dry we got absolutely drenched bringing the boat back.

After lunch we sailed towards Lymington, catching more rain on the way. Crossing Bournemouth Bay and rounding the headland at Christchurch we were pleased that we had accurately calculated the tides through the run at Hurst. Roger gave a cheery wave towards his home in Barton-on-Sea which we passed just before the Hurst narrows.

Tied up in Lymington, Judith and her friend Jayne came aboard for dinner and an evening of entertaining anecdotes. By this time, we had quite a few! We were now back in the Solent and only about 20 miles from Hythe, where we had started out the previous year. There were four days to go until Saturday when we were expected to arrive in Hythe, and where a large welcome party was planned. We reckoned that we would easily be on time!

The following morning Peter, Roger's neighbour, came to visit us at the town quay where we were berthed. A former Merchant Navy officer and employee of HM Coastguard, he had been a keen follower of the blog and had posted several comments on *Blue Star*'s Facebook page. It was good for Mike to meet him in person.

Whilst wanting to arrive back at Hythe on time, we did not want to arrive too early either, as that would spoil the welcome party somewhat. Therefore, we had time to kill and planned to use it by visiting a few high spots in the Solent area.

Leaving Lymington, we sailed for Newtown Creek on the Isle of Wight, where we anchored for lunch amongst many other boats. Newtown has an interesting history. There is some evidence that it had been attacked by the Danes, but by the mid-14th century it was a thriving commercial centre, perhaps the de facto 'capital' of the island. Then the plague struck, after which the French ransacked the town; it never recovered. Today it is owned by the National Trust and is a sanctuary for wildlife. Evidence of the old quay can still be seen, but there are no buildings left. The creek is rather narrow, and the entrance extremely tight. What appeared to be sandbanks were in very close proximity on both sides as we motored in. It looked as though we might run aground, but with a charted depth of around two and a half metres there was ample clearance.

Inside, the surrounding land is very flat and marshy. There, silence reigns. Indeed, it is the very tranquillity of the place that attracts so many visitors. It is a favourite of ours. Yacht crews pick up one of the mooring buoys then take their dinghy upstream. Disembarking at a small wooden jetty, they can then walk to the nearby pub.

After lunch we proceeded to East Cowes Marina for the night. Here we met up with Mike's sister, Pat, who lives on the Isle of Wight.

On Thursday we witnessed Ben Ainslie's America's Cup team practising in the Solent. They sailed within a few metres of *Blue Star*. We had a great view of the catamaran as it lifted its hulls above the sea to sail at incredible speed with just the dagger board foils and rudders in the water! In the afternoon we returned to Lymington to collect Judith. She was to join us for the final few days. Jean-Francois and Joan returned home; we would see them again at the party.

The night before our long-anticipated arrival in Hythe we were tucked into the pleasant marina at Buckler's Hard. This allowed us to time our departure the following morning to make the short hop to Hythe. Buckler's Hard is set in the most attractive landscape, on the Beaulieu River in the New Forest. Ships that fought at the battle of Trafalgar were built there, as well as torpedo boats used in World War Two. Nowadays, it is partly a museum with cottages of former boatbuilders, all well restored, lining the 'high street', actually a grassy bank! There is a visitor centre towards the top of the hill and the Master Builder's Hotel, close to the river, at the bottom. It is a favourite stopping place for yachts. There we met Diane's sister, Susan, and her husband, John, who were staying at the hotel in readiness to attend *Blue Star*'s formal return 'home' at Hythe the next day.

We left Buckler's Hard at 0900 hours on Saturday, 17 September and motored gently down the Beaulieu River. It is an incredibly scenic and peaceful stretch of water. We passed woods and marshy ground before crossing over the bar and out into the Solent. There was a fair wind so we hoisted the mainsail and showed off our 'Woolcool' logo once more! Off Calshot, the northwest wind and waves came at us from all the way down Southampton Water and it became difficult to make progress against them. Slowly, under engine and mainsail, we inched our way forward. Finally reaching Hythe, we saw the crowd of supporters and well-wishers standing on the quayside to welcome us in. Yellow Cystic Fibrosis Trust banners were streaming in the wind. The weather had one last laugh as we got roughly tossed around in the lock before passing through into the marina.

Everyone migrated to the pontoon where we had tied up. Mike, standing on the foredeck, leaned over *Blue Star*'s bow to kiss Diane and then danced a short 'victory jig' to Elvis singing 'Return to Sender' on the iPod. Meanwhile, Roger broke open the champagne! The party sprang into life. Many photographs were taken and everyone joined us on board for a celebratory drink.

In the evening we held a 'Sail Home' dinner, at the Boathouse Hotel beside the marina. We thanked everyone for coming to greet us and spoke about our amazing adventure. Cliff made a speech, congratulating us on our achievement and said how well the fundraising had gone. Keith presented us both with a splendid 'Woolcool GB Challenge Trophy' and Bob Hillyer gave us 'Shipping Forecast' mugs! True to his word, Roger had ordered *Blue Star* medals for the skippers, Mike's also in recognition of his encounter with the Weymouth triathlon; these were presented by Jamie. Three trophies in one day – not a bad haul!

It had been an incredible voyage, and one we will remember for the rest of our lives! We had enjoyed some exhilarating sailing, seen amazing sites of historic interest, superb scenery and wonderful wildlife. Of course, we had also experienced and overcome many obstacles – rough seas, cold weather and fog, to name but a few. We had also spoken to countless interesting and supportive people and made many new friends. Best of all was the money we had raised for the Cystic Fibrosis Trust!

***

Joke
'I went on a sailing trip to Poole'
'In Dorset?'
'Yes, I highly recommend it.'

***

Above: The Old Harry rock stacks (and black fishing-pot marker!)

Below: Jake prepares *Roamer* for the return trip to Alderney

Above: Arriving back at Hythe.   **Right: Mike's victory jig**

Left and below: Celebrations on board

Below: Receiving the Woolcool GB Challenge Trophy from Keith and Angela

Above: Roger with his Shipping Forecast mug

Epilogue

From Barton and Stone we came together,
To sail the seas whatever the weather,
We cruised canals and rounded capes,
With fun and adventure for charity's sake.

Roger Colmer, 'The Challenge'

As we said farewell to friends and well-wishers and commenced taking all our personal kit off the boat, it really felt like the end of a great adventure. For the last time under the *Blue Star* banner we wheeled our boat bags away. She had been a good boat and, for us, 'home' for most of the two preceding summers.

Some days later, with Jean-Francois and his friend John, Roger sailed the boat the short distance from Hythe to Swanwick Marina, where it had all begun in early 2015. The boat had been purchased especially for this venture with an understanding that either of us could buy out the other at the end of the trip. For various reasons we both decided to dispose of *Blue Star* and therefore she was put on the market through the good services of Clipper Marine, Swanwick.

On 28 September the boat was hoisted out of the water and placed on the hard; there was minimal fouling on the hull. During our adventures there had been the odd minor bump and scrape and these needed addressing. The hull was vinyl wrapped and therefore we felt the most expedient way to bring it back to good condition was to re-wrap. None of the surface marks, which in places had torn the vinyl, had penetrated the gel coat. Eventually the wrapping contractor carried out his responsibility but not without a lot of chasing!

Next task was to address the repairs and maintenance needed. The first job, replacing the leaking hot-water heater, was reasonably straightforward. Access was simple and the job was completed in a day. It is a credit to the build quality of the boat that during our two years of ownership and all the miles sailed, the only unplanned maintenance issues were the replacement of the leaking domestic fresh-water pump, the water heater and the starter battery – probably all the original units. Other than that we just had a little stitching done to the mainsail, had a repair made to the cooling water pump and replaced a few light bulbs. Routine servicing of the engine and saildrive were also on the final jobs list.

Over the autumn weeks and into the winter of 2016/17 regular trips to Swanwick were made to check that *Blue Star* looked marketable. By early 2017, after three months on the market, we had received two enquiries but these did not translate into a sale. A few months later we had a serious enquiry. With the brokering skills of Clipper Marine we settled on a price – slightly lower than we wanted but still acceptable. The buyer could see that she was in excellent condition and did not even request a test sail! We'd loved owning *Blue Star* and were sure that her new owner would be pleased with her too.

Sadly, within four years of finishing the project, several of the crew who sailed with us died. Margaret, Chris and Graham all passed away. We salute their contribution to the *Blue Star* project and take solace in the enjoyable time we all shared together on board.

Roger:

Whilst in Peterhead, Scotland, I had spied a lovely looking sailing boat with a deck saloon, a Sirius 35 DS. During 2016, with the prospect of our circumnavigation coming to an end, Judith and I decided we would like to continue sailing and the Sirius seemed to fit the bill. They are built in Germany, just north of Hamburg. We had set our hearts on their smallest yacht, the 310 DS, but whilst on our first visit to the yard the company owner suggested we should look at a 35 DS which they had prepared for the Dusseldorf Boat Show. Within a few hours the decision was made – we would order the larger yacht. The company builds around 15 yachts annually and all are custom-built to order, so we had a 15-month wait for her to be constructed and launched in the Baltic. The experience with the Bavaria was invaluable and helped inform a number of decisions. Mike kindly agreed to me taking some of the specialty items off *Blue Star* for our new boat in exchange for a donation to the CF Trust.

The final link between *Blue Star* and our new yacht, *Star Mist*, was the kind offers of help I had from crew who had sailed on *Blue Star*, to assist me in bringing the new yacht back to the UK from the Baltic in 2017.

Judith and I, together with Jean-Francois and Joan, brought the boat from the Baltic through the Kiel Canal to Cuxhaven. From there Kevin joined me together with one extra hired crew member. We sailed along the German and Dutch coasts, then across the North Sea from IJmuiden to Harwich. Back in British waters, we did a crew change and I was pleased to sail again with Rob Hollins and Graham Rennie. I should add how grateful we were to Rob's wife, Val, who did our shopping. What we did not know was that she had to drive many miles to reach a supermarket in Harwich – we were in Shotley Marina on the other side of the river! The final leg took us across the Thames Estuary to Ramsgate, then Eastbourne and eventually the Solent. The total trip from the Baltic to Swanwick was nearly 700 miles. Since then we have had many happy days exploring the South Coast of England, once again joined for various passages by good friends, Rob, Mike and Diane and Jean-Francois and Joan. Through these friends we were able to keep the good memories of *Blue Star* alive.

Living close to the Solent on the South Coast, it seemed natural when I wanted to expand my volunteering activities, after our sailing adventure, to join the National Coastwatch Institution (NCI). Established 25 years ago it now has some 56 operational stations around the coast and about 2,700 volunteers. The organisation's slogan is 'Eyes Along the Coast' and, by manning many of the relinquished coastguard stations, volunteers are able to actively support the Coastguard.

Through a rigorous training programme, some stations and their volunteers are able to gain 'Declared Facility Status', which means the Coastguard formally recognises the level of expertise, local knowledge and competency they bring to maritime safety. As the Coastguard has become more centralised, that local knowledge can make a vital difference when an emergency develops. One valuable service and a plea to all recreational sailors is the radio check facility which can be accessed by calling the NCI on VHF Ch65 leaving Channel 16 free for emergencies.

I am based in the NCI centre at the top of the Calshot Tower, a familiar landmark for those sailing in the Solent. With a recreational water centre nearby, we are kept extremely busy monitoring all types of activities for potential incidents. In contrast to some of the ports and harbours we visited on our trip, Southampton Water, which is extremely busy with all types of water craft, is largely unrestricted. With cruise liners, super tankers, container ships, car transporters, high-speed ferries, low-speed ferries, and often hundreds of recreational sailors, we are kept glued to our binoculars when on watch!

Mike:

I agonised long and hard about whether to keep *Blue Star*. The adventures we'd had with her will remain with me for the rest of my life. My heart really wanted to keep her, but the head said that, living so far from the sea, regular trips to the boat for maintenance and sailing would be difficult. I had to be realistic. Sadly, I agreed that she should be put up for sale.

Of course, that was not the end of my sailing – far from it. As well as taking trips with Roger aboard *Star Mist* I have organised several charters with sailing club members and friends. There are many advantages to chartering – no maintenance costs, you can sail in many different types and sizes of craft, and in different places around the world. We have sailed not only in the Solent, but also in the warm climes of the Mediterranean, off the South Coast of France and off Corfu. I discovered that skippering larger boats, with bigger crews, brings a fresh challenge. On yachts of around 50 foot, with all the extra room that that entails, I found that the on-board heads and showers have so much space that even I need not worry about shoreside facilities!

One of my earlier passions, teaching, re-entered my life a few years after the *Blue Star* project. After qualifying as an RYA instructor I delivered my first navigation course on behalf of Stafford Coastal Cruising Club. The excellent success rate and the lovely feedback from the students was very gratifying.

We chose to raise funds for the Cystic Fibrosis Trust because my son, Daniel, suffered from the disease. Sadly, Dan lost his life to CF in 2017. He continues to inspire and motivate me to raise money for the Trust. Many of my activities and sailing expeditions have a challenge associated with them, enabling funds to be generated. Woolcool have continued to be excellent supporters.

Whilst we have lost Dan, Diane and I have a wonderful daughter-in-law. Dan's widow, Jess, who also suffers from cystic fibrosis, is a very special member of our family. She works for the Cystic Fibrosis Trust. The Trust has helped to fund the development of new drugs, based on gene therapy, and has lobbied for the new treatments to be made available on the NHS. There is hope that these will be a 'game changer'. The first patients are currently taking the new medication but it remains to be seen how effective it is long term. It is hoped the medication will enable patients to live a more normal life. Unfortunately, the new drugs are not suitable for some patients. More research is needed to develop treatments that all those with CF can benefit from. I hope that I can continue to help make a difference.

***

We do hope that you have enjoyed reading our book!
Please give us a review, e.g. on the Amazon website – it will help us to sell more books and raise more funds for charity. Thank you.
Best wishes,
Mike and Roger.

***

<u>OK, a final joke</u>
Be careful if you use Velcro on your sail bag – it's a rip-off!

***

Above: We find an apt sign in Douglas, Isle of Man

Statistics relating to the voyage

Sea miles logged	2015: 1,158 2016: 1,468 Total: 2,626
Longest legs	Pwllheli to Milford Haven: 90 miles Milford Haven to Padstow: 72 miles
Shortest leg	Dartmouth to Brixham: 12 miles (discounting cruising in Solent, waiting for our planned arrival home time)
No. of ports visited	71 different ports
No. of days at sea	2015: 33 2016: 45 Total: 78
Engine hours	2015: 177 2016: 217 Total: 394
Hours under sail	135
Fuel consumption	Average of 2.2 litres/hr = 860 litres
Estimated time spent under way	534 hours
% of time with engine on	Estimated at 75% (Much higher than we expected, due to the large number of days with wind on the nose!)
Number of additional crew	35
Furthest north	N 058° 48.0', Stromness (Same latitude as Stavanger, Norway)
Furthest south	N 049° 55.4 (off Lizard Point, Cornwall)
Furthest east	E 002° 07.0', off Northeast Scotland
Furthest west	W 006° 59.6', off Rathlin Island, N. Ireland

List of ports visited

2015
Hythe (start)
Gosport
Brighton
Eastbourne
Dover
Ramsgate
Queenborough
Burnham
Bradwell
Harwich
Lowestoft
Wells-next-Sea
Grimsby
Scarborough
Whitby
Hartlepool
Newcastle
Amble
Eyemouth
Arbroath
Peterhead
Whitehills
Inverness
Fort Augustus
Cullochy
Banavie
Corpach
Dunstaffnage
Crinan
Tarbert
Portavadie
Port Bannatyne
Lochgoilhead
Greenock
(TOTAL 34)

2016
Greenock
Portavadie
Cairnbaan
Bellanoch
Crinan
Lochaline
Tobermory
Mallaig
Kyle of Lochalsh
Gairloch
Lochinver
Kinlochbervie
Scrabster
Stromness
Wick
Lossiemouth
Inverness
Aldourie Estate
Fort Augustus
Gairlochy
Banavie
Corpach
Dunstaffnage
Crinan
Port Ellen
Glenarm
Red Bay
Bangor (N. I.)
Douglas
Conwy
Port Dinorwic
Pwllheli
Milford Haven
Padstow
Newlyn

2016 (cont.)
Falmouth
Fowey
Plymouth
Salcombe
Dartmouth
Brixham
Weymouth
Poole
Lymington
Cowes
Lymington
Buckler's Hard
Hythe (finish)
(TOTAL 48)

Acknowledgements

We would like to record our gratitude for the support provided by the following people who have helped us to publish our book.

First and foremost, our wives. They let us buy a boat and go off sailing, leaving them behind for weeks at a time to get on with the real work of running a home and family! We are most grateful that we had their support. Without it, the project would have been a non-starter. Diane also helped enormously with proofreading, editing and redrafting of the manuscript. The book is undoubtedly a far better document for all of the hours and days she spent on task! Judith too was incredibly diligent in her proofreading, checking continuity and suggesting redrafts which helped tremendously.

Angela Morris and Keith Spilsbury of Woolcool have given amazing support, and not just for the sailing part of the project. Once the idea of a book was mooted they were immediately on board, providing encouragement and, together with their media consultants, Verso Creative, freely giving their time to produce a marvellous cover design and map showing the route that we took.

We are grateful to the many crewmates who sailed with us. Their recollections of the voyage, and their photographs, helped us to produce the book. We thank them, not only for accompanying us on the voyage, but for giving us every encouragement with writing it all up. Most wanted to place an order as soon as possible!

We are grateful to everyone who helped us with the fundraising. Although it did not impact directly on publishing the book, it undoubtedly helped to drive us on with the voyage and made it much more worthwhile.

Information sources

We had a large collection of nautical charts and pilot books on board during the voyage, too many to list here. Several were used in helping to draft our text, particularly the port details provided in the pilot books.

Reeds Nautical Almanac was used to confirm some of the port data and instructions for entering specific harbours. It also enabled us to check tidal-stream data.

The Scottish Canals online guide for skippers transiting the Caledonian Canal was used to refresh our memory of the various stopping points, and of the rules that skippers and boats need to conform to. A similar online guide was used to help us draft our accounts of passing through the Crinan Canal.

We have used online sources to check the background facts relating to the various coastal features that we navigated past, be it a historic relic or a modern coastal town. Wikipedia was frequently consulted but this was far from the only source.

We made notes of the historical data on public display at several ports of call. Often there would be a plaque intended to inform tourists, providing much thought-provoking data.

Blue Star's log book was invaluable in reminding us of some of the particulars relating to specific passages.

We kept a blog during our voyage. This was used to refresh our memories of specific passages, and of our thoughts at the time.